MASTERS OF PAINTING AND
THEIR CONCEPTS OF ART

MASTERS OF PAINTING AND THEIR CONCEPTS OF ART

from the eighteenth to the twentieth centuries

Amir Reza

ISBN: 0692946845
ISBN 13: 9780692946848

Table of Contents

Literature and artistic creation are among the intellectual expressions that give us a better knowledge of ourselves and of the human condition in general. To comprehend the intellectual message of a master painter, we need some knowledge of evolution of his or her art and to read through his or her choices of color, line, form, brushstroke, and the play of light and shade.

At the end of the eighteenth century, the effects of the French Revolution spread over the whole European continent, and the turbulent age of the nineteenth century, with its chain of revolutions punctuated by counterrevolutions, reflected the desire for freedom from age-old boundaries and the search for new values in all aspects of life. But proponents of tradition, who stood fast against aspirations for change, were hostile to any new art aesthetic.

Despite this attitude of the academy, the nineteenth century witnessed the emergence of a wide range of new concepts in painting. Romanticism was followed by realism, which gave way to impressionism and postimpressionism; and at the close of the century, the concept of reality was challenged by the symbolist movement, which replaced sensation with idea and thought.

With the beginning of the twentieth century, reactions and changes that came over the continuity of painting were unprecedented.

Critical discussion of new styles challenged the principles of the academy and expanded the knowledge of art and the range of aesthetic appreciation. Consequently, modern painters moved toward the concept that the poetry of their painting did not derive from what they represented but from the way they served the elements of picture making to represent their own specific poetry.

Part 1

The Move toward Modern Times

With the Renaissance turning away from ideas of a supernatural orientation, the curious phenomenon of the secular humanism of Petrarch joined to the Christian humanism of Saint Frances appeared in Europe, which, armed with these humanistic values, considered any civilization having a different world view and ideals as barbaric.

The expansion of contact with other cultures through colonization, commerce, and religious missions stimulated the curiosity of Europeans. Along with that, printing, which multiplied books, and the opening of universities induced the desire to discover new ideas. Consequently, Europeans began to question their existing values.

In France, contemplating the variety and fluctuations of beliefs in law, morality, philosophy, and religion led Montaigne to skepticism. He was the first to ask, "What do I know?" It was a question that thereafter every philosopher would ask. His liberty of not adhering to any one idea but to exploring them all influenced the most prominent thinkers of the West. Voltaire and Diderot considered him a precursor of the free thought of the Enlightenment. In England, Francis Bacon repudiated the reliance upon tradition and authority and offered the development of experimental science as a basis for progress. Under these movements—coupled with the reaction of Europe to the conservative agricultural civilization founded on adaptation to the perpetual rhythms of nature, and with limited refinements based on experience—modern Europe took form.

The Age of Louis XIV

During the reign of Louis XIV, known as Louis the Great, from 1643 to 1715, France became the leading power of Europe. French language, literature, and art exercised dominance over European culture.

Confiscation of fine works of art gathered by Mazarin and Fouquet, and judicious purchases of the king that increased the number of paintings in the royal gallery from two hundred to twenty-five hundred, provided a rich basis for the conversion of the Louvre Palace to a place for displaying the royal collection at the end of the seventeenth century, a decision that expanded education and development of the art of France.

In 1648 Mazarin founded the Académie de Peinture et de Sculpture. In 1664 Colbert reorganized this academy as the Académie Royale des Beaux-Arts, in which painters were classified according to their specializations. First came history painting, followed by genre painting concerned with intimate subjects, and then by portraiture, landscape painting, and still life. Within the academy, the power of decision was conferred upon the officers, who determined the academy's aesthetic orientation. Among the academy's members, only history painters could attain the rank of officers. Le Brun, as the director of the Académie Royale de Beax-Arts, by exalting line above color and discipline above originality, established the principles of the classical style and set the standard for French art. Raphael among Italians and Poussin among French painters became the favored models. Polished form and elegant expressions of this art, which were the ideals of the king, lost contact with the life of people and actuality.

In 1666 Colbert and Charles Le Brun set up in Rome the Académie Royale de France. The academy regularly organized competitions, for which it chose the subject and awarded the prizes. The first prize called Prix de Rome, entitled the student to three years of study at the Académie de France in Rome at the expense of the French government. It offered the student the opportunity to study classical and antique masterpieces, making copies and drawings at the Académie de France in Rome.

Because at that time museums did not exist, painters had no access to private collections, and churches constituted the only source of knowledge of the art of the past, the Prix de Rome was an opportunity for an aspiring young painter to become familiar with the art of the masters.

Under Louis XIV, the academy began to organize art exhibitions called salons. From 1740 on, the organization of annual exhibition of submitted paintings and sculptures turned salons into the most prestigious art exhibitions in the world. Selection of the jury of the salons gave the academy a tremendous controlling power over the art of France.

Part 2

The Eighteenth Century

A work of art is both matter and mind, both form and content.

—HENRI FOCILLON

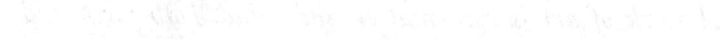

Section 1

The Age of Enlightenment

The first half of the eighteenth century was a time of transition. Advancements in technology and the expansion of trade increased the wealth of the middle class and paved the way for the rise of the bourgeoisie, towns grew, interregional trade accelerated, and the bourgeoisie enjoyed more economic power than ever before. The application of the steam engine to industry and transportation transformed the nature of European life. The century became a period of scientific activity. Along with those changes, absolute rule of monarchies diminished.

Social and philosophical thought in the age of reason, and the debates of writers and thinkers of the Enlightenment, a European intellectual movement of the eighteenth century, over the nature of reform, progress, advancement in science, and secular thought had a deeper social and intellectual effect than material circumstances. The sharp contrast of the realities of actual society with the idea of Enlightenment intellectuals of government as a social contract,[1] and their belief that the human race could attain perfection through the application of common sense to social problems, triggered attacks on established European civilization. Glorification of the power of

---

1 A theory in political philosophy, the social contract describes an agreement between the ruled and their ruler, defining the right and duties of each of them. It stipulates that, to retain its essentially moral character, government must rest on the consent of the governed.

the individual—and above all the desire for freedom, which is fundamental to human improvement—instigated revolutionary developments in politics and arts.

The discerning minds of France, the leading cultural center of the Enlightenment in Europe, opened into public discourse issues that used to be the domain of abstract philosophy. This aspect of the Enlightenment is most apparent in the publication of *L'Encyclopedie*. Diderot, a French philosopher with a materialistic and atheistic view, with the help of other French philosophers undertook *L'Encyclopedie*, an organ for radical and anticlerical opinion and a massive enterprise that tried to codify accumulated knowledge from the past and current ideas in the present.

The second half of the century moved toward the French Revolution, which became the opening of the modern epoch. Rejection of the absolutism of kings and the Church triggered revolutions in different aspects of European society and set new social values. At first it was a time of "Trust your heart rather than your head," the slogan of sensibility preached by Jean-Jacques Rousseau. Then the heroic emotions of the French Revolution summoned the self-sacrificing virtues of Greek and Roman history. From both of these movements emerged an attitude of mind called romanticism, which Baudelaire equated with modernism. The modern mankind, in search of a more realistic image of himself, repudiated the humanistic values of the Renaissance.

VOLTAIRE (1694–1778)

Voltaire, the most amazing and influential thinker of the eighteenth century, was a writer of an incredible quantity of quality dramas, stories, poems, and matters of religion, philosophy, and politics. His sharpness and the clarity of his mind were unparalleled. His library of over six thousand volumes of subjects, with his marginal comments, reflected the range of his intense curiosity. He examined legends, traditions, and ideas with skepticism. Among his vices were flattery of the politically powerful, vanity, and jealousy. Generosity to friends and needy people that he had never met, the moral courage to attack the Church, willingness to fight against injustice, loyalty to friends, and above all humanity were his virtues. His three years of exile in England influenced his thinking, during which he became attracted to Deism[2] and social contract theory and was greatly impressed by the liberalism of English institutions.

Frederick of Germany and Catherine the Great of Russia were among his correspondents. Voltaire's writings and activities influenced the direction taken by European civilization. There was scarcely a subject of importance on which he did not speak or write; religious tolerance, respect for the rights of humans, freedom of thought, and development of knowledge were his constant chosen themes. He demanded the revision of French law, freedom of the press, subordination of ecclesiastical to civil law, and distinguishing sin from crime. He believed that reason and educating the masses would lead to progress and that "the more enlightened men are, the more they will be free." He held that feeling and passions were not significant in discussions of life and experience.

---

2 In England, Deism was a philosophical synthesis form of God, reason, and nature.

Section 2

Jean-Jacques Rousseau (1712–1778)

Rousseau was a Swiss-born philosopher, writer, and music composer whose writings inspired the leaders of the French Revolution. His writings in *L'Encyclopedie* attracted admiration. His *Discours sur les Science et les Arts* (1750) attacked arts and progress as responsible for the corruption of morals. In 1752 Rousseau's operetta was presented before the king and later for the public in Paris. In his long article *Discours sur l'Origine et les Fondementes de l'Inégalité parmi les Hommes* (1754), he considered man to be naturally good, but social institutions corrupt him. He argued that despite all defects, the family, the most ancient society, was the happiest of all and that private property and the laws and institutions to protect it marked the start of inequality. In 1755, in his long article *Discours sur L'Économie Politique*, in *L'Encyclopedie*, showed some divergence from earlier discourses. Here, he honored society, government, and law. His sentimental novel *La Nouvelle Héloïse* (1761), in the form of letters between two lovers, was a great success. Through the novel he sublimated nature and expounded on his ideals of a happy marriage and his view of the education of children. *Du Contrat Social* (1762) opens with "Man is born free, and he is everywhere in chains." He argued that the social contract is not a pledge of the ruled to obey the ruler but an agreement of individuals to subordinate their powers to the judgment of their community as a whole.

In *Emile* (1762), which is halfway between a novel and a treatise on education, he rejected the method of teaching of his time directed by the Church. He recommended moral education, but said that intellectual and religious education must wait until age eighteen. Harsh reaction followed the publication of *Emile*; it was condemned in Paris and Geneva. The parliament ordered the book burned, and a decree for Rousseau's arrest was issued. It was the beginning of a fugitive life for Rousseau. His *Dialogues* (1772) was an attempt to answer his enemies. His most beautiful book, *Les Reveries du Promeneur Solitaire* (1778), exemplifies the eighteenth-century movement as the age of sensibility. The effect of Rousseau's ideas upon literature, art, philosophy, politics, pedagogy, and morals began after his death. His writings opened the eyes of men to the beauty of nature, fostered a love of nature, and matured the romantic movement as a revolt of sensibility against reason, subjectivism against objectivity, and imagination against reality.

Section 3

When Louis XIV died in 1715, his successor Louis XV, was five years old. Philip Duc d'Orlean, the regent from 1715 to 1723, moved his court to the Palais-Royal in Paris. Redecoration of the Palais-Royal with sinuous designs and naturalistic carved flowers, carved to be deliberately asymmetrical, foreshadowed the rococo style.

The court move to Paris and was followed by the French nobility and refurbishing of their Parisian homes. The new interest in the "salon," an elegant but less formal room as a gathering place for conversation led largely by women, became fashionable.

The prevailing style during the reign of Louis XV (1723–1774), known as rococo style, emphasizing elegance and delicacy, was a backlash against the formality of the baroque style. (The word *rococo* is a combination of the French word *rocaille*, meaning "shell," due to its similarity to shell-like curves, and the Italian word *barocco*, for the baroque style.) This graceful style, with its tall and slender moldings carved asymmetrically into C and S shapes and its predominant colors of pastel, ivory, white, and gold, was a transformation of the grandeur and austerity of the style of Versailles to a more intimate style. Centered around the life of the aristocracy, rococo was not an art preoccupied with the political and economic realities of the time, nor did it mirror the rising tide of reason and the simplicity of the Enlightenment.

In the early eighteenth, France enjoyed great prestige throughout Europe, and consequently the rococo style, which first emerged in interior design and the decorative arts, was adopted in other countries, principally Germany and Austria.

Among painters of the rococo period, Watteau and Chardin stand apart. The emotion and the sensibility of Watteau's art and Chardin's intimate poetry of the life of the middle class distinguish them from the sensual paintings of the rococo period.

JEAN-ANTOINE WATTEAU (1684–1721)

Watteau was born at Valenciennes, a town of the Spanish Netherlands that had recently passed to France. In his earliest youth, he used to go to the main square of the town to make sketches of people. His father, a roof tiler, with reluctance was persuaded to place Antoine as an apprentice to a local painter. But to force Antoine to follow his profession, he did not provide the expenses to study painting for a length of time. At about age eighteen, Antoine left home and went to Paris. At this time, dealers in the provinces demanded devotional pictures. Watteau, obliged to make a living, attached himself to a painter who had a few pupils whom he employed like manual laborers to copy from an original of a devotional picture.

In 1703 an acquaintance of Gillot, a painter of theatrical and opera designs, changed the direction of Watteau's life and art. Gillot, who loved especially *commedia dell'arte*, after seeing Watteau's drawings and paintings invited Watteau to work for him. As a result of an affinity of character and taste, a friendship grew between them. When they parted on bad terms, Watteau expressed gratitude to his old master, and Gillot admitted that his pupil had surpassed him. The experience of this period left an everlasting influence on Watteau's art. He returned frequently to the theme of *commedia dell'arte*, and the balletlike movements of his figures are reminiscent of ballet.

In 1708 he entered the studio of Claude Audran, whose principal study was ornamentation. Audran was the most famous decorator in Paris and the curator of the Medici Gallery in the Palais du Luxembourg. It was due to Audran's activities that the heavy tastes of his predecessors were set aside. Working with Audran gave Watteau a taste for decoration and lightness of brushwork. At the palais, Watteau studied the Venetians and copied Rubens, and his drawing of the trees in the beautiful gardens of the palace subsequently served him for his pictures. However, Watteau had no wish to remain in another employment. The pretext to visit his family was an honorable excuse to leave Audran, who had treated him with consideration.

Back at home, he made sketches of scenes of soldiers returning from battle who were camped in the countryside. From these sketches he painted a few pictures that found favor with the public. After a short stay in his hometown, he returned to Paris. In 1709, with a desire to visit Rome to study the works of the old masters, he enrolled in the competition for the Prix de Rome. He won the second prize but not the journey to Rome. In 1710, as a guest of art dealer Pierre Sirois, he met Sirois's son-in-law Gersaint, who became a faithful friend for the rest of his life. Watteau, who had never renounced study in Rome and who could not make the journey without financial assistance, submitted two pictures executed in his personal style in the competition of 1712. The colors, harmony, and novelty of the style of the pictures that he submitted, suggesting the work of a master, attracted the attention of the members of the academy. They accepted him as a full member of the academy. The imaginary world of Watteau's paintings, featuring figures in ball dress in a lush outdoor setting, which was a move toward intimacy and away from the grandeur of previous periods, was new to the academy, so to describe Watteau's paintings, they created the term *fêtes galantes*. The honor he received and the originality of his style attracted more commissions than he could deal with.

In 1715 Pierre Crozat, a rich financier art lover invited Watteau to take quarters in his residence. Gersaint stated that one of the reasons Watteau decided to accept the invitation was the knowledge of the priceless collection of drawings of this art collector. At that time royal or important private collections were not readily available to the public. Watteau's experience of drawings from the scenery of Luxembourg Ggarden had served him in becoming an inventive landscape painter. While staying in Corzat's country house, he painted a landscape in which he transcended the natural aspects of the scene he was depicting. Despite comfort and pleasure, out of a desire for independence, he eventually left Corzat's residence and went to live in a small lodging of a friend's house, where he asked that his address not be revealed.

Watteau did not submit his acceptance piece, *L'Embarquement pour l'Ile de Cythere*—Cythere, a Greek island, was thought to be the birthplace of Aphrodite, the goddess of love—to the academy until 1717. The elegant figures, their distinctive poses, and the graceful, balletlike movements of figures in this painting, which is considered his masterpiece, were carefully studied. The fragile beauty of the figures and the nostalgic melancholy that slightly shadows the theme of love and happiness reflect the temporary nature of happiness and the precariousness of life. The landscape, immersed in the golden light and subtle haze of sunrise, is a romantic yearning. Despite the title referring to embarkation on a pilgrimage to the birthplace of Aphrodite, a place of love and happiness, it seems the people are leaving the island rather than arriving. In the foreground of the picture are three couples. One couple, still sitting, are absorbed in their love conversation; the man of the second couple is helping the woman to rise; and in the third couple, while they are on their way to join the group down the hill, the woman turns her head to look back to the place she is leaving.

In 1719, for unknown reasons, he painted a second version of *L'Embarquement pour l'Ile de Cythere*. In this version, painted at a time when his health was failing, the blue sky of noon has replaced the golden sky of sunrise of the first version, and the haze of early morning has dissipated.

Watteau was a very fine draftsman. He himself valued his drawings more highly than his paintings. He did his drawing in a bound book so that he always had a rich supply of drawings available for his paintings. His drawing book shows that, in order to find the smoothest and most refined of attitudes, he observed and drew the slow movements and refined attitudes of his figures from different angles. Gersaint considered Watteau's subtle and graceful drawings as the best that France had ever produced.

Watteau had had fragile health since childhood and was all of his life a sick man. In 1719 he went to England to consult a famous physician, but London's air aggravated his health condition. On his return to Paris in 1721, he took up residence in Gersaint's house, which was above his gallery. He asked Gersaint, in order to take the numbness from his fingers, to allow him to paint a signboard for Gersaint's gallery. Although his delicate health constrained him to paint only in the mornings, *L'Enseigne de Gersaint* was the work of eight days. Contrary to his other paintings, which werepainted from drawings, this picture was from nature; the only exceptions are the figure of the lady in a lavender dress, from a study that may have been done earlier, and a hasty sketch of the packers. He grouped his figures within a setting as a box, and in the foreground a checkered design leads in the eye. Its colors are gradated in such a way as to achieve magical transitions. The natural attitudes of the figures in the picture fascinated artists and passersby.

Soon after painting *L'Enseigne de Gersaint*, which was his last painting, he relapsed into a state of languor. Fearing that he might become an inconvenience to Gersaint, he begged Gersaint to find him a suitable abode in the country. At Nogent, a secluded area in the house of Le Fevre was arranged for him. There, he was struck with remorse for his impatience in attending to the advancement of his pupil, Pater. He begged Gersaint to have Pater come to Nogent to work under his inspection, and he devoted his entire last hours to him. When the curé of Nogent presented him with a crucifix, he said, "Take this crucifix away from me. I pity it. Is it possible to have so ill served my master?" Worn down by tuberculosis, he died at the age of thirty-seven.

Although Watteau lived most of his life under Louis XIV's reign, his art typifies the graceful style of rococo and epitomizes the elegance of the Regency. The poses and gestures of his figures suggest easy movement, while the structure of his pictures is severe. Watteau's art was more than a transformation of a style; he was the first painter to sense the fatigue of his time from the old civilization. His art was a signal of the impending changes that took place in French civilization.

Though Watteau had received no education, reading was his great recreation. He was fastidious judge of music and arts, he spoke little but well, and he also wrote well. Goncour considered Watteau to be a painter-poet. Watteau's airy foliation of trees, elegant figures with vague corporality, and delicate color nuances, turned the *fêtes galantes* into poems of love.

He returned frequently to the themes of the *commedia dell'arte*. To unfold the cruel realities of the human condition, he often painted the character of Gilles, the sad clown exploited by everyone, who with arms dangling to his sides, a fading smile, and a questioning expression on his face as he looks at the viewer.

The elegance and grace of Watteau's figures had an undeniable influence upon the attitude and dress of women in Paris. The women realized that elegance, charm, and coquetry are beyond mere physical beauty. Watteau's artistic legacy pervades French art up to the emergence of neoclassicism. During the French Revolution, his art was associated with the aristocracy and considered as frivolous, but gradually, interest in his art was revived. Poets and writers were among those who sensed his greatness. Watteau's sober melancholy and his sense of the futility of life contrasted with the erotic frivolity of Boucher and Fragonard, the two French rococo painters who followed him.

JEAN-BAPTISTE-SIMÉON CHARDIN (1699–1779)

Chardin, the son of a well-known carpenter, is considered the greatest still life painter of the eighteenth century. He started his study of painting at the studio of Cazes, where the teaching was limited to copying the masters. Coypel, a well-known painter who called him as an assistant, instructed him to paint a gun in the portrait of a huntsman. The care that Coypel gave to the placing and lighting of the gun opened Chardin's eyes to the secrets of painting.

A surgeon friend of his father asked him to paint a signboard for his shop. Chardin, tempted to paint a lively scene from Paris similar to Watteau's *L'Enseigne de Gerdaint*, painted a fifteen-foot-long sign crowded by a general bustle in a lively scene of Paris. The sign was beyond the expectation of the surgeon, who was on the point of anger but disarmed by the public's admiration. Through this signboard Chardin's ability as a painter was discovered.

In 1728, at the exhibitions of the Place Dauphine, he exhibited a few pictures. The members of the academy admiring his *La Raie*

("The Skate") urged him to submit his name for membership of the academy. His application was approved amid general applause.

Still lives became Chardin's specialty. He painted still lives with love and treated the objects with the same respect as living beings. Vigorous drawings, carefully composed objects bathed in a softly diffused light, reflecting neighboring objects and establishing a link between them, raise this secondary branch of painting to the highest level of art. For a long time, Chardin continued to paint still lives before approaching the human figure.

Goncour brothers in their study of Chardin's life and art, presented him as being content with the scant prices paid for his art. He lived a hard life throughout his youth, and even at the height of esteem of connoisseurs and critics for his art and his fame in Paris and Europe—when his pictures were included at the Gallery of Vienna, and the Empress of Russia commissioned his pictures for the Hermitage—he did nothing to fetch a reasonable price for his works. But according to Georges Wildenstein's documented study, Chardin kept a shrewd eye on his finances and saw to it that he had a regular income in his old age.

In 1731 he married Marguerite Saintar. Four years after their marriage, his wife died of a lung disease, leaving Chardin with a son. His second marriage, to a widow with a small fortune, relieved him from a hard life and permitted him to work at his ease.

He always lived as a modest bourgeois in his native quarter of Saint-Germain-des-Prés. He confined his art to an intimate poetry about his family and the objects of his humble world. His models were his wife on her return from the market or busy with everyday housework or taking care of the children, his children with their grace and full of the joy of infancy, their vessels, and the vegetables, fruit, bread, and meat that they were going to eat. The honesty that prevails in these pictures and their charm reflects Chardin's pleasure in family life.

He painted human figures with the same calm and collected simplicity of objects. The success of this intimate realist art, a sincere mirror of the life of the French middle class, was neglected for a long time in France and established Chardin's reputation. He had a remarkable treatment of light and a luminous quality of paint. He boldly applied contradictory tints side by side. His sense of spatial order made him comparable to Vermeer. Cezanne called him "A wily old boy who knew every trick of the trade." Chardin has been quoted as saying, "One uses colors but paints with feeling."

Toward the middle of the century, critics began to display disappointment at his repetition of old subjects with insignificant alterations. Even Diderot, an advocate of his art, stated, "Chardin's art is dead." In 1770, with failing sight and trembling hands, he took up the art of pastel. These pastels were the last triumph of an old master. The death of his son and his own physical suffering and infirmities of old age, added to the wounds inflicted by criticism and severe judgement, embittered the last years of this very tender and sensitive person.

Chardin developed his pictures without separate sketches or drawings. Although his style has all the refinement and charm of his period, both in technique and subject matter, with carefully constructed still lives and intimate domestic scenes that portray the private lives of the middle-class eighteenth century, he stands apart from his contemporaries.

After the Renaissance, the art of the West was deeply rooted in humanistic values, and still lives played a subordinate role in the art of great masters. But Chardin's art proved that still lives could be a vehicle for great painting. Pascal, in a famous reflection, had said that paintings that could attract admiration for their resemblance to things of which we do not admire the originals was a vanity. But

Chardin's art is not a simple creation of resemblance. Through the plastic language of painting, he stresses beautiful aspects of the object, drawing our attention and reminding us that we are surrounded by a world of beautiful objects, an awareness that refines our judgment and elevates our thoughts.

WILLIAM HOGARTH (1697–1764)

William Hogarth was born in Bartholomew. His father, Richard, was a Latin schoolmaster and a minor classical scholar. In 1703 Richard opened a Latin-speaking coffeehouse. Failure of the coffeehouse led to his confinement to the Fleet Prison for debt. During Richard's five years of confinement, his family lived in an area outside the prison.

William grew up in an era of growing dominance of the middle class and a redrawing of all social strata. In 1713 he was apprenticed to a silver engraver. Seven years later he opened his own engraving business. His graphic virtuosity attracted the attention of booksellers and was employed to produce illustrations for literary books.

In the eighteenth century, interest in books exploded in England. In the evolution from text to image, Hogarth's early works, in which pictures were subordinated to text, played a considerable part. Although the presence of text in the margins or in the pictures, as well as the literary form of his compositions, built his reputation as a verbal artist, his art asserts the independence of the image.

In 1725 Philippe Mercier transformed Watteau's *Le Bal Champêtre* into small-sized paintings of informal portraits of groups of people in a domestic interior or garden, called conversation pieces. In this kind of picture, which had been evolved to meet demand from the new middle class, the emphasis was shifted from an individual to his position among his own milieu. Hogarth, who had decided that his art should serve a moral purpose, chose this kind of painting to render facets of London life, but in contrast to the French rococo pictures, for his numerous "conversation pieces," he selected closed scenes resembling the stage of a theater.

It was the age of English satirical writing. Hogarth, admiring satire, began to publish satirical prints in 1724. To follow a character in his encounter with social problems, he began to paint serial story-pictures that could be read like a book. He also made drawing for engravings of twelve plates for "Hudibras," Butler's satiric poem. For his paintings of several scenes of John Gay's *Beggar's Opera*, by borrowing from stage lighting and the gestures and positioning of characters in the theater, he became close to the world of the London stage. In 1731 he initiated sales by subscription of the engravings of *A Harlot's Progress*, a collection of six scenes depicting the fate of a country girl led to prostitution. His *A Rake's Progress* is about a merchant's son who wastes his inheritance, ending up in prison, and *Marriage à-la-Mode* depicts a marriage for money that leads to tragedy.

In Hogarth's narrative serial works, plural pictures unfold successive events that take place in time or space. With representations full of life and motion that criticize various forms of the social relationships of his time, he came to public attention and established his reputation as a master of graphic expression.

Hogarth painted some outstanding portraits. His masterpiece, the delightful *Shrimp Girl*, is a portrait of a smiling young girl with cheeks reddened by the sea wind. This portrait, painted as an impression, and its free brushwork are unusual among Hogarth's portraits. Hogarth, with his uncompromising fidelity to truth rather than to flatter the sitter, was not the kind of painter that aristocrats expected to stress their elegance or to enhance the beauty of their ladies.

Despite his anti-French sentiments, he chose the rococo style for his works and even made a trip to France to see the latest French rococo paintings. He wrote *The Analysis of Beauty*, a treatise in which he argued that the undulating lines and S curves prominent in rococo style are the basis for grace and beauty in nature and art. In this treatise, he valued female beauty as superior to the classical male beauty, and he considered the geometrical style of perspective set up by the Renaissance as too rigid to express the flexibility of the forms of nature.

Traditionally, England imported painters from the continent. Hogarth, the first great English painter, had a middle-class upbringing. His style owes something to France, yet his subject matter is English. He was against the academy's restrictions, yet his works were within its framework. Through a series of narrative paintings and engravings, he brought art to the common man. He chose moral subjects while satirizing the English society of his time.

Section 4

Neoclassicism

The excavations of Herculaneum in 1738 and Pompei in 1748 and the writings of J. J. Winckelmann (1717–1768), the German art historian and archaeologist who was the first to apply the modern classification and description of art based on general stylistic traits that change over time, turned the romanticizing taste of Europe to a new style called neoclassicism. In his writings Winckelmann articulated the difference between Greek and Roman art, characterizing Greek sculpture as a manifestation of noble simplicity and calm grandeur. In his reflections on aesthetic theories, he considered beauty to be the purpose of art. Neoclassical painters lacking sufficient access to ancient painting chose ancient sculpture as their prototype. The importance of the neoclassical for modern art is that, for the first time in modern history, it propounded the principle of plastic[3] figuration of the subject matter.

JOHN FLAXMAN (1755–1826)

Flaxman, a sculptor, designer, and book illustrator, was born in York, England. As a young boy, he worked in his father's plaster-casting workshop. In 1770 he entered the Royal Academy school In 1775 he began working for the potter Josiah Wedgwood.

---

3   - Plastic = the art of modeling.

The neoclassical reaction to the rococo and baroque styles reached its heights in 1780 and attracted Flaxman. In 1787, he went to Rome to study antiquities and he stayed there for nine years.

In Italy, he illustrated the works of Homer and Dante's *Divine Comedy*, which brought him international fame. Flaxman inspired by classical Greek and Etruscan vase painting, limited his forms to purely linear outlines with no chiaroscuro. The elegance of Flaxman's designs, which inspired Ingres, led Goethe to describe him as "the idol of dilettanti."

JACQUES-LOUIS DAVID (1748–1825)

David's father's side came from a family of tradesmen, but his mother's side included some men of artistic talent. David was only nine years old at the time that his father was killed in a duel. His mother retired to Normandy, and he was entrusted to the care of his uncles. At the age of sixteen, he wanted to study painting with Boucher, his grandmother's cousin, but Boucher was too old to teach and sent him to Vien, a professor at the academy. Around midcentury the frivolity of the prevailing trends in French painting came under attack, and Vien was one of the first advocates of a return to classical antiquity.

After four unsuccessful attempts, in 1774, David was awarded the Prix de Rome. In Italy, he made drawings from old masters, antique bas-reliefs, and statues, as well as studies from nature that nourished his contact with nature and human life. The frescoes discovered at Pompeii, and Winckelmann's influence at its height, affected his thoughts about art. His early painting displays solidity of drawing and balance of colors. After his return to France, the exhibition of his works at the Salon of 1781 spread his fame beyond France's border. His travel to Flanders acquainted him with the art of the Flemish masters.

For a picture on a large scale, David selected the subject of the Horatii, a story from republican Rome. In a war between the cities of Rome and Alba, it had been decided that the result of combat by three champions from each city would settle the dispute. The drama lay in the fact that one the sisters of the Horatii brothers, champions of Rome, was married to one of the Curiatii brothers, champions of the city of Alba, and one of the sisters of the Curiatii was married to one of the Horatii. To immerse himself in antiquity, David went back to Rome in 1784. For the clarity of composition of *The Oath of the Horatii*, he rejected the single-viewpoint horizon of linear perspective and instead used a solid background across the picture plane, similar to the background of a frieze or classical relief. The picture with its intense emotional conflict between patriotic sacrifice, represented by the rigid forms of men, and love and grief, represented the by curvilinear shapes of women, the harmony of colors, and the clarity of composition, was a total triumph. With this picture, he was recognized as the leader of the neoclassical school. As he felt sure of his standing, he applied for appointment as director of the Académie de France in Rome. Since he was considered too young for this position, his application was rejected. Yet the aristocracy and men of finance captivated by his fame commissioned him for portraits and historic paintings.

At that time France favored republican Rome with its virtues as a model society. David's admirably composed *The Death of Socrates* looked beyond Rome to ancient Greece. But his composition of this picture, suppler than *The Oath of the Horatii*, was less in harmony with David's character. A vast archway that opens on one side of the solid background gives the picture a feeling of depth.

The revolution plunged France into a new era. David was a member of the privileged class, but as a revolutionary he aspired to the principles of the Roman Republic. In 1789 he painted *Lictors*

Returning to Brutus the Bodies of His Sons, which showed Brutus, a hero of the history of the Roman Republic, who condemned his two sons to death for joining in a conspiracy against the Roman Republic. The scene is composed of three parts, divided by light. Brutus sits alone in shadow, absorbed in thoughts, while lictors bring in the bodies of his sons, and a beautifully designed group of grieving women cling to each other.

The Tennis Court Oath was an assertion that political authority derives from the people and their representatives, not the king. David was invited to paint a picture commemorating the event. This large-scale drawing of portraits was his first work of a contemporary historical event.

The academy had offered David certain opportunities but not enough to rise to high levels. In his studio, he encouraged young artists to rebel against the academy. His minor war against the academy became more bitter, and in 1790, he made a final break with the academy and set up the Commune des Arts.

After the monarchy was overthrown and the Legislative Assembly was replaced by the Convention. David, a revolutionary, and a friend of Robespierre and Mara, was elected as deputy to the Convention. He voted for the execution of the king and signed with his colleagues nearly three hundred arrests, most of whom would be guillotined. His wife, unable to tolerate his conduct, divorced him.

During this period, his artistic activity was considerable. The Convention, according to David's proposal, abolished all academies, but after the fall of Robespierre reestablished the École de Rome. In light of his proposals and his activity, he was one of the founders of the first museums in France.

On July 1793, Marat was stabbed to death in his bathtub. David's *The Death of Marat* is an emotional picture of the death of a friend. Marat's face is marked by suffering. The soft light that falls on his features becomes harsher as it illuminates the assassin's petition.

Following the fall of Robespierre, David was arrested. After he was moved to the Luxembourg, he painted *View from the Luxembourg* and completed the first sketch for *The Intervention of Sabine Women*. In 1795, with general amnesty for crimes related to the revolution, David recovered his freedom and remarried his former wife.

David returned to his plan to paint *The Intervention of Sabine Women*. The subject, from the early days of Roman history, was more devoted to reconciliation than glorification of heroic values. The Sabines, to avenge the abduction of their daughters, attacked Rome. Hersilia, the daughter of the leader of the Sabines, had been married to the Roman leader and had two children. In David's picture Hersilia adjures both sides not to separate families. The subject was Roman, but David's sculptural treatment of body of the figures were Greek, and in order to attain greater simplicity, he painted his heroes nude. In 1799, when the painting was completed, he organized an exhibition of his works that continued for five years. Napoleon Bonaparte, visiting the exhibition, criticized the lack of action of the warriors of *The Sabine Women*, whereas David's intention was that the bursting of Hersilia between the two leaders, and the actions of the women, had frozen the clash of two armies.

As the revolution was over and France was in danger, General Bonaparte became David's hero. David met Napoleon in 1797. His first portrait of the general was a passionate sketch of the face. Napoleon, as the first consul, asked David to paint his portrait and said that he wanted to be painted calmly, on a fiery horse, and insisted on the likeness of his favorite horse but was not concerned about his own likeness. The subject David chose was of *Bonaparte Crossing the Alps at the Saint-Bernard Pass*. The soft tones of the background accentuate our attention on the horse and on Bonaparte.

David was invited to witness the ceremony of the coronation and was asked to paint scenes from the ceremony. The horizontal view of *The Coronation of Napoleon and Josephine* gives clarity to his spacious and balanced composition, and it captures the grandeur of the ceremony. The emperor and empress, the two focal points of the picture, are distanced from each other, so that the viewer's attention moves from one to other. Several days after the coronation, David was named first painter to the emperor.

David worked on *Leonidas at Thermopylae* over two separate periods: one from 1799 to1803 and one from 1813 to 1814. Leonidas was the king of Sparta who, to delay the advance of the Persian army, led three hundred men for the defense of the pass at Thermopylae. David, whose son almost perished during a campaign in 1813, seeing France threatened on every side, chose this subject as a model of civic duty and self-sacrifice. The composition of this picture, the most Greek of all of his works, forms a star so that the viewer's attention focuses successively on each one of the major heroes. With the return of the Bourbons in 1814, David decided not to send any pictures to the salon, and he exhibited *Leonidas at Thermopylae* in his studio.

After his return from the Island of Elba in 1815, Napoleon elevated David to the rank of commander of the Legion d'Honor. After the collapse of the empire in 1816, the chamber enacted a law denying amnesty to the signatories of the Acte Additionnel to the constitution of the empire and gave them one month to leave France. David, one of the signatories, rejecting the favors of the king, who was willing to exempt him from this law, proved the consistency of his beliefs. As allied against France had barred him from living in Italy or Switzerland, he emigrated with his wife to Brussels.

He lived in Brussels until his death in 1825. Saving his art for France, he refused the proposal of the king of Prussia to settle in Berlin to establish a new museum, rejected bids for his work from the king of the Low Countries and the king of Bavaria, and refused to paint a portrait of the duke of Wellington. Louis XVIII made certain gestures, ready to give David permission to return to France, but David rejected a pardon. He wrote to his friend, "I was exiled by a law. I shall return only by a law."

David's *Mars Disarmed by Venus and the Three Graces*, painted between 1822 to 1824, is far from the spirit of *The Oath of the Horatii*. The subject, chosen from Greek mythology, is the love affair between the god of war and the goddess of love. The scene takes place above the mountain of Olympus. The attitudes are graceful, the body of Venus is exquisitely painted, and the colors are translucent.

In 1822 Stendhal wrote, "His misfortunes do not seem to have defeated his strength of character, which in the past enabled him to fight against and triumph over bad taste."

The death of childless Charles II in 1700 ended the rule of the Habsburg family and started the succession of the Bourbon kings in Spain. In 1759 Charles III, a wise man with twenty-four years of experience of reigning in Naples and Sicily, became the king of Spain. He was an intelligent leader who selected men of outstanding qualities, such as Floridablanca, to his government and gave them freedom of action, and during his reign enlightenment ideas gained ground in Spain.

Charles III, who had no training in art, summoned to Spain two famous foreign painters: Tiepolo, the last great representative of a vanishing epoch, whose paintings of great elegance and grace with bright colors were suited to rococo architecture, to paint in the new royal palace, and Mengs, a celebrated German neoclassical painter, who believed that great art was to imitate the antiquity, as the first painter of the chamber to organize the Academy of San Fernando, and to direct the Royal Manufactory of Santa Barbara, responsible for the decoration of the King's palaces. But the arts of these foreign artists were not congenial to the Spanish temperament. Mengs returned to Rome in 1769, Francisco Bayeu succeeded him, and Tiepolo died in Madrid in 1770.

In 1788 Charles IV succeeded his father to the throne of Spain. Unlike his father, he lacked qualities of leadership. Perpetually hunting, he left the affairs of government to the queen, Maria Louisa. Manuel Godoy, a young petty officer, was the lover of the queen; the count of Floridablanca, the prime minister, took it upon himself to acquaint the king with what all Spain knew. For the queen, it was time to test her force. Floridabalanca was dismissed and thrown into prison, and the count of Aranda, an old man with liberal ideas, replaced him.

The French Revolution touched off a panic in the Spanish court. Count Aranda urged the king to prudence. But the ambitious queen, disregarding the delicacy of the situation, pushed aside Aranda under the pretext of old age, and Manuel Godoy, a man with no knowledge of management or of politics, became the prime minister. The execution of Louis XVI aroused all Spain. Godoy did nothing to avoid a losing war. In contact between the two armies, French revolutionary ideas made headway among the Spanish army, and the Spanish commenced to doubt their cause. The war became unpopular, and the treaty of Basle, by the terms of which Spain was forced into alliance with the French Republic, brought peace to Spain.

FRANCISO GOYA (1746–1828)

Beyond any doubt, Goya is one of the most profound painters of all time. He paved the way for the painting of the nineteenth and twentieth centuries. In the immense body of Goya's work, man is always present. His fight against ignorance, superstition, injustice, despotism, and ecclesiastical dominance makes him a man of the Age of Enlightenment. Whereas his art, penetrating into the deepest layers of the human psyche, more to reveal human nature than to criticize it, and giving form to its obscure forces, belongs to romanticism. He was the last great classical painter, but his art laid the groundwork for mpressionism, expressionism, and surrealism. Goya's career and the high points of his art can be divided into three periods:

- Artistic development from 1775 to 1792: His tapestry cartoons were painted during this period.
- Artistic maturity from 1792 to 1819, after an attack of an illness that left him deaf: The frescoes of San Antonio de la Florida, *The Family of Charles IV*, *The Shootings of May* were painted during this period.
- The third period, from 1819 to 1828, after the second attack of his illness. *The Caprices*, *The Disasters of War*, *Black Paintings* and the *Disparates* are creations of this last period.

Goya was born in northern Spain at Fuendetodos, a hamlet of the province of Aragon. His father was a master gilder, and his mother belonged to the petty nobility. After the family moved to Saragossa, Goya began to study at a religious establishment, where learning was limited to reading and writing. Martin Zapater, his classmate, became his long-life confidant, and Goya's letters to Zapater are the only authentic documents of his intimate life.

At the age of fourteen, he started a four-year painting apprenticeship in his hometown. His first teacher in Saragossa, Don Jose Juan Luzan, had spent several years in Italy, where he had acquired a mastery of design and a coloring borrowed from Tiepolo. His teaching consisted of copying from plaster casts and from prints.

A myth of Goya's youth presents him as chief of a band, but the two rival gangs that disturbed the public peace were not organized until long after Goya left Saragossa. Research of documents also invalidates a narrative of his involvement in a night quarrel.

In 1763 he left for Madrid and competed twice for a scholarship, without success. The exact date of his entering Bayeu's studio or how long he stayed there is unknown. He went to Rome at his own expense to study painting. In Italy, he participated in the competition of 1771 at the Academy of Palma. Although his painting received some votes, it was set aside. Goya was a contemporary of David, and despite his study in Italy, his art has no sign of neoclassicism, the prevalent style of Rome at that time, and he never accepted the cult of the "beau ideal" of Greeks.

The old church of Our Lady of the Pillar, in Saragossa, had become too small to accommodate the number of pilgrims. After the celebrated architect Ventura Rodriguez completed the vast building operation that had started at the end of seventeenth century, the painting of the high dome was entrusted to Antonio Gonzales Velasquez; but for the painting of the small choir in 1771, the chapter looked for a more assuming painter among local painters. Goya accepted the price that was offered, and the condition to submit a finished sketch that had to be approved by the Academy of San Fernando. His project was liked so much that the chapter did not ask the approval of the academy. These early paintings are in the baroque style. Ramon Stolz, who restored and studied these frescoes closely detected parallel streaks of red, gray, and green merging optically at a distance, a technique that Goya later used extensively in San Antonio's frescoes.

In 1773 Goya married the sister of Francisco Bayeu, the court painter of Charles III. In 1775, Bayeu obtained for Goya a commission for a set of tapestry cartoons for the royal palace. Charles III, a tapestry lover, had issued orders to the royal manufactory that the themes of tapestries should be scenes of hunting or of Spanish life. Goya's first commission was of a hunting scene, in which Goya conformed himself to the prosaic type of painting required by the academy. But in his cartoons of 1776 of the scenes of Spanish pastimes, Goya showed originality and his lyrical vision, and his palette became warmer and more varied. The nature of the subject matter of these cartoons connected him to a world in which the aristocracy and common people lived side by side. Being a keen observer, while watching the activity of people, he learned from their body movements and their attitude. He was always a fast worker. He painted approximately sixty cartoons from 1775 to 1792, which matured his technique. At this stage, the subjects and warm colors of Goya's paintings express his joy of life. In 1777 he suddenly fell ill, possibly a first warning of his future nightmare, but he recovered quickly.

With the intention of Charles III to make the treasures of the royal collection known to a large public, in 1778 several artists were assigned to the reproduction of the masterpieces of this collection. Goya's task was to make a set of etchings after Velasquez. Access to the royal collection was a great opportunity for him to study Velasquez, Rembrandt, and the Venetian masters. These etchings were more fruitful than all his previous studies in Spain and Italy. Based on his study of Velasquez, he learned to recognize and isolate what was essential in a face. His cartoons of 1786–1788 demonstrate the effect of this study at the royal collection.

In 1779, in order to submit his work, Goya was given an audience with the king. Full of joy, he kissed the hand of Charles III, the hand of the prince, and that of his wife. He wrote to Zapater, "I have kissed their hands. Never have I experienced such happiness."

With the protection of Bayeu and his help in the reception piece for the academy, Goya was elected to the Academy of San Fernando in 1780. Opposed to the aesthetic of the day, and conscious of his own talent, Goya resented being regarded as a Bayeu protégé. He was looking for an opportunity to break free of the supervision of Bayeu, whose frigidity of character was irreconcilably opposed to Goya's temperament. Painting frescoes for the cathedral of El Pilar at Saragossa in 1780 presented him with an opportunity to make a stand against Bayeu.

Bayeu was assigned to painting two vaults in the cathedral of El Pilar. There were other vaults to be painted, but Bayeu had many obligations in Madrid. His suggestion that his brother and Goya carry out the decoration of other vaults under his supervision was approved. Goya's sketches were a success, but trusting his own inspiration of the moment, Goya neglected to prepare a full-size cartoon and began to paint with his usual impetuosity, rendering faces with a few strokes. On the scaffolding, Bayeu, shocked, reproved him for careless and faulty work. Goya told him that seen from the below all would fall into place. There was a stormy scene between the two until the intervention of a monk calmed down Goya. He made changes, but the incident rankled in his mind. Ramon Stolz confirms that the technique of these Goya's frescoes was far in advance of any of his contemporaries. Seven years later, the frescoes of San Antonion proved that Goya was right.

The construction of San Francisco el Grande, a church attached to a Franciscan monastery, was something in which all madrid took interest. Apparently, Ventura Rodriguez, its architect, who knew Goya at the time of his work at Our Lady of the Pillar, called attention to him, and one of the seven altars was assigned to Goya.

His first official portrait was, in 1783, of the count of Floridablanca, the prime minister. Always uneven in his work, Goya painted this portrait with clumsiness. He painted with all light on the count and himself in the shadows, much smaller than the minister. He had high hopes of this picture, but the count did nothing for Goya—a bitter experience that served him in understanding the realities of life.

In 1783, recommended by Rodriguez, he spent a month at Los Arenas de San Pedro to paint portraits of the Infante Don Luis, the king's brother, and his family. He painted fifteen portraits of them.

The infante and his family were very pleased with the portraits, and Goya was flattered to have been close to his highness. He wrote to Zapater, "These princes, they are angels." The patronage of the infante was a turning point in Goya's career, and orders from influential men began to come in.

Painting portraits in 1783 was a new development for his art, and within a few years he became the favorite portrait painter of the Spanish aristocracy. Due to the exigencies of this branch of painting, a rapid improvement in Goya's technique took place, and he developed a technique and style of his own that represent his evolution and herald the portraits of his mature period, the subtlest portraits that West has known.

In 1784 Josefa gave birth to Xavier, the only child to survive of many children that she had brought into the world. Goya, who always loved children, had greeted the birth of each of his children with happiness, and with their deaths had kept silence in his grief.

Gaspar Melchior de Jovellanos, a politician and at the same time a poet and playwright, was a man of vast culture with knowledge of French ideas and above all a Spaniard. Jovellanos, who must have met Goya in a formal session of the academy, called upon Goya for the decoration of four altars in the church of the Calatrava College at Salamanca. That call was the beginning of a lifelong patronage and friendship that along with the friendship of Rodriguez opened the doors of Madrid high society to Goya, and he became in touch with the most enlightened circle of Spain.

The year 1785 was the great turning point of his career. He was elected the assistant director of painting at the academy. He painted the portrait of the duke and the duchess of Osuna, and in 1789 the portrait of *The Family of the Duke of Osuna*. Despite the lack of intimacy of a family portrait, they liked it, and the duchess continued to recommend Goya.

The second series of tapestry cartoons that he painted between 1786 to 1788, enriched by his self-confidence, are full of charm and reflect the realistic tendencies of the eighteenth century. He chose the subject of the four seasons for four of these cartoons. In the *Spring*, a charming and graceful girl offers a rose to a young lord. In the *Winter*, a little company is moving forward, shoulder to shoulder, under harsh weather.

His paintings between 1785 and 1792 reflect his joy of life and his happiness before his dreadful illness. He painted seven anecdotal painting whose freshness of colors is delightful. Among those are *The Swing* and *The Greasy Poles*, and *The Prairie of San Isdro*, a cartoon of the festivals of all social classes mingled together, was created by means of minute brushstrokes, dark touches that balance light tones, and an inverse-triangle composition. This painting, more a tableau than a cartoon, never submitted to the royal manufactory, was purchased by the Osuna family. In a few works of this period related to the life of common people, for the first time a social concern emerged, which foreshadows the etching of his mature period. With the accession of Charles IV to the throne in 1789, Goya was appointed court painter.

Although the year 1792 could be considered the dividing line for Goya's art, he had achieved the perfection of his style before his illness. His portrait of Don Sebastian Martinez inaugurated his "pearl-gray period."

While Goya visited his fried Sebastian Martinez in Cadiz in 1792, a serious illness left him so deaf that without using sign language he could not communicate with people. The deafness, which deeply affected his thinking and his judgments of himself and of people, started a new era in his life and his art. He revolted against orthodox art and all set rules. Goya had always been a rapid and impatient painter, but now his creative flame burst forth in the violent movement of forms and a more personal palette. Incapable of hearing people's words, Goya found that their gestures and facial expressions took on new significance. Imprisoned in his inner self, he listened to himself. All the memories of the past changed to bitter experiences, and the mediocre man who felt honored to kiss the hand of royalty, the painter of the portrait of the Count Floridablanca, passed away.

Back in Madrid he started his real career as the painter of the life of Spanish people. He painted eleven pictures for the Academy of San Fernando, regardless of the rules and opinions of the day. In the cover letter to the director of the academy, he wrote, "To occupy an imagination mortified by the contmplation of my sufferings and to recover, partialy anyhow, ...I fell to painting a set of pictures in which I have succeeded in giving observation a place usually denied it in works made to order, in which little scope is left for fancy and invention."[4] *A Scene from the Inquisition* and *The Madhouse* are possibly part of that group of paintings. In *A Scene from the Inquisition*—the ecclesiastical tribunal to control freedom of thought—high walls separate the tribunal from the outside world, where the sun is shining, but the scene takes place under the heavy atmosphere in a closed space. *The Madhouse* is a tragic depiction of the loneliness of man and the absence of reason; its space, with the vaulted ceiling, high walls, and limited sunlight, have a similarity to *A Scene from the Inquisition* that very possibly was intentional.

In his self-portrait of 1793, he placed himself against the light of a window. This is a portrait of a confident painter, far from the man he painted at the side of Count Foridablanca. The subject matter of his mature period reflects his intellectual view of mankind and its acts. In terms of light and color, his new technique, with its shorter

---

4 - Goya, by Pierre Gassier, Translated by James Emmons, Albert Skira, page 40

and more agitated brushstrokes leaving splashes of color, formed a new dynamic style that presages modern painting.

The portraits represent the advancement of his technique. His expressive brushwork and the refinements of his palette after 1792 attain to astonishing perfection. The delicate range of pearl-gray colors of the magnificent portrait of *Francisco Bayeu* in 1795 is a fine example of the extreme subtlety of his admirable palette. Contrary to the minutely detailed and busy English portraiture, Goya avoids inopportune details, and his unadorned background emphasizes and enhances the overall quality of the portrait.

During this period Goya was the most in-demand portraitist of Spain. He painted portraits of aristocrats in their elegant costumes but took no account of their social standing and refrained from any flattery. As a realist portraitist and a keen observer, he perceived the most characteristic features of face, body, and manner of the model, revealing them as Goya saw them. The portrait of the Countess del Caprio (1792) is the perfect image of the proud, self-imposed restraint of a melancholy Spanish noblewoman; or the stern face of the portrait of Bayeu reveals an upright person oppressed by a narrow mind. But affected always by the love or revulsion of his sitter, his portraits could not be equal. The Countess of Chichon was the daughter of Infante Don Luis, married to Godoy. Goya had painted her as a little girl, while he was staying with the family at Los Arenos de San Pedro. Now, after seventeen years, he was painting the portrait of an innocent noblewoman, who had to live in the corrupted environment around her. He painted the slender woman with fatherly affection. After the death of Bayeu in 1795, the academy elected Goya to succeed him as the director of the School of Painting.

He painted portraits of the duke and duchess of Alba in 1795. The duchess is in a white gown with a mass of black hair. The portrait of the duchess of Alba started a romantic period in Goya's life.

The duchess of Alba, the duchess of Osuna, and the queen were the most famous women of eighteenth-century Spain, and of the three, the duchess of Alba was the most provocative, the most beautiful, woman of the Spanish aristocracy. The duchess's beauty, elegance, and strength of character impressed Goya to the point of falling in love. After the death of her husband in 1796, the duchess retired to her Andalusian estate of Sanlúcar. Goya followed her, stayed several months with her, and painted another full-length portrait of her, this time in black gown, with two rings on her right hand, one bearing the name of Alba, the other Goya, and with her index finger pointing to the name of Goya on the ground close to her feet. The portrait is dated 1797. But the truth of his relationship with the duchess, a woman with liberal upbringing, is unknown. There are no written records of Goya's leaving for Sanlúcar, but he kept an intimate journal of rapid drawings of his sojourn at Sanlúcar. In these drawings, he follows every step of the duchess of Alba, as if by a lover's eye. The notebook of Sanlúcar also contains the first sketches for *The Caprices*.

In 1982 the duchess died under mysterious circumstances. The queen hated the sight of her, and Godoy had accused the duchess of conspiring against him. In 1808 two portraits of the duchess painted by Goya, both in the same reclining position and one of them nude, were found in Godoy's assets. These portraits are known to visitors to the Prado as *La Maja Vestida* and *La Maja Desnuda*. The duchess had a slender figure, while the bodies of the two majas are plump, and the awkward adhesion of the heads to the bodies implies that Goya had recourse to two models. Regardless of who posed for these portraits, *La Maja Desnuda* has attracted the attention of art critics. André Malraux considered *La Maja Desnuda* an erotic portrait without being voluptuous, painted to suggest, not to represent.[5]

---

5 Saturn, Andre Malraux, La Galerie de la Pleiade, 1950, page 68

In 1797 Jovallenos served eight months as the minister of justice. Opposed to the Inquisition, Godoy send him to exile and to prison. With the fall of Jovallenos any hope to shake off the grip of superstition, and the power of Inquisition in Spain came to an end.

In 1799 Goya published eighty-two etchings, each with a caption, under the name *The Caprices*. The preparatory drawings for these etchings show that their quality is comparable to his paintings and had been prepared off and on during previous years. Two days after the publication, apparently under pressure from the Church or his fear of the Inquisition, the album was withdrawn from sale. Etching number forty-three, originally intended as the frontispiece, with the caption of *The Sleep of Reason Produces Monsters*, points to the selection of subject matter for *The Caprices*. Through these etchings, Goya, a devotee of the Enlightenment, depicted the dark side of the human mind. He demonstrated that the sleep of reason opens the door to all kind of irrational human behavior and all idiotic individual and collective vices, weaknesses, and particularly superstitions that make possible the monstrous dominance of ecclesiastical institutions over the mind of man, hand in hand with the government, to keep man in perpetual ignorance. Etching number forty-three divides the album into two sections: almost all the etchings of the first section imply the falsities in human relations, while in the second section, with an accentuated ironic character of the drawings, most of the subjects are related to witches and demons. He started to cover the face of some of his figures with a mask and then replaced the mask with the head of an animal or to give the animals the figure of human beings. No doubt living in the Age of Enlightenment and friendship with the leading Spanish advocates of the Enlightenment affected his thoughts, but surely living in a silent world gave him time for more intellectual thinking. *The Caprices* take us beyond the domain of the Enlightenment and plunge us into the world of irrationality that dominated Spanish life. For the kind of art that Goya had in mind, he chose light, shade, and line as his means of expression. The expressionist drawings of human figures in these etchings foretell the distortions of the San Antonio frescoes. Malraux wrote that Goya's art "has no light but lighting"—as lighting is used in theaters to emphasize a part of the stage. The gloom of these etchings was not a creation of Goya's dreams; it was the reality of social conditions, as well of the mind of Spanish people of the eighteenth century. The interest that we show in these two century-old etchings indicates that *The Caprices* picture the human condition of all civilizations of all times and that there has been no fundamental change in human behavior or the dominance of controlling powers over our lives and minds. The humanistic value that had flattered European society for centuries was an obstacle for the betterment of human character. Goya's *The Caprices* was a great step toward changing this illusion.

The duchess of Osuna commissioned Goya to paint a series of pictures of the type of *The Caprices*. "Witches' Sabbath," with the enormous figure of the goat among the witches, is one of that series. In France, *The Caprices* attracted the attention and admiration of the French romantics.

In 1798, during the brief ministry of Jovellanos, by a royal command, Goya was commissioned to paint the frescoes of the church of San Antonio de la Florida, a small new church in Madrid built in the neoclassical style in the form of a Greek cross. The church of San Antonio de la Florida, which is now converted into an art sanctuary and mausoleum, was originally outside of the city.

The frescoes of San Antonio were an opportunity to give free rein to his imagination, to paint one of the most typical paintings of his style and of his freedom of technique. For the subject matter of the frescoes, Goya chose the tale of the resurrection of a dead by

San Antonio to testify to the innocence of his father. Disregarding the place of the miracle in a court of Portugal, as described by the tale, Goya chose an open space for the scene, with witnesses of all ages and of different social strata of people in the very district of Madrid, where the church is located, gathered around a circular wooden railing resembling the fence of a bull ring. In these frescoes, with the intent to transpose his vision of art into form and color, Goya moved beyond the illustration of a religious legend. He dissociated the art of painting from its subject matter, and his expressionist interpretation of human figures breaks with traditional idealistic art. The diversity of witnesses, chosen for their characters and their human significance, and the extreme differences of their reactions to the miracle—from indifference to rapture—could have impaired the overall unity of the scene, but Goya's unity of execution holds the whole composition together. To produce one of these miracles of art, he disdained the meticulous drawing and smooth brushwork of the neoclassical, the prevailing style of the day. He used his own style based on line, splashes of colors, and feverish and expressive contrasting brushstrokes that link diverse witnesses, with their different reactions to the miracle, to each other.

He inverted the layout of the traditional decorating of church domes. In lieu of a depiction of the heaven, with all the favorite heavenly devices of the Renaissance and the baroque painters, at the summit of the dome, he painted the scene of the miracle up in the cupola and painted charming angels below the cornice.

The portrait of the *Family of Charles IV* and the *Countess of Chinchon* were the culmination of Goya's mastery of the portrait. The suffocating atmosphere of the room, in which the family stands, subtly alludes to the lack freedom in Spain. In spite of splendid attire and dazzling jewelry, *The Familly of Chales IV* (1800) is the most critical portrait ever made of a royal family. The authoritarian figure of the ugly queen, who creats a void around her and dominates the scene, and the dull-witted face king look like actors facing the public. Allegedly the only objection of the king to the portrait was over the turned-away face of the princess, which Goya refused to change. Considering no other objection to the portrait, it has to be assumed that Goya, constant in his style, portrayed them realistically as they looked, and the family was not intelligent enough to realize that Goya's painting is mercilessly suggestive of their stupidity and vulgarity. Goya himself, dimly discernible in the shadows, is looking beyond the group toward the observer.

Despite his dazzling fame and success, when in 1808 he applied for the office of the director general of the Academy of San Fernando, only eight members of the academy voted for him. Other members voted for a rival painter. Regardless of their reasons, it was a vote for mediocrity.

In 1807, following a treaty with Imperial France for the conquest and partition of Portugal, French troops entered Spain to invade Portugal, but on their way occupied Spain's major fortresses. Intrigues of Prince Ferdinand against his father and Godoy furthered Napoleon's intention to give the throne of Spain to his brother. He summoned the king and the prince in Bayonne, compelled both of them to abdicate, and appointed his brother Joseph Napoleon to the rule of Spain.

On May 2, 1808, the people of Madrid, unaware of the decisions of Bayonne, heard the news that the last members of the royal family were leaving the capital. Their pride already hurt by the presence of foreign soldiers in the streets, a disorganized throng rushed into the streets. The French cavalry pushed the mob to the Puerta del Sol. There the appearance of the French platoon of Mamelukes, whose oriental costumes reminded the Spaniards of the Moors, provoked an angry response. Armed with daggers, they attacked the Mamelukes, and the combat lasted the whole day. The fusillade of the night of May 3 put an end to the revolt in the streets of Madrid.

An uprising against the occupation broke through in Spain. In 1810 Cortez of Cadiz, a revolutionary body dominated by liberals, was assembled, and in 1812 a constitutional monarchy, inspired by the constitution of revolutionary France, was declared. The fight between the revolutionaries and the French army took the shape of outbidding in ferocity. An insurrection of the people of Saragossa led to the siege of the city. After several unsuccessful assaults, when they made their way into the city, they faced a frenzied defense. Needing all French troops, Joseph Bonaparte ordered them to abandon Saragossa and retire. A message was sent to Goya that the glory of Saragossa had to be immortalized through paintings. The ravages and atrocities inflicted by war that Goya saw on his journey to Saragossa were so nightmarish that he could never release himself of the horrors he had witnessed.

Goya's early paintings had a polished view of the working class of Spain. In his mature period, when he had discarded the false aspects of his works, his *The Water Carrier* and *The Knife Grinder* bear witness to the reality of working people's hard lives. *The Pest- House*, painted in 1810, is one of his masterpieces. The light through a window, which hardly penetrates the heavy and gloomy atmosphere of the space, throws a dim light upon the isolated and sad world of the diseased figures.

During the siege of Madrid from 1811 to 1812, famine ravaged the city, and more than twenty thousand people perished from starvation. Goya and his family survived the year of famine, but in 1812 his wife died, and he became alone.

Goya had retained his position of court painter during the reign of Joseph Bonaparte, but in his solitude, he began drawings of what he had witnessed of the violent and tragic events of war and its ravages. *The Disasters of War* are eight-two aquatint etchings, each followed by a caption, drawn between 1810 and 1820. The etchings are depictions of the atrocities of war and its absurdity, not a glorification of national struggle. These scenes of rapes, executions, and burnings that are evocative of thousands of years of human atrocities to each other and their indifference to the misery or death of other human being, reveals the brutal nature of human beings. Compositions are reduced to essentials, with broad plane of light and dark, and their powerful design strengthens his message. The collection, executed in secret, was not to be known to the general public during Goya's life. The academy published it in 1865. The eighty-two plates of the set are divided into three groups. The first group depicts brutalities committed during a war, such as torture and mutilation of captives by the French army or Spanish resistance groups, and scenes of assault and rape of Spanish women. In the early plates, Goya, a patriot man, sympathizes with the Spanish resistance, but he later rejects any heroic dignity and blames any brutality. The second group depicts scenes of death from starvation during the Madrid siege. The last group expresses his disappointment at seeing the encouragement of the clergy by Ferdinand VII. An etching of a preaching priest with a parrot head is a return to the subject matter of *The Caprices*.

At the end of war, in 1814, before Ferdinand VII returned to Spain, Goya, afraid of the precariousness of the victory of the Spanish people, decided to commemorate the uprising of 1808 against the French army, and he painted two pictures: *The Charge of Mamelukes* and *The Shooting of May Third*. These are the first paintings in the history of art that depict contemporary historic events. *The Charge of Mamelukes* depicts the ferocity of man, who kills to survive. For the location of his *The Shooting of May Third*, he chose a hill outside of Madrid and a lantern for the source of light. The French firing squad, seen only from their backs, stand shoulder to shoulder, forming a massive unity of bodies compacted to each other, and their repetitious line of rifles contrasts with the muddled and distressed Spaniards in front of them, while another groups of Spaniards, one covering his eyes, and others with terror on their faces, are walking to the execution area. In the group facing the soldiers, a man in a white shirt kneels amid an already executed group, his eyes wide open in terror, staring toward the rifles with flung-up arms. He becomes the focal point of interest in the picture. A wound on the palm of his hand is reminiscent of the wounds of Christ. In this masterpiece, without any theatrical or anecdotal aspects in the composition, Goya combines realism with expressionism. Goya's agitated brushwork and splashes of colors intensify the effect of the brutality of the subject matter of both pictures. These two masterpieces exalt the heroism of the Spanish people against the French aggression, while *The Disasters of War* are his intellectual reaction to the irrational brutality of man.

Spain was already a century behind other European countries. Ferdinand VII, his restoration to the throne of Spain a step backward, initiated a ruthless persecution of the Spaniards who had served the government of Joseph Bonaparte. Goya, as the court painter, was included in this group, but for the commission appointed to examine every individual case it was hard to condemn the painter of the uprising of *The Charge of Mamelukes* and *The Shooting of May Third.*

Bullfighting, known as tauromaquia, had always been one of Goya's old favorite themes. In 1815, he began a collection of drawings for *The Tauromaquia.* In these drawings, full of light and movement, he breaks up movement into successive phases. From 1817 he lived withdrawn from the world. In 1819 lithography was introduced to Spain. This new technique, more direct than etching, attracted the inquiring mind of the old Goya. He made twenty-three litho-graphs: ten in Spain and thirteen in France.

In February of 1819, he purchased the *Quinta del Sordo* ("House of the Deaf Man"). The dates of his moving to the house and the start of the painting of fourteen frescoes on the walls of its rooms are unknown. In this house, a distant relative, Dona Leocadia (bring-ing her two children) joined him as half mistress, half housekeeper. The presence of Leocadia's little daughter, Maria del Rosario, whom Goya loved with fatherly tenderness, was comforting for him.

One of the amazing features of Goya's works is their simulta-neous diversity. He painted two pictures for the Escuelas Pias de San Anton, whose mystic longings and religious emotion are absent in Goya's previous works. In the *Last Communion of Saint Joseph of Calasance*, one of his masterpieces, the ecstatic face of the saint is bathed in light, and his clasped hands produce a religious effect ab-sent in Goya's work. At the end of 1819, Goya had another attack of his illness, but as soon as he recovered, he started working.

The nationwide revolt of 1820 compelled Ferdinand VII to re-store the constitution. Goya made his last appearance at the acad-emy to swear allegiance to the constitution. Two major works belong to the next three years: the wall paintings of the *Quinta del Sordo* and the *Disparates* etchings.

As the frescoes of the *Quinta del Sordo*, which are the culmina-tion of Goya's mural work, were neither a commissioned work nor for public view—at least during his lifetime—he gave free rein to his imagination and his style, covering the walls of his residence with horrifying pictures. Questions arise about his purpose or even the sanity of his mind. Did he intend to leave a message through fres-coes, a more powerful medium and with wider scale than etching, for posterity? As to the sanity of his mind, these gloomy pictures are not far from modern thoughts. These wall paintings, called *Black*

Paintings, were transferred to canvas and are displayed at the Prado Museum.

The *Black Paintings* are painted with a diminished palette, expressing the chagrin of a disillusioned old man who used his art for the purification and advancement of the human mind. Some of them are extensions from the themes of the *Caprices*. The *Meadow of San Isidro*, painted thirty years earlier, was the depiction of a day full of the joy of life, while the *Black Painting* of the *Pilgrimage to San Isidro* depicts a group of intoxicated pilgrims of various social strata of Spain, with faces devoid of human intelligence. The scene of the *Gathering of the Witches* reflects the grip of superstition over the mind of man. The *Fight of Two Men* with each other while they are trapped in a quagmire is possibly an allusion to Spanish society under the despotism of Ferdinand VII. *The Dog*, having no caption and no name, has left the door open to interpretation. *Saturn Devouring His Son*, which illustrates the Greek myth, the most horrific of all the *Black Paintings*, comes from the depths of the fears of men. The bold brushwork with splashes of color of the *Black Paintings* is similar to Goya's frescoes of San Antonio. Despite the limited range of dark colors in most of the pictures, which reminds one of colors of a few figures of the frescoes of the church, their expressive powers are unequaled.

Goya's enigmatic works of the *Disparates* (meaning nonsenses or stupidities), are a series of expressionist etchings of nightmarish visions of the problems of human existence. The academy published them in 1864 under the name *Proverbs*. Despite the apparent incoherence of subjects with each other, the unity of the series derives from the profound links between different problems that enchain human life.

Liberalism that Ferdinand VII had reluctantly accepted was short-lived. In 1823, with the blessing of the Congress of Vienna,

French army restored absolutism in Spain. With the rule of Ferdinand VII, as an absolute monarch, terror of a despotic regime raged over Spain. The man who was flattered to kiss the hands of royalty could no more accept the despotic government. In 1823, Goya gave the *Quinta del Sordo* as a present to his grandson Mariano. Dona Leocadia, whose son was on the blacklist as a liberal, fled with her son and daughter to Bordeaux. Goya, as the court painter, had to ask for permission to leave Spain. It seems that he justified his leaving under the pretext of taking the waters at Plombieres. In 1824, he crossed the frontier and went to Bordeaux. In Bordeaux, he decided to go to Paris. Gericault's *Raft of the Medusa* and Delacroix's *Massacre of Chios* dominated the Salon of 1824. Their spirit was close to him, but his technique and his coloring outdistanced the young romantics. Back from Paris, he lived again with Dona Leocadia and the little Rosario, who was now ten years old, near his liberal Spanish friends.

The portrait of *Milkmaid of Bordeaux*, a charming young figure with a faraway look, painted with luminous colors, was his last homage to women, and the portrait of his friend Don Jose de Molina, built up of light and shade, was his last painting. He died on April 1828 and was buried in the family tomb of a friend. In 1888 Spain remembered her illustrious son. The tomb was opened, the bodies of Goya and his friend were laid side by side. The bones of the two men were mixed, but the skull of Goya was missing. The men in charge, having no instructions, closed the tomb. In 1899 the bones of Goya, mixed with his friend, were brought back to Spain and buried under the dome of San Antonio de la Florida.

Goya, who had no other master than his observations of the art of great painters, toward the end of life said that his only masters were nature, Velasquez, and Rembrandt. A revolutionary in political inclination and in his art, not only because of the power of its contents but also by the potential of its pictorial values and the quality of its brushwork and colors, his work is one of the apexes of the art of painting. His execution, radically diverged from the lines of eighteenth century art, dissociated the subject from the actual painting and proclaimed a painting with its own proper law. His achievements profoundly affected painting movements from romanticism and realism to impressionism in the nineteenth century, to expressionism and surrealism in the twentieth century. Goya considering fidelity to model an absurdity, and his rejection of the humanistic ideals of the Renaissance, which had sublimed man above the human conditions, was a turning point for the painting of the West.

Section 6

Romanticism

Simultaneous with the neoclassical movement, a romantic movement in search of a more primitive attitude of mind reacted against the refinement of the elegant art of France.

The word *romantic* derives from the literature and language of Romance, a mixture of Latin and native languages spoken in the old Roman provinces of Southern Europe. Romance languages became the vehicle for medieval tales based on legend, chivalry, loyalty, love, adventure, and a fascination with mystery. Gradually, particular qualities of these tales were attached to the word *romance*. The growing middle class of the eighteenth century, rediscovering medieval tales, found in them reinforcement of their own attitudes of mind against the intellectual Enlightenment.

The romantic spirit first manifested in the works of English writers and poets in 1750. Development of romantic ideas that took place in England, Germany, and Scandinavia found in romanticism the appropriate mode to express confused forces that had been repressed after the Middle Ages. In Germany, *Sturm und Drang* ("Storm and Stress") a proto-romantic movement in literature and music influenced by the works of English poets and the thoughts of J. J. Rousseau, was characterized by individual sensibility, high emotionalism, and rejection of the rationalism of the Enlightenment. Its principal representatives were Schiller and Goethe in literature and Wagner in music.

Individualism, a salient feature of the romantic spirit that had a profound effort on the arts, released artists from the boundaries of the standards set by the whole corpus of the Renaissance and academism traditions. Consequently, the imaginative, the inner emotions, and the irrational replaced logic. Romantic painters, discovering the appeal of color to our senses, chose coloristic effects to express their emotions, and for their compositions, they reverted to assymetry and diagonal recession in depth. The demonic and macabre subjects of Fuseli, a Swiss man who settled in England, emphasize the mysterious dark side and irrational aspects of the human mind, while the serene works of Blake, the English poet and painter, contrast Fuseli's tormented paintings.

Believing that nature is full of a spirituality of its own and that it had to be contemplated with devotion, romanticism lifted landscape painting to the level of first importance.

Part 3

The Nineteenth Century

The history of the nineteenth century does not reflect a political and cultural unity. Political and social transformations that the French Revolution had started continued with much force. Stimulated by the sentiment of independence and individualism, a chain of revolutions in all aspects of experience, punctuated by counterrevolutions, liberated man from the confinements of traditions. The modern era that began with the French Revolution at the second half of the eighteenth century took shape in the course of nineteenth century.

In France, as a reaction to the French Revolution, in 1814 the reign was restored to the Bourbons. In 1830 the rising bourgeoisie instigated a revolt against the absolutism of the Bourbon Restoration. Charles X was deposed, and Louis-Philippe became king of France. The Revolution of 1848 led to the abduction of Louis-Philippe, although the revolution was followed by a quick restoration. But as the Revolution of 1848 was a consequence of new conditions of life and of people, its effects went far and spread through the whole of Europe. The Second Republic was proclaimed, and Napoleon III was elected president. An ambitious man, he assumed the imperial title and waged war against Prussia. After his defeat in the

Amir Reza

Franco-Prussian War, the Third Republic was proclaimed. The period of peace that followed the Franco-Prussian War brought economic prosperity and cultural activities to Europe. In retrospective to the horrors of World War I, the period between 1871 to the outbreak of World War I in 1914 is called "La Belle Époque."

For the man of the nineteenth century, living in a world characterized by change and lacking the cohesiveness of past cultures, all values became open to question. Individualism led to the consciousness of man of his loneliness and a refusal to follow traditions set by collective experiences. The individual experience became the basis for a search for new forms in all aspects of culture and civilization of the West.

For the arts, these changes meant liberation from the supervision of the Church and the state. But the rising bourgeoisie that had replaced the aristocratic class, lacking proper aesthetic judgment, held fast to the pale shadow of an art stranger to their own values. Despite this problematic environment for avant-garde artists, who had started a continuing debate over the nature of art, a succession of new theories and new movements appeared in the nineteenth century. By the middle of the century, the dominant presence of subject matter gave way to artistic matters: form, color, and brushstrokes came to be regarded as means of judgment of a painting.

Baudelaire, the first to advance the concept of modern life, declared, "Modernity is the transient, the fugitive...There had been a modernity for each former painter." At the second half of the nineteenth century, along with changes in the structure of European societies, all sorts of public entertainment—opera, theaters, concerts, cabarets, music halls, cafés and bars, shadow-theater plays, and the circus—became aspects of modern life in Paris and subjects for painters, who followed the concept that art should mirror contemporary life. To explore possibilities of line and color, these painters began to break with tradition. As a result of their varied approach to the art of painting, the art of Paris became multifaceted.

Now that the revolution had given it an increase of political and cultural prestige, France became the principal center for artistic activity in Europe, and a great number of highly creative artists of various nationalities made it a practice to participate in the artistic activity of Paris.

Changes in the structure of European society, the invention of the camera, and new concepts of art prompted a new type of portraiture aimed at exploring character instead of the sociopolitical position of the sitter. Mass-produced printmaking and poster art attracted young painters at the end of century.

Realism, a response to liberal values following the Revolution of 1848, and the revolutionary concept of impressionism to capture nature of light, were followed by symbolism, whose roots go back to Baudelaire. Stephane Mallarmé, whose poetic goal was "to describe not the thing itself but the effect it reproduces" influenced symbolist painters to use the emotive power and abstract language of color and line to explore the irrational world.

In the second half of the nineteenth century, the achievements of three genius painters with mighty individuality produced three different concepts of painting that influenced the course of the development of painting in the twentieth century. The art of Cezanne, Van Gogh, and Gauguin took form outside of the academy's approval and public taste and was a response to the exigencies of their intellectual and spiritual demands, not to seek a profession.

- Cezanne did not produce a school of painting, but isolated elements of his intellectual vision of the world, such as his research into fundamental forms of space and volume, became the foundation of new movements.

- Van Gogh, by way of his intense colors and expressive movement of forms, influenced fauvism and expressionism.
- Gauguin's intellectual concept of art, his synthesis of subject and idea, showed the way to represent a profound and mysterious sense of the world through images.

Section 1

Jean-Auguste-Dominique Ingres (1780–1867)

I ngres was born to a humble family in Motauban, a minor city near Toulouse. His father, an architect, painter, and sculptor, provided his son instruction in painting and sculpture. In 1891 Ingres enrolled in the Académie Royale de Peinture of Toulouse. In 1797, after the end of his formal training in Toulouse, he set out for Paris and entered David's studio. David, as a great enemy of the academy, while making corrections on the drawings of his students, used to comment on his views of art. Students also discussed with each other, but Ingres witnessed the discussions without participation. While following David's training, forms of archaic civilizations attracted him. After two years of study under tutelage of David, he enrolled at the École des Beaux-Arts.

In 1801, he submitted *Achilles Greets the Ambassador of Agamemnon*, a classical piece for the Prix de Rome. He won the Grand Prix de Rome, but because of the disarray of state finances, his study at Rome was postponed, and he had to wait in Paris until 1806.

Ingres painted only three purely classical pictures. The rest are classical in content but not in style. For David line determined the contour of his model, while for Ingres, whose approach to art was intellectual creation, line translated a natural reality. Flaxman's purely linear outline style appealed to Ingres, but Ingres's line had a power that conveyed relief.

In the Salon of 1806, Ingres exhibited two of the three portraits of the Riviere family. The linear character of the portrait of *Madame Riviere* are an application of his study of Greek vases. The complex arrangement of curves and the adaptation of the body of the sitter to these curves are the earliest example of anatomical anomalies of his mature works.

In 1806 Ingres painted *Napoleon I on His Imperial Throne*. As he had not attended the coronation ceremony, he based his portrait on David's *Napoleon I in His Imperial Robes*. The overly autocratic pose of Napoleon and the unbounded attention to detail of the picture, exhibited at the Salon of 1806, faced the indignity of critics.

When he left for Italy, he had already created a personal aesthetic that foretold romanticism and pre-Raphaelism. In those years, any work of art made earlier than Raphael's mature works was considered primitive. The critics reproached Ingres that for inspiration he was appealing to the immobile format of medieval portraits and to the clarity of detail of the Flemish masters of the fifteenth century. Later Baudelaire judged him as a "revolutionary in his own way."[6]

Each year, boarders in the Academy of Rome were required to send an imaginative work to Paris." The flattening effect of interior modeling of *Oedipus and the Sphinx*, painted for his initial envoi in 1808, was closer to the spirit of Flaxman than to David. His fourth envoi was *Jupiter and Thetis* (1811), in which the massive and masculine body of Jupiter contrasts with the sinuous forms of the long body, elongated boneless arms, and long neck of Thetis. The academicians of Paris, not approving the peculiarities of Ingres's works, rejected the application to extend his boarding at Rome.

---

6 Ingres et Ingrisme, Albin Michel, 1950, page 33

During his boardering in Rome, he painted portraits of Granet, an ex-student of David, and of Madame Devaucay. The portrait of Garnet is composed of the pyramid of Garnet's body against the vertical and horizontal lines of the background building. The stormy sky of the painting defines the character of the sitter. For the portrait of Madame Devaucay, he used a different procedure than for Garnet. Through linear stylization and subtle distortions, a characteristic of his design for female figures, he expresses the complex psyche of Madame Devaucay. Her attitude and enigmatic smile have been likened to Mona Lisa.

With the expiration of his pensionnat, to be able to remain in Italy, he began to paint commissioned portraits of the growing community of French expatriates. These portraits bear witness to his tendency to grasp the essential psychic and moral character of the sitter. Of his dozen portraits painted between 1810 to 1814, the admirable portrait of Madame de Senonnes is one of his best. The sitter has an attitude of abandon over the cushions of a divan. The harmony of shawl, cushions, soft fabrics, and the pleats of her dress, along with the pose of the sitter, is the essential element of this picture. Lack of modeling of the figure emphasizes the purity of contours.

Besides the desire to perfect his art in Italy, the receptivity of the French administration in Rome, in contrast to the hostility of Paris, was a deciding factor for Ingres's decision not to go back to Paris. From 1809 to 1814, Rome became the second capital of the Napoleonic Empire. General Miollis, the governor of Rome considering Ingres, who had gained the esteem of the French administration of Rome as the painter of the French colony, commissioned him to decorate the bedroom of his private residence and was instrumental in commissioning Ingres for two monumental decorations for Quirinal Palace.

In the life classes of the École des Beaux-Arts in Paris and in the French Academy in Rome, the male nude model was preferred to the female nude. As the graceful forms of a woman's body are better suited to distort and adapt to an abstract linear style, Ingres always preferred nude women for his paintings.

Caroline Murat, the queen of Naples, ordered the celebrated *Grande Odalisque*. In this almost unmodeled, boneless body, which is the culmination of Ingres's deformations and rhythmic patterns, only the line is essential. The careful composition of this picture bears witness to Ingres's marvelous sense of construction. The curtain on the right balances the head and the rise of the upper torso of the figure, and the accessories create an oriental atmosphere. Critics accustomed to the anatomy of figures and unable to understand the intellectual creation of Ingres and his intention that anatomy should not disturb the form of his odalisque, criticized the lack of bone and muscle in the body of the woman.

Prior to his departure for Rome, Ingres had become engaged to Julie Forestier. The long separation led to a cooling of the relationship and cancellation of the engagement. In December of 1813, he married Madelaine Chapelle. The following year, the fall of the Napoleonic Empire prompted the evacuation of Rome by its imperial representatives. That was the worst timing for the newlywed couple. Deprived of his financial supporters, Ingres relied on commissions for portrait drawings of tourists and allied nations. To these portraits of unknown sitters, he gave the clarity of a charming design. The French royalist, replacing imperial representatives, demanded narrative historical subjects, which Ingres preferred to portraits. To adopt the style of the historical subjects to that of the period in which the subject took place, his style became eclectic for these pictures.

In 1820, when he was dreaming of returning to Paris, his friend, the Italian sculpture Bartolini, encouraged him to go to Florence.

For a while, he lived with Bartolini, and then he established his own residence and studio. Life in Florence was more difficult than he expected. The commissions he received were numbers of portraits and a historical genre picture. He stayed in Florence until his return to Paris in 1824.

In 1820, he received the commission for the painting of *The Vow of Louis XIII*. From the very beginning regarding this picture as an opportunity of salvaging his languishing career, he abandoned his anatomical distortions, and painted a picture derived not from the Quattrocento[7], but from the mature Raphael. With this picture, he returned to Paris.

His picture was exhibited in the same salon that was exhibiting Delacroix's *Massacres of Scio*. After a long absence and often harsh critics, Ingres received a welcome reception. He was regarded as a restorer of the classical tradition. At the closing ceremonies of the salon, Ingres received the ribbon of the Legion d'Honneur from the king, and a few months later, a seat in the Académie des Beaux-Arts.

He opened a teaching atelier in 1825. His students defined him as wrapped in the doctrine that he had elaborated in Italy, intolerant in discussion, but without contradiction. Commissions followed the success at the salon. As he had painted historical subjects in Italy, he was invited to decorate one of the newly expanded rooms of the Louvre containing antique vases of Egyptian and Greco-Roman collections. The subject assigned to Ingres was the *Apotheosis of Homer*. Ingres saw the decoration as an opportunity to manifest the supremacy of line to color. He selected *The Parnassus* of Raphael as a source of inspiration, but Ingres's painting lacked the grace and harmony of Raphael's, and critics found the picture lifeless.

---

7   Quatrocento was a Fifteen century cultural and artistic movement in Italy. The term is used for early Renaissance art.

The reactionary policies of Charles X led to street fighting in 1830 and the overthrow of his regime. Louis-Philippe d'Orlean, the liberal cousin of Charles X, was elected the king of France. His reign, called the July Monarchy, was a period of dominance by the wealthy bourgeoisie.

Ingres was always sensible to human contact, so his portraits are among his best works. Louis-Francois Bertin was a celebrated newspaperman and a defender of the July Monarchy. Ingres's portrait of Monsieur Bertin casually sitting in his chair with spread legs, his expressive hands on his knees, and with a challenging, direct look, resumed the spirit of the dominant bourgeoisie of the period. Ingres's portraits reveal a fidelity to nature that made him a forerunner of naturalism.

Ingres's religious painting of *The Martyrdom of Saint Symphorien* for the cathedral of Auyun, exhibited in the Salon of 1834, created a polarized reaction. As always, the critical reaction had less to do with the aesthetic qualities of the picture than with personal and political opinion. Within weeks of the opening of the salon, Ingres announced his retirement from public life, and until the end of his life he abstained from participating in the salon. He solicited and was appointed to the post of director of the French Academy of Rome.

Preoccupied by the management of the Academy of Rome, from 1835 to 1841, he painted few major pictures. A major work of this period was *La Stratonice*, commissioned by the duke of Orleans. The story of Antiochus and Stratonice had already been the subject of one David's canvases. Antiochus, the Seleucid prince, heartsick over his love for Stratonice, his father's second wife, resolved to die rather than to reveal his love was taken to his bed. The increased palpitation of Antiochus's heart with the entrance of the queen revealed his secret to the physician. In this picture, Ingres used the movements of Stratonice's hand and head, Antiochus's arm, and the physician's right hand as means of expression. With Ingres's persistent refusal to participate in the salon, the picture was exhibited to a limited number of invited guests in the apartments of the duke of Orleans. Critics announced the picture as one of the greatest achievements of modern art.

Ingres considered line the essence of painting and nude women the most appropriate for giving shape to expressive lines. In *Odalisque with a Slave* (1840), another of the major works of this period, painted with a different concept than *The Grande Odalisque*, the line acquires a life of its own. Interestingly, critics were still unable to understand the originality of Ingres's sinuous lines.

With the expiration of his directorate of the academy in 1840, Ingres returned to France. In Paris, he chose a semipublic exhibition for his work. In 1846 an association of artists organized an exhibition of paintings, as a survey of modern French painting since the mid-eighteenth century. In this exhibition Ingres was represented by eleven paintings. For the first time, critics were confronted with an array of Ingres's works side by side. They already had knowledge of Ingres's anatomical distortions, but to discover obvious flaws and errors by a master designer who was strongly identified as an adherent of classical tradition, was beyond their imaginations. The critics had to recognize these intentional flaws as an integral component of Ingres's art. The display of his most celebrated portraits, mostly of beautiful and rich women in this exhibition, increased the appreciation of his capabilities as a portraitist.

The Universal Exposition of 1855 also included international contemporary art. Ingres was requested to end his boycott of official exhibitions. He accepted and agreed to participate under the condition that he be given a separate gallery. By 1855, romanticism had ceded place to realism, an art responsive to social problems and involved in politics. With no concern about promoting social, religious, or political causes, and affiliated with the *l'art pour l'art* aesthetic[8], Ingres's art was exhibited in the same exposition with the realists, provoking the old polarized reactions.

A few days after catching a chill, Ingres died in 1867. His love for the abstract value of line and his inventiveness within the realm of the female nude influenced the avant-garde painters of the modern period. He was admired by Renoir, Seurat, Gauguin, Matisse, and Picasso

---

8 L'art pour l'art is a 19th century concept, that art is created for its own sake with no need to consider moral, or social purposes.

Section 2

JOHN CONSTABLE (1776–1837)

Constable was born in East Bergholt, a valley on the border of Suffolk and Essex. His father was a successful country merchant. As a boy John was introduced to Sir George Beaumont, who showed him a landscape by Claude Lorrain in his collection. The boy, who was meant to enter his father's business, was so impressed by the picture that he decided to pursue the career of an art painter. Persuaded to let him to pursue his wish, in 1799, his father gave his son the permission and a small allowance to go to London to study painting at the Royal Academy School. At the time art classes stressed history painting, but Constable's interest was in landscape. To have a good grasp of the art of landscape painting, besides taking classes, he studied and copied landscape paintings of the masters. In 1802, to continue his study of landscape, he refused a post as drawing master at a military academy.

Constable, who became the first naturalist landscape painter, passionately loved the beauty of nature. Deeply attached to the scenes of his boyhood, he painted them with more emotion than his other works. As reader of poetry, Wordsworth's belief that nature has a spirituality of its own appealed to him. Through close observation of nature, his landscapes represent the Wordsworthian romantic worship of nature.

From 1803 he exhibited landscapes at the Royal Academy. As he was unsuccessful in selling his landscapes, his parents urged him to try another branch of painting. Despite his dislike, he turned to portraiture, but the problem of earning money was persistent. In 1809 he met Maria Bicknell, a girl he had known as a child. He fell deeply in love with her, but considering John not good enough for Maria, her family prevented their marriage. The inheritance that he received upon the death of his parents, within a year of each other, meant financial independence—and marriage with Maria in 1816.

In classical landscapes, dominance of a single idea prevents disturbance of distracting details, observed by landscape painter. Constable, a naturalist painter faced with the infinite variety of nature, recognized the importance of subordination of the variety of nature to a dominating factor. To solve this problem, he used his oil sketches to record his first sensation of the subject in terms of a drama of light and shade.

After his marriage, he began to paint large pictures from Stour Valley. To turn his first sensation captured by his oil sketches into large finished pictures, he began with detailed drawings from nature and a large oil sketch to study the effect of local color and tonal relations. To paint the final picture, he used stormy strokes of the palette knife. *The White Horse*, his first large picture shown at the Royal Academy, was well received by the public and by critics. A few month later, he was elected an associate of the Royal Academy.

In 1821, he painted *The Hay Wain*. After seeing the picture at the academy, amazed at the beauty of Constable's work, Gericault arranged for this picture to be sent to the Salon of 1824, where it won a gold medal awarded by the king. After seeing *The Hay Wain*,

Delacroix repainted the background of his *Massacre of Scios*. The landscape also became a source of inspiration for the landscape painters of the Barbizon, who shared Constable's love of nature.

In contrast to the considerable admiration of his art in France, in England his art was not much appreciated. At that time, British art was moving toward pre-Raphaelism, away from Constable's opinion that painting should be scientific as well as poetic.

In 1819 Maria exhibited signs of tuberculosis. The family moved to a suburb of Hampstead where she could have fresh air. There, Constable focused on the study of the changeable quality of clouds. The storm blowing up in the sky of his *The Leaping Horse*, a masterpiece painted in 1825, is a sign of his anxiety. His wife died in 1829. He never married again and took care of his seven children. In 1829 he was made a royal academician.

In his stays in Salisbury with the Bishop of Salisbury, an old friend of the family, he painted three magnificent Salisbury landscapes. He believed *Salisbury Cathedral from the Meadows*, the last of the three pictures painted in 1831, to be his masterpiece, and he went on retouching it for years.

After the death of Maria, his paintings show signs of melancholy. A year before his death, he expressed his deep melancholy in *The Cenotaph* and *Stonehenge*. Despite the rainbows of *Stonehenge*, a symbol of hope, the stones standing on a remote barren land denote his mood at the end of life.

The first to discover the art of naturalism, Constable emphasized a scientific approach to the study of nature. Solidity of the construction, balance of composition, emotional content, and intensity of poetic response to the scenery are characteristics of Constable landscapes. His ability to keep his agitated brushstrokes and palette knife under control gave unity of effect to his pictures. To convey the freshness of nature, he bathed his landscapes in an atmosphere fresh with dew or rain, moved by a breeze. He used tiny dabs of pure white scattered over the picture to create a sparkling shimmer of light across the surface of the canvas. To indicate the difference in the texture of wood versus foliage, he made the pigmentation of leaves thinner. His studies of the sky under various weather conditions indicate the importance he attached to the skies of his landscapes. He said the best lesson on art he ever had was this: "Remember, light and shadow never stay still."

J. M. W. TURNER (1773–1851)

Born in London, Turner was the son of a barber. As a youth, he spent much of his time among the ships of the harbor. At the age of fourteen, he studied painting with Thomas Malton, followed by the study of painting at the Royal Academy Schools from 1789 to 1793. In 1790 critics praised his watercolor exhibited at the academy.

In 1795 he traveled widely, sketching the landscapes of England and Wales. Collectors and engravers were buyers of these drawings. In 1796 he sent ten watercolors and his first oil painting to the annual exhibition of the Royal Academy. Despite signs of inexperience, the paintings received positive comments. The Royal Academy was limited to forty members, governed by an elected council of eight. Turner was elected as an associate of the academy in 1799, as a full member in 1802, and as a member of the council in 1803. Then he was elected as professor of perspective at the academy in 1807. In 1804, following a power struggle between members of the academy, he withdrew for some time from the academy's activities and established his own gallery.

In 1799 he was impressed by Claude Lorrain's *Sacrifice to Apollo*, displayed in the house of a collector, but he had no real sympathy for the classical style. Witnessing an actual thunderstorm inspired him for the storm of *The Fifth Plague of Egypt* (1800).

The signature of the Peace of Amiens between England and France in 1802 gave Turner the opportunity to go to Paris to study old masters in the Louvre. After a brief stop in Paris, he went to see the Swiss Alps. In front of the majestic Alps, he perceived that traditional landscape compositions were not capable of conveying the power of nature and that new means of expression were needed. Back in Paris he studied and made sketches from the old masters in the Louvre. His notes show that Titian and Veronese were his favorite painters. For some years to come, engaged in an imaginary challenge, he tried to surpass the old masters of landscape painting by means of exaggeration. Meanwhile, he began to paint pictures of the sea in its every mood, which became his favorite subject.

Over the course of years, Turner's style continued to change. In the early landscapes, he balanced descriptive realism with poetic imagination. In his middle period that pessimism turned him toward catastrophe in nature, and forms in the middle distance are dissolved into the mist. In his great and original later works, that misty atmosphere absorbs the foreground and middle ground, and he moved toward abstraction. His sketches testify that distorted visual impressions were arbitrary, and despite distortion he gave the illusion of truth. Although Turner abstained from exhibiting his most original works whose move toward abstraction was beyond the comprehension of his time, critics were unable to understand the pictorial concept of even his relatively conservative works or to see that the intentional lack of precision in the foreground was to give unity to the picture.

Both Constable and Turner were influenced by English poetry. Turner's early works were in the vein of Wordsworth. But the stupendous effects of his later works in search of the sublime resemble Shelley's poems. As his continuous search for the sublime in nature was not understood by critics, from 1803 on, he faced some hostile criticism inside and outside of the academy, that he has departed from standard imitations of nature.

Persistent criticism by Sir George Beaumont, one of the benefactors of the British National Gallery, caused a decline in sales of Turner's pictures, and consequently Turner had to live in the most modest manner. His father, who was living with Turner and was taking care of all domestic affairs, had to keep an eye on expenses. Sir Beaumont's attacks brought Ruskin to Turner's defense, and despite their difference in age they became friends.

Despite the opinion of that time that watercolor was not a medium for serious painting, Turner had a predilection for watercolor. From experiments in this medium, he had learned that washes over white convey a luminosity that is wanting in traditional oil painting. As the object of Beaumont's attack was Turner's oil painting, he moved toward watercolor, which became a source of income for him. Another source of income for him were his drawings. Turner was an excellent draftsman and his pencil drawings were ideal for printmakers. It was a preoccupation with color that had moved him away from line.

Turner's quest to convey the force of the elements and their constant movements had to ignore traditional composition, which was based on verticals, horizontals, and diagonals. In *Hannibal Crossing the Alps* (1812), the vortex of cloud and mist is composed of intersecting arcs. The composition of *The Shipwreck*, exposed at his gallery in 1815, is based on an agitated diamond shape in the middle of a mass of conflicting directional lines. Turner's composition was beyond the understanding of his critics, who analyzed his picture in terms of traditional landscape compositions.

Although Turner's study of color began with his copies of Titian and Veronese in the Louvre, it was the light of Venice and reflected and refracted colors in their atmosphere that liberated his color. In his trip to Venice in 1819, he found the light that he carried all his life in his mind's eye. In 1828, 1835, and 1840, he returned to Venice, this world of light and color.

Turner was the first painter to realize the appeal of color to our senses, independent of subject matter. He made an extensive study of color and its theories, and he subjected his art to the sensations of light and color. Due to his creation of shimmering light through color, he had been considered the precursor of the impressionists, but Turner was a painter of the world of dream and did not belong to the objective world of impressionism.

By stripping away everything considered unessential in his later pictures, Turner's art came close to abstraction. This abstract approach, which made light and color the basis of his designs, is the most admired characteristic of Turner's art in our time.

The death of his father in 1829 and his friends from 1825 to 1833 left a void in Turner's life. Lord Egremont, a generous patron of art, always welcomed Turner at his Petworth country mansion in West Sussex. Turner, who loved the informality of the mansion, stayed there frequently after his father's death and painted a great deal.

In 1834 a fire started in the Houses of Parliament. As soon as Turner learned of the fire, he rushed to the scene. He spent the whole night making numerous watercolor sketches, which he expanded into two paintings.

The Snow Storm (1842), an exceptional landscape in European art, is a picture of a terrifying storm of upheaved masses of water that replace the waves of his early paintings. Despite the abstract appearance, the picture had been painted based on careful observation. In order to render the destructive power of nature, he decided to observe and experience it for himself, so he got the sailor to lash him for four hours to the mast of a ship. Turner's extraordinary memory assimilated his four hours of observation into his poetic vision. The swirling composition of the picture moves beyond the limits of the baroque's sweeping movements. The color in the center is cool; only in the dispersing smoke and its reflection on the waves are some warm colors.

At a time when railways were considered an abomination, Turner, who had traveled in stage coaches, admiring the comfortable system of railways, painted *Rain, Steam, and Speed* (1844). In the 1840s sunrise and the rising mists of early morning that unite the earth and sky shifted his interest from sunset to sunrise.

Toward the end of his life, he became more withdrawn and had no close friends. When John Ruskin, forty years younger than Turner, met him in 1840, Turner had become old and lonely. Drinking too much rum caused a decline in Turner's health. On December 19, 1851, the weather for days had been cloudy. On that day the sky had cleared, and lamenting the absence of sunshine, Turner struggled toward the window. He was later found dead on the floor.

THEODORE GERICAULT (1791–1824)

Gericault was born in Rouen. His father was a prosperous businessman. After finishing his studies, he entered the studio of Carle Vernet, and after two years, the studio of Pierre Guerin, a painter inclined to the Davidian neoclassical style.

Part of the generation of the French Revolution and the Napoleonic era, in his first canvas, *The Charging Chasseur*, submitted to the Salon of 1812, Gericault showed signs of the romantic admiration for fierce powers. The ponderous forms of his *Wounded Cuirassier* disappointed critics. In 1816, after failing to win the Prix de Rome, he went to Rome at his own expense. In Italy, he was impressed by Michelangelo's *Last Judgment* and influenced by the baroque masters. Fascinated by the traditional race of riderless horses called Barberi horses in the Corso at Rome, he began to develop large-scale compositions of *The Race of the Riderless Horses*, but he left it unfinished and returned to France in 1817.

In 1816, the *Medusa*, a government vessel, foundered off the West African coast. The incompetent French aristocrat captain, who had gained his position through connections to the Bourbon government, abandoned 147 people on a hurriedly constructed raft, and with his officers sailed away on lifeboats. When the raft was rescued after thirteen days, of 147 people only fifteen were still alive. Some had died of starvation; others, crazed by starvation, had been killed or thrown overboard into the sea by their comrades or themselves. An account by survivors agitated public opinion for both humanistic and political reasons. The event attracted the attention of Gericault, who was against the Bourbon government. Trying to achieve a maximum of authenticity, he interviewed survivors, studied corpses in the morgue, and had a model of the raft built. Of several episodes of the event, he drew detailed compositions: *The Mutiny of the Crew*, *The Outbreak of Cannibalism*, and *The Sighting of the Rescue Vessel*. At the end Gericault chose the dramatic moment when the frantic castaways attempt to attract the attention of a distant ship. He made the pictorial composition upon two pyramidal structures. The perimeter of the mast forms the larger pyramid, and the black man waving vehemently at the rescue ship is the apex of the second pyramid. From a foreground piled with corpses and motionless figures of desperate men, the groups of signaling men rises as with one motion. The powerful light and dark of contrasts enhance the dramatic effect of the subject, and raise its expressive power. *The Raft of the Medusa*, a continuation of the trend that David initiated toward contemporary events, shows the realistic tendencies of Gericault's art.

The government construed Gericault's depiction of the horrible event as a political attack. The painting was badly hung in the Salon of 1819, and discussions reflecting more political than art issues depressed Gericault, who was already exhausted by his lengthy work.

He left for England in 1820. The exhibition of *The Raft of the Medusa* in England was a success, and he remained there for two years. Some of his watercolors of this period show his interest in aspects of horsemanship. He also made a series of lithographs for English publishers. Some of these lithographs of the lives of the poor show his concern with social matters.

Gericault returned to Paris in failing health. He continued to draw lithographs. The intensity of realism and the expressive power of his art reappear in a few portraits that he made at the request of his psychiatrist friend, Dr. Georget, of insane patients. For these portraits, he made many studies of inmates of hospitals and institutions for the criminally insane. Gericault, a deeply pessimistic person, attempted to commit suicide while in London. He cared for nothing but riding the most dangerous horses, and after a fall from a horse, he died in 1824.

EUGENE DELACROIX (1798–1863)

Charles Delacroix, a minister of France in Holland and medically certified in 1797 as incapable of having children, could not be the father of Eugene Delacroix, who was born in Paris in 1798. Presumably, Talleyrand the famous politician of the nineteenth century, who served as the minister of foreign affairs for Napoleon and Louis the XVIII, was his father.

Delacroix started to study painting at the age of seventeen. While in the Beaux-Arts at Guerin studio, he met Gericault, whose art and friendship profoundly influenced him. With *The Barque of Dante*, a picture full of movement and expression, he broke with the neoclassical training of Guerin. The tormented and damned figures of this picture have the spirit of Michaelangelo, and the fiery dynamism of its composition has the vitality of Rubens. In matters of color, he was influenced by the Venetian masters. The picture was accepted by the Salon of 1822, and it received a hostile reaction from the public, but Adolphe Thiers, a journalist and a future chief of state, defended him, and the picture was purchased by the state for the Lille Musée des Beaux-Arts.

Delacroix was an individualistic artist and a master of color, imbued with classical training, whose direct painting—instead of classical sequences of drawing, modeling, and coloring—and his sharp contrasts and visible brushstrokes defying carefully graded color transitions of the classical style, sacrificed accuracy to expressiveness. In his little *Portrait of Paganini*, unconcerned with the likeness of Paganini's physical form, Delacroix presents gestures that reveal the emotions of the great violinist while performing. Considering his brushstrokes of juxtaposed pure colors and his studies of color, he was a forerunner of the impressionists.

At that time Greece was fighting for its liberty against the Turks. The massacre of the people of the island of Chios by Turks inspired Delacroix's *The Massacre at Chios*. Against the luminous background—influenced by the colors of Constable's *Hay Wain*, which was exhibited at the salon—in the foreground he painted the figures of sick or dying people. Exhibited in the Salon of 1824, the picture attracted interest but was criticized by artists and critics. With this painting, critics distinguished Delacroix's art from neoclassicism and applied the term *romantic* to his work.

Delacroix's high culture, intelligence, elegance and charming manners opened the doors of Paris high society to him, and he became intimate with the finest spirit of his time. A brilliant and exuberant writer, he recorded his observations over nature, man, and spirituality, and his judgments of the great masters of painting, both of the past and contemporary, in his *Journal*. Voltaire was his preferred writer of the eighteenth century, and his writings reveal a Voltairian skepticism. He appreciated the poetic sentiments of J. J. Rousseau for nature, but he did not agree with his view of civilization. He was not religious, yet his *Pietà* and *Christ on the Cross* interpret Delacroix's sadness and suffering. Legend, epic, historic events, and literature were his sources of inspiration.

An intellectual person, Delacroix had a taste for literature and continued to build on the literary education he had received at high school. His painting and lithographs of Hamlet, and his *Death of Sardanapalus*, inspired by Byron's tragedy, confirm his attraction to English literature. In his trip to London in 1825, a performance of *Faust* attracted him to the world of Goethe. His lithographs for *Faust* delighted Goethe himself.

The Death of Sardanapalus, inspired by Byron's poem about the tragic end of the Assyrian king, was exposed in the Salon of 1827. The picture depicts the last hours of Sardanapalus, who, informed of the defeat of his army and the fall of the city, decided to be involved in his own death and the destiny of everything that had given him pleasure in life. He set up a pyre, and from over his funeral pyre, he watched impassively the execution of his order to kill his women, slaves, and horses, and to destroy everything dear to him. The contrasts of light and dark of the composition, the sumptuous colors, and the tumult of the scene intensify the calm of the king, despite the violence and suffering around him. The painting provoked hostility from critics and officials.

Delacroix's most memorable work is *Liberty Leading the People* (1830). About the political upheaval of 1830, the picture is Delacroix's only major picture inspired by a contemporary event in France. The picture is dominated by the majestic and beautiful figure of Marianne, the allegorical figure of the spirit of liberty and the national emblem of the French Republic, carrying the tricolor banner of the French Republic and leading the revolution; at her sides are a man in the top hat and waistcoat of the middle class, a man in a white shirt brandishing a sword representing the laboring classes, and a street boy. The picture represents the forces of a new order and modern aspirations in France and the entirety of Europe in the nineteenth century, in opposition to the old order. But later in life, Delacroix became skeptical about politics and revolutions.

Delacroix's visit to Morocco and Algeria in 1832 was a turning point for him. The exuberant sight of nature, wild animals, colorful interiors, Arab dress, and a life of unbroken tradition vastly different from European civilization impressed him so profoundly that their effects lasted all his life. He recognized it as being more ancient and more dignified than the classicism of the salon. He was allowed to enter a harem to observe and sketch the Arab women in their private environment, and he also attended a Jewish wedding. He came back with abundant drawings, sketches, and watercolors that later served his paintings. Among pictures reminiscent of that trip are: *Women of Algiers*, *A Jewish Wedding in Morocco*, and violent scenes of wild animals with expressive movement of forms. In *Women of Algiers*, painted with a different temperament from *Chios* or *Sardanapalus*, he admirably reproduced the silence and torpor of the inside of a harem.

Lions and tigers occur in the drawings of other painters. But it was Delacroix who used lions and tigers as symbols of wild passion and the animal vigor of human nature. He believed that by nature man is a savage. He portrays this violence in his marvelous paintings *Arab Horses Fighting in a Stable*, *Combat of the Giaour and Hassan*, and *Lion Hunt*, in which he connects the worlds of human and animal to each other.

For one of his rare pictures from Greek mythology, he chose Medea, the heroine of Euripides's tragedy, a passionate and vengeful woman whose husband betrayed her for the love of the daughter of the king of Corinth. Torn between sorrow, hate, love, and an intense anger she decided to murder her twin sons. For the place of the murder, Delacroix chose a grotto, where Medea holding fast to squirming children in her grip form an animated pyramid. To show Medea'sanxiety, he arrested the time of his picture at the turn of Medea's head toward the opening of the grotto. The animation of the children, the shadow across half of Medusa's face, and the chiaroscuro effects make *Medea* a well-conceived picture.

Adolphe Thiers, the journalist who believed in the genius of the young painter of *The Barque of Dante*, now a minister, commissioned Delacroix's great decorative works in 1833 and thereafter. For the ceiling of the library of the Palais-Bourbon, the fragility of civilization and the contrast of peace against the destructive forces of war, became Delacroix's theme. At one end Orpheus brings the benefits of art and civilization to the Greeks still left to a savage life. At the other end, Attila and his barbarous hordes annihilate the culture of Italy. The composition of *Orpheus Bringing Civilization to the Barbarian Ancestors of the Greeks* is static and serene. Its dominant colors are light blues, greens, and mauves. *Attila bringing Savagery to the Ravaged Italy* is full of dynamism, and violent contrasts of colors. The decoration of the two hemicycles and its five cupolas, with the help of assistants, took almost ten years

In 1840, he painted *Crusaders Entering Constantinople*. The canvas was commissioned by Thiers for the Versailles. This picture, which Delacroix called his "third massacre," is different in spirit from *Chios* and *Sardanapalus*. The exhausted look of the conquerors and the sorrowful looks on the conquered people show the fatigue of violence. The smoke of the burning city has darkened the sky, and the blue of the Bosporus in the background is like a distant relief.

Delacroix's "three massacres" express his judgment of the human's behavior. The desperate, dying people in the foreground of the first picture, while a Turk soldier is about to slaughter a woman, is a condemnation of man's atrocities. Sardanapalus's detached witnessing of the killing of the woman who gave him love and pleasure and the slave who served him is the apex of egotism. His final "massacre" shows the absurdity of conquest.

A refined and intellectual man, he believed in the force of spirit. For decoration of a chapel at Saint-Sulpice, he selected the subject of *Jacob Wrestling with the Angel,* symbolizing the combat of man against spiritual forces. The heavy build of muscular and brutal Jacob contrasts with the lightness of the angel. The great oaks under which this encounter takes place symbolize the antiquity of the struggle.

Human figures and animals were his main interest. Yet in the later years, he made a few studies of flowers and of landscapes that are harbingers of the impressionist's plein air[9] paintings. In 1857, the old and ailing master was finally elected to the academy and became a member of the salon jury. But as he was in the minority, he was unable to prevent the rejection of Manet's paintings.

Delacroix was one of the most intelligent and intellectual men of the nineteenth century, a great poet, and a passionate and individualistic person who vigorously expressed his ideas and romantic emotions through violent and expressive movements of brushwork and warm, imaginative colors. Many of his works are scenes of ferocity and bloodshed. But there is another side to Delacroix's art: his self-portrait in the costume of Hamlet, and a set of lithographs of Hamlet, show his interest in the question of the destiny of man. For him nature was a vast dictionary for reference, but he believed that through imagination art assumes the quality of poetry. He was a great original colorist. He did not build up harmonies for their own sake, but as a means of dramatic expression. His contemporary

---

9 - Painting en plein air = painting outside of studio

critics did not grasp the importance of Delacroix's art, yet great was the respect in which he was held by the following generations.

The musicality of expressive colors and movement were his major technical concerns. His study of optical effects created by juxtaposing of complementary colors paved the way for the impressionists and postimpressionists. By disregarding anatomical proportions, he was a precursor to the expressionists. His contemporaries remarked that he resembles the tigers that he painted with so much admiration. Baudelaire described him as "the last of the great artists of the Renaissance and the first modern."

Section 3

Jean-Baptist-Camille Corot (1796–1875)

Corot was born in Paris and came from a prosperous family. When he was in the College de Rouen, M. Sennagen, a cultivated man and friend of family, was charged with looking after the boy. Sennegon, in love with nature, used to take him for long country walks that left a lasting impression on young Corot. After college, he worked as an apprentice in the clothing business of colleagues of his father, and he attended evening drawing classes at the Académie Suisse.

In 1822, he obtained his father's consent to devote himself to painting, along with a yearly allowance. He began his study under Achille Michallon, a young and talented painter who followed the neoclassical school of painting. After Michallon's early death, Corot continued his study with J. V. Bertin, also a neoclassical painter, who in parallel of neoclassicism exposed Corot to the tradition of careful composition of Claude Lorrain and Poussin.

A trip to Rome was indispensable to his neoclassical studies. In his visit to Italy, between 1825 to 1828, although captivated by the forms of classical architecture, he confined his Italian studies mostly to landscapes. A balance of light and shade, subtle handling of values, and a thick impasto replacing the smooth finish of neoclassicism characterize these landscapes. While sketching en plein air, he sensed the superiority of outdoor work to the artificiality of painting in a studio. In a letter from Rome, he mentioned the conflict he experienced between working outdoors and in the studio. He visited Italy in 1834 for the second time and again in 1843 for the last time.

Back in France he divided his time by working in Paris and traveling in the summer to the provinces to paint landscapes. His landscapes of this period followed the style that he adapted in Italy. Perfect drawing and clear values are evident in *Chartres Cathedral* (1830), his masterpiece of this period.

His father had bought a country house at Ville-d'Avray, ten miles from Paris. Corot was enchanted by the house and the nature of the region. From time to time, he would go to stay with his family at Ville-d'Avray. Early mornings before the sun dissipates the mists or late afternoons when evening mists began to gather were his favorite times to contemplate and paint.

Back from his second visit to Italy, he chose historic and mythological themes for his landscapes. An emphasis on figures, which was an influence of Poussin, created incongruity between the poetic content of his landscapes and the classical figure. Ten years later the soft and diffuse light of *Homer and the Shepherds*, which fused together the two tendencies, solved this problem.

In 1846, he received the Cross of the Legion d'Honneur, but still there were no buyers for his paintings. In 1847 a meeting with Delacroix drew him to a more romantic conception of painting. During this meeting, he gave hints to Delacroix about how to handle a tree.

Morning, the Dance of Nymphs (1850), inaugurated a new phase in Corot's art. This picture indicates a change of subject from ancient history to romantic literary content supported by stylistic changes. A subtle light diffused by mist dissolves the precise contours of earlier forms to lyrical, atmospheric effects. Broader and more flexible brushwork replaced short and firm strokes, and from few colors he obtained an infinite variety of harmonic silvery gray tones. This new style brought fame to Corot—and sales of his works.

After the death of his mother in 1851, he went to Arras in Northern France to stay with his friend Dutilleux, whose family became a second family to him. Northern France, with its soft and misty light and damp climate corresponding to his new style became his favorite region in France. Subsequently, every year he went to visit his friend. In 1852 Corot met Daubigny, whose art, criticized by Theophile Gautier as mere "impressions," aroused Corot's interest in the fluctuations of light.

Corot's art was not based on theory but on contemplation. He handled his outdoor sketches with remarkable freedom. His rendering of variations of outdoor light and atmosphere anticipated the plein-air paintings of the impressionists.

Corot had a versatile talent. His earlier portraits of women were well observed and graceful. After 1850, his portraits of young women, deep in a melancholic reverie, have the same monumentality and delicate poetic charm of his landscapes. His *Woman with a Pearl* (1868), with a similar pose to the *Mona Lisa*, brings Vermeer to mind.

A major work of his mature period is *The Bridge of Nantes* (1868–1869), in which he has wedded poetry and reality. With perfect harmony between atmosphere and volume and a subtle counterpoint of vertical, horizontal, and slanting lines, the picture has a stunning compositional precision.

One of the first to show that sketches had qualities of vitality and spontaneity that a more finished picture lacks, Corot alternated between plein-air and studio work. He was admired and respected by the impressionists. Pissarro exhibited at the salon as "a pupil of Corot." Renoir said of Corot, "With a bit of a tree he gives us everything." He influenced Monet, Degas, Renoir, and Sisley, and he gave a few lessons to Berthe Morisot. Delacroix considered him the father of modern landscape.

The softening of contours, an inclination to reverie in his lyrical landscapes, and the way his figures are lost in thought are all melancholy expressions of a sensitive man tired of the long struggle for recognition and loneliness after the death of his parents. Corot was a kind and generous man, and fame and fortune did not change his way of life. When he heard that Daumier was living in a damp and dilapidated house that the landlord refused to heat until Daumier paid his back rent, Corot sent money to Daubiny to purchase the house and to install new flooring in the room.

Section 4

Realism

THE BARBIZON SCHOOL

The classical landscape painters, subject to the laws of academic traditions, always made djustments to nature. In the years between 1830 and 1860, in all of Europe, there appeared a taste for reality and objective observation. The Barbizon school, a group of painters settled in the village of Barbizon at the edge of the Fontainebleau forest and inspired by romanticism, had the opinion that nature, under its banal appearance, contained a harmony that the artist had to divulge. Their pictures, a balance of sensibility and intellect painted in realistic terms, became a representation of close observation of nature, a procedure that led to impressionism.

In 1836, discouraged by a continuous lack of success at the salon and to get away from Paris, Theodore Rousseau was the first to settle in the village of Barbizon. Millet, Daubigny, and a few other painters joined him later. Although each of them had a concept and method of his own, yet their devotion to nature and disregard of historical or anecdotal subjects were held in common. After long years of struggle, from mid-1860 the Barbizon painters began to receive official and critical recognition, and their paintings were exhibited at the Universal Exposition of 1867.

THEODORE ROUSSEAU (1812–1867)

Beginning in 1831 Rousseau began to exhibit regularly at the salon. But between 1836 and 1841, the jury rejected all of his entries. Then by settling in the village of Barbizon, Rousseau distanced himself from the life and art of Paris. He had a static response to nature. His landscapes, made on various excursions, of clusters of trees, pools, and forest clearings, were not the result of a fleeting glimpse but were made over a protracted period of time. He was a meticulous draftsman, and his pictures represented accumulated thoughts and reactions. After the Revolution of 1848, the salon became more liberal, and Rousseau received official recognition as a major landscape painter.

JEAN-FRANÇOIS MILLET (1814–1875)

Millet, like Courbet, came from farming origins, but the two had fundamentally distinct characters. Courbet was politically active, while Millet loved the peace of village life. A student in the atelier of Paul Delaroche at l'École des Beaux-Arts, after his unsuccessful competition for the Prix de Rome, he left Delaroche's atelier and tried his hand at historic subjects and portraiture. However, humanitarian sentiments inclined him to rural imagery. Following political unrest after the Revolution of 1848 and the outbreak of cholera, he moved to the Barbizon village. There he found the peace of peasant life, and a firm friendship bound him to Rousseau. Extending the landscape to figure painting, Millet painted with tenderness pictures of the labor of a group or of isolated peasants. Among his most well-known pictures are *The Gleaners* and *Angelous*.

CHARLES-FRANÇOIS DAUBIGNY (1817–1878)

Daubigny was an honest observer whose paintings show great attention to nature, without turning it into a vehicle of self-expression. Of all the Barbizon painters, he was the one who worked en plein air, and his art was the first to be criticized as impressionist, while others were content to make outside sketches for pictures and execute the pictures in their studios.

HONORE DAUMIER (1808–1879)

Daumier was born in Marseilles. His father, a glazier with literary aspirations, seeking his fortune as a poet, left his wife and his seven-year-old son in Marseilles and went to Paris in 1814. There he discovered that being appreciated for his gifts was not an easy task. In 1816, he found a job and sent for his family. At the age of twelve, his father's breakdown forced Honore to seek paying work. First, he became a messenger boy, which familiarized him with world of law. Next, he worked for a bookseller. His father, noticing his passion for painting, asked his friend Alexander Lenoir, an artist, to keep an eye on his son. At the age of sixteen, Daumier received lithographic training and studied at the Académie Suisse, where students could make drawings from live models.

At that time, the majority of French people were illiterate. Pictures were the best medium with which to communicate, and lithography used for mass production was quite suitable to that purpose. To the contrary of painters of the Barbizon school, who had little concern with the political and social unrest in Paris, Daumier was in close touch with the events of Paris. Unable to live on painting, Daumier who was embracing the political inspirations of the working class, began to produce satirical lithography published in *La Silhouette*, the first satirical weekly, founded in 1829.

The common people who had put Louis Philippe on the throne soon realized the bourgeoisie were reaping the rewards. Stern measures of the regime of Louis Philippe against the working class created an overheated political atmosphere. A few months after the ascension of Louis Philippe to the throne, the Philipon brothers launched the opposing journal, *La Caricature*. Daumier became a contributor to *La Caricature*, using cartoons as a deadly medium to attack the government. Following the publication of *Gargantua*, a lithograph showing a gigantic Louis Philip receiving tributes, Daumier was sentenced to six months' imprisonment and payment of a fine; however, this time he was not jailed.

The Philipon brothers commissioned Daumier, who had already practiced sculpture, to do a series of small busts of the leading deputies of the Conservative party, modeled in terra cotta, to be displayed in the window of *La Caricature*. Later, to preserve these busts, since their plastic quality was beyond their caricature value, a few of them were cast in bronze.

Daumier's lithograph of *La Cour du Roi Petau* was beyond the government's tolerance. He was sentenced to six months in prison, but Philipon persuaded the authorities that Daumier should instead serve some seventy days in a mental hospital. Heavy fines ruined *La Caricature*. Consequently, the publication of the journal stopped in 1834, and Philipon launched *Le Charivari*, a journal that became a republican organ and the target of harsh judicial measures.

In 1834 the silk workers of Lyon revolted in protest of unfair salaries. The Lyon revolt had immediate repercussions in Paris. In Lyon barricades were erected in a few streets. One of them was the Rue Transnonain. A shot from one of the buildings in that street wounded an officer. The soldiers rushed into the building and stabbed everybody in the building with their bayonets. Daumier's lithograph *Rue Transnonain*, of the morning following the massacre, memorializes the slaughter of the uprising of 1834. Under the morning sunlight, we see the bodies of the innocent victims in nightshirts, blood still dipping from the nose of a child under the body of an adult.

A law to silence the opposing press was enacted. The press had the choice of keeping silent or making a pretense of loyalty to the regime. Daumier, who had joined *Le Charivari*, was obliged to turn to less aggressive themes. In the theme of Robert Macaire as the symbol of the business and financial class that was borrowed from a satirical play suspended by the government, he found an indirect means to ridicule the backbone of the regime for two years.

Having had experience working as a messenger boy for a process server, Daumier was familiar with the legal world and the manners of judges and lawyers. From 1845 to 1848, he executed lithographs of judges and lawyers. Through the motion of their bodies under their large lawyer gowns, he shows us his antipathy for their theatrical and affected manners.

The Revolution of 1848 in France led to the abduction of Louis Philippe. The revolution had major consequences. Revolts against authoritarian regimes broke out in all of Europe. After proclamation of the Second Republic, artists were invited to compete for an allegorical figure to represent the new republic. Twenty sketches were approved, including one by Daumier. The artists were asked to expand their sketches. But a clash of opposing interests, which led to four days of uprising in June, set aside the project.

Foreseeing the collapse of the Second Republic and the advance of the Second Empire, as a warning, Daumier made his statue of *Ratapoil*. The crumpled trousers and frock coat and the wicked expression on the face of the statue evoked the insolence and the ignominy of the mercenary legion of the first Napoleon.

In 1846 Daumier married Alexandrine Dassine, who had given birth to his child, and to earn his living he turned back to lithography. The year 1848 became a dividing line for Daumier's works and life. Before 1848, he was a lithographer and sculptor of satirical subjects. From 1848 to 1871, he devoted his time to painting.

Favorite heroes of this man with deep compassion for the poor and simple people were women carrying heavy bundles of wet linen, and passengers of the third-class wagon, caught unaware of the painter's observation. His choice of subjects of everyday activities of simple people provoked discussion of social issues. His pictures of scenes of urban entertainment cafés, café-concerts, ballets, and theaters, which conveyed the social contrasts inherent in urban life, allowed him a shrewd psychological analysis of the performers and spectators. Fascinated by Cervantes's hero, he painted several versions of Don Quixote's adventures. His paintings show an interest in movement, in the effects of light and air, and in some of them we see the same expressive treatment as in his sculptures. After meeting Corot, Rousseau, and Millet at Valmondois in 1853, he often visited them at Barbizon.

As painting could not support his life, he had to turn back to lithography. But the public had lost interest in Daumier, whose real interest had become painting. In 1860 *Le Charivari* stopped taking his lithographs, and as he could not find any interest for his paintings, his financial situation grew worse. In 1864 *Le Charivari*, unable to replace Daumier, offered him a new contract. Two years later, with the deterioration of his eyesight, his output of lithography dropped.

This adversary of kings was a modest republican, living a humble life, never asking for anything. During the Franco-Prussian Wars and the year of the Paris Commune, he lived on borrowed money. In 1865, he moved from Montmartre to a modest house at Valmondois. When Corot learned that Daumier was unable to pay for his rent, he purchased the house and gave it to him as a gift. The Third Republic granted a monthly pension to this defender of liberty and unfortunate people, and it offered him the medal of the Legion d'Honneur. But Daumier, who had declined it under the Second Empire, declined it again. In 1878 an exhibition of his work was organized at the Durand-Ruel Gallery. The exhibition did not meet the expenses, but it helped him to be recognized as a great artist.

Along with Courbet and Millet, Daumier initiated an art that was consistent with their broad and profound sentiment of human life as well as the aspirations of their time. They painted a reality that went deep beneath the thin layer of the surface.

GUSTAVE COURBET (1818–1877)

Courbet was born in Ornans, in a prosperous farmer family. Free from financial worry, he devoted himself to his art. He began painting at the studios of Steuben and Hess. As he believed that painting should be a living art, and translates ideas of his time, he decided that following the spirit of the current system of painting was a waste of time. He left his teachers, and went to the Louvre to copy masters to learn technical bases of the art of painting, and studied the old masters with profit. Particularly he benefited from Spanish paiters. He said: "I studied art of ancients and art of moderns, outside of any sprit of system."[10]

The Revolution of 1848 ushered in a new liberal sprit. In the prefaceof her Francois Champi (1850) George Sand announced an art neither classic nor romantic, that would respond to the modern idea of man. In the nineteenth century, the spectacle of contemporary life had attracted some painters, but they lacked the humanity and audacity of Courbet and his respect for the majesty of life. Courbet's art was response to the utter need of an honest art, expressing social problems in the second half of the nineteenth century; and he became the leader of the school of realism.

Courbet, a born painter, through brush, palett knife, or using his fingers, he conveyed the subtlest tone or the richest substance.

---

10   - La Peiture aux XIXe et XXe siscles, Henri Focillon, Librairie Renouard, 1928

He painted admirable portraits, and his landscapes opened the way for impressionism. He was a man of powerful personality, and despite his utter implicity, he was a friend of many intellectuals of his time. His realism was closely related to his democratic and materialistic world view. Believing that a work of art should express ideas and be judged according to its function within society, Courbet used his paintings as social commentary. He abandoned the imaginary and abstract subjects of romanticism and classicism in favor of scenes of contemporary life, without any idealization. He said, "I did not make art for art's sake but to vindicate my intellectual liberty." He maintained that there was beauty in simple, ordinary, everyday life, and except for his *The Atelier*, he avoided allegory. Courbet entitled *The Atelier* an *allegorie reelle*. In the center of the picture, Courbet is painting a landscape, while his model and a boy are watching him with admiration. To the righr are his friends and supporters; to the left are allegorical figures. Sitting on the ground beside the left side of the canvas is the figure of ultimate poverty, and behind her are allegorical figures of people he disapproved: priests, prostitues, merchants responsible for exteme poverty, and grave diggers.

It was a period of great social movements, demanding an art endowed with a profoun humanity. Courbet, an artist with a plebian personalit, had compassion forsy simple and hard-working people. *The Stone Breakers*, an image of two men—one very young and the other too old for such hard work—painted one year after the Revolution of 1848, was his protest against social conditions.

An admirable unity of execution links his vast composition of *A Burial at Ornans*. The pictue, which " does narrate, but presents", is a vast portrait of simple people, whose faces express various responses to the situation. The figures are composed like an architectural relief, parallel to the picture plane.

Following the refusal of all his pictures for the International Exhibition of 1855, Courbet constructed at his own expense his "Pavilion of Realism," close to the official building. Delacroix, visiting Courbet's exhibition, was impressed by *The Atelier* and said, "They have rejected one of the most extraordinary works of the age."

At the end of 1861, a group of students of Picot and Couture, dissatisfied with the methods of teachings, asked Courbet to accept them as pupils. Courbet told them every artist ought to be his own master, but he was willing to tell them how he himself became a painter. A studio was rented, and the model was in turn a horse or a bull. Soon, both teacher and students grew tired of repeated explanations, and the studio was disbanded.

Courbet's dynamic personality stimulated young painters to break with the past, and his art, which opened painters' eyes to the visible world, contributed to the formation of impressionism. Courbet's *Les Demoiselles au Bords de la Seine* (1856), a painting of two girls reposing en plein air, inspired Monet and Renoir to study the reflections of light and the shadows of foliage. His marine landscapes render the majesty of the scenes and reflect Courbet's powerful personality.

Following the collapse of the Second Empire, the Paris Commune ruled Paris for a few months. During the short period of their rule, they voted for the destruction of the Column of Vendôme that was built by Napoleon Bonaparte to commemorate his grand army. They also elected Courbet as president of the Republican Art Commission. After the suppression of the Paris Commune, Courbet was held responsible, since under his watch the Column of Vendôme was pulled down. All of Courbet's possessions, including his paintings, were seized. He crossed the border, and after four years in exile, he died in Switzerland.

Courbet's trial and condemnation symbolized the end of an era. By the end of nineteenth century, the view that art should be concerned with social interests or should respond to the aspirations of society started to fade, and a move toward art that relied on sensibility alone began. The experiments of the impressionists stimulated painters to explore a wide range of different styles.

Section 5

Color Theories

The three primary colors – red, yellow, and blue (RYB) became foundation of color theories in the eighteenth century. Investigation on variety of color effects, in particular the contrast between complementary hues, were summarized in two documents in color theory: *The Theory of Colors* by the German poet J. W. von Gothe, and *The Law of Simultaneous Color Contrast* f (1839) by the French industrial chemist M. E. Chevreul.

Chevreul's *The Law of Simultaneous Color Contrast* was an artistic milestone, that many painters from Delacroix to Matisse attemted to apply in their art. Chevreul claimed that if two color areas are seen close together in space or time, each will shift in hue and value, as if the **visual complementary color** of the neighboring or preceding color were mixed with it.

Color Harmony:

Colors seen together producing a pleasing response are said to be in harmony. However human responses to color involve emotional response and judgement. Hence our responses to the notion of color harmony is open to the influence of a range of different factors.

Warm vs. cool colors:

Warm colors are hues from red through yellow, with brown and tans included; they generally seem to advance or prject. Cool colors are hues from blue-green through blue-violet, they generally seem to recede.

Section 6

Impressionism

Before the nineteenth century, landscape panting was committed to improve nature in the interest of ideals. Early in the nineteenth century, in the concept of landscape painting changes took place. Constable discovered the art of naturalism, Corot fundamentally a classical painter, his art convey sensation. Courbet considering beauty a part of nature said artist has no right to change nature. In the second half of the nineteenth century, a few young painters, rather than following the path set by older generation, were concern with producing their immediate sensation of nature. From collaboration of Monet and Renoir a new movement, which trusted unreservedly to visual sensation was born

Impressionism was not a movement founded on theories; it was the result of the research and contributions of a few young painters, each with a different background, character, and temperament. Benefiting from Delacroix's studies of optical effects of color, the works of Courbet, the painters of the Barbizon school, Corot, Boudin, and Manet, their revolutionary concepts carried painting to naturalism, the apex of realism.

Discovering that everything was in perpetual motion and changing in value, they recorded the attractive features of the ephemeral and momentary. These painters, by their naturalistic mode of vision, relied entirely upon their impressions and renounced looking up to the past, which took classicism as its model, or took refuge in the reveries of romanticism. They decided, in order to have a sincere and honest encounter with the problems of painting, to bypass linear perspective, the artificial interpretation of volume, and the artificial source of light, which were heritages of the Renaissance. As the introduction of metal-tube color in 1841 had made painting out of the studio a possibility, in their endeavor to depict nature more truthfully, they painted en plein air. Part of their struggle to capture the fleeting instant was the problem of color and how to transfer light into color. In their study of light and color, they noticed that the color of every object perceived by the eye is a combination of its hue with the reflection from its surrounding colors and atmosphere.

Light, as one of the most important elements of nature, has always been the subject of study and analysis by painters. To suggest light, the most intense suggestion is obtained by contrast of white and dark areas through etching. While trying to transform the light as a colorless tonality into color, and to render the intensity of light, impressionists discovered that although pure colors are darker than light, nevertheless they are more capable of conveying the intensity of light to the eye than white. They intuitively applied Chevreul's principles. They limited their colors to the components of light, juxtaposed pure colors, banished gray and brown tones that did not vibrate, and when blending colors, preserved all the potency of their vibration intact, letting the diversity of color components appear. They also realized that the profusion of mixing white with other tones reduces the vibration of color. Through their observations they learned that shadows are colored; therefore, instead of making shadow of an object from the color of the object with some brown or black added, they broke up any color with its opposite color. An important consequence of painting en plein air was the effect of atmosphere over form, volume, and the space of the picture. Impressionism was not limited to the out-of-door landscape. Some of their best pictures are portraits or indoor scenes. Their research into light and color not only opened their eyes to the marvelous world of light and color, but it also led to the study of form, space, and composition.

The purpose of portraiture, from the Renaissance to the early nineteenth century, was to combine likeness with assertion of authority. The change of structure of European society prompted a new concept of portraiture aimed at exploring the character of the sitter. The impressionists, not concerned about likeness or the character of the sitter, painted portraits in their private environments to heighten a sense of immediacy.

Painters whose later research led to the impressionist movement, gathered in Paris around 1860. These years, coinciding with protests against the intransigence of the jury of the salon, inspired them to resist the constraints of the older generation. They became close friends, but each of them retained his/ her identity. The joy of depicting the beauty and freshness in the life of people and nature around them bound them together. From the beginning Monet and Pissarro influenced two fundamentally different tendencies, which matured in Argenteuil and Pontoise. Monet was more marine, and Pissarro was bound to earth. The years before 1874 were a period of slow and consistent research to establish the technical principles of impressionism. The culmination of their consistent evolution manifested in the historic impressionist exhibition of 1874.

The year 1880 was a turning point for the impressionist movement. The initial spontaneous intuition gave way to a more systematic approach with scientific overtones. Monet started his series, Pissarro changed to pointillism, and Renoir followed Cezanne's example and returned to the tradition of classical painting.

The development of impressionism took form in the period of the Franco-Prussian war, the fall of the Second French Empire, and establishment of the Third Republic of France, followed by a phase of prosperity.

*   *   *

After two centuries of national seclusion, in 1853, Japanese ports were reopened for trade to the West. Among the exported items were woodcut prints of Japanese masters, which became a source of inspiration for impressionist and postimpressionist painters. Although none of the impressionist painters imitated Japanese art, Manet, Degas, and Monet looked to it for suggestions related to their own research: Manet for contrasts of a clear and dark surface, Degas for placing the subject off center, and Monet for light with no shadow. And the expressive dynamic lines, pure flat colors, and two-dimensional Japanese prints impressed Gauguin and Lautrec.

EDOUARD MANET (1832–1883)

Manet was born in Paris to a well-off family. His father was a reputable judge, and his mother was the daughter of a diplomat. His father wanted him to study law, but the young man's desire was to become a painter. His uncle, a connoisseur of art supporting Edouard's wish, advised him to enroll in a special drawing course and to visit museums. From 1850 to 1856, he studied painting in the studio of Couture and made copies at the Louvre. Despite fundamental differences with his teacher, he owed his grasp of pictorial technique to Couture. In 1856, he opened his own studio.

The International Expositions intensified the exchange of artistic styles between European countries. The exotic themes and rich colors of the Spanish painters created a Hispanic trend in France. The

Salon of 1861 accepted two paintings submitted by Manet. Although badly hung, the vivid colors and the loose and broad brushstrokes of Manet's *Spanish Singer*, compared with the meticulous paintings of other participants at the Salon, attracted the attention of young artists, and the picture was highly praised by Theodore Gautier.

Baudelaire, a poet sensible to visual impressions and a critic who participated in the art activities of his time, stated, "The pleasure which we gain from presentation of the present derives from the beauty with which it may be possessed as well as its essential quality as present." Manet, by spirit an innovative painter, was mindful of Baudelaire's observations about modernity. With a sophisticated notion of "realism," he painted the *Musique aux Tuilleries* (1861). His modernity was not limited to the selection of theme or the clothing of gentlemen. He turned away from theatrical composition and chose realistic arrangements.

Manet, a Parisian dandy and a cultivated and brilliant conversationalist, was a friend of Proust, Zola, Baudelaire, and Mallarmé. His close friendship and daily contact with Mallarmé reveals his yearning for poetry. After painting feverishly in the studio, he used to go to the fashionable Café de Bade, but he soon abandoned this place for the Café Guerbois in the Grande rue de Batignolles, where he chatted with writers and artists. They were soon known as the Group of Batignolles.

Manet, Degas, and Bazille came from wealthy and educated bourgeois families. Cezanne, despite a fortune amassed by his father, neglected his appearance and liked to exhibit rough manners. He would sit in a corner and listen, and when an opinion radically opposed to his own was discussed, he would leave the gathering without taking leave of anybody. Monet was more concerned with listening than contributing to the discussions. Reading through many nights and studying the masters of the Louvre had helped Renoir grasp the essence of the discussions, but he was not concerned with theories. Pissarro, a convinced atheist with anarchistic ideas who was conscious of the social problems of the time, was interested in political discussions. The group's opinions concerning the salon were divided. Painters who had sufficient resources preferred to participate and wait. Manet argued that the salon was the only place where they could present their art, so they had to accept the challenge and wait. Cezanne believed that the painters should depart from established custom and send their most offensive pictures to the salon. The subject of shadow was one of the artistic topics of discussion at Café Guerbois. Manet maintained that a single tone is sufficient to convey light, and it is preferable to move abruptly from light to shadow. But painters who painted en plein air disagreed. For them, shadow was rich in complementary colors.

In the mid-nineteenth century, the progress of Western societies and the chain of revolutions had accelerated movements to unsettle the foundations of old values and replace them with new orders. The rising bourgeoisie, which had supplanted the aristocracy and the Church as patrons of the arts, lacking art education, clung to an art alien to their time. They did not realize that new waves of art and the bourgeoisie class itself were both products of the progress of society and changing values. Blindly following the judgment of the jury of the salon, not only did they refuse to buy pictures rejected by the jury, but they even returned pictures they had previously bought. As rejection or acceptance of a painting by the jury of the salon had financial consequences for the painter, many painters who had no need to look for customers did not exhibit in the salon. Unfortunately, except for a few enlightened ones, the art critics of the time were not helpful. They were so deeply rooted in the past that they were unable to realize that the changes that had taken place in all aspects of European life were born out of a necessity to progress, to which art was no exception. They did not realize that the original messages of old masterpieces had lost their meaning. Now their value resided only in their play of form and color. In fact, they were defending messages of the past, while nobody was attacking the timeless values of the art of Raphael, Titian, or Rembrandt. Consequently, many innovative painters of the second half of the nineteenth century suffered from the hostility of the defenders of old orders and the lack of knowledge of critics.

The year 1863 had crucial importance in the history of modern painting. Following the rejection of some four thousand paintings by the jury of the salon, and the resulting protests of the artists, Napoleon III ordered the establishment of the Salon des Refuses. Manet, whose *le Dejeuner sur l'Herbe* had been rejected by the jury, exhibited his canvas at the Salon des Refuses. Although he had adapted his theme from a Louvre painting attributed to Titian as well as Giorgione, a naked woman sitting in the company of two men in contemporary clothing, as well as Manet's technique, shocked the public and critics. In fact Manet repeatedly borrowed themes from the old masters, but his style made a new piece of art of the borrowed work.

With his indifference to subject matter and his rejection of the Renaissance conception of a picture as a window into an illusionary world, Manet asserted painting as a two-dimensional surface covered with colors, the only reality of a painting, and inaugurated the age of modern painting. The jeers of the crowd and the admiration of the young generation revealed the passage of one generation to another. Manet, strong enough to follow his vision, showed indifference to the irony of the public and the guardians of old values, but each rejection by the jury of the salon was an agony for him.

Purely representative art of Manet, that disregarded social implications of the realist school of painting, necessitated a new definiation, therefore the name *naturalist* was coined for painters whose art was to reproduce figures or nature without interpretation.

Manet's revolutionary approach to painting, which began with *Musique aux Tuilleries* and was followed by *Le Dejeuner sur l'Herbe*, culminated in *Olympia* (1863). This female nude had numerous precedents; among them are Titian's *Venus of Urpido* (1538), Velasquez's *Venus and Cupid* (1647), Goya's *La Maja Desnuda* (1800), and Ingres's *Grand Odalisque* (1814). But Manet's *Olympia* is once more a transposition of a mythological theme into the world of his own time. Olympia, a reclining nude female, with a ribbon around her neck that accentuates her nakedness, stares with a passive boldness at the viewer. The strong light on the nude suppressed transitional values and flattened her forms, which were only functions of color and light. The picture was exhibited at the Salon of 1865, and as before the followers of old orders took arms against Manet. But for avant-garde painters, it was an epoch-making piece of art. They realized Manet had not translated the outside world, but the picture had a language of its own.

Tired of constant rejection, Manet decided to follow Courbet's decision of 1855 by building his own pavilion. He built a pavilion at the World's Fair of 1867. The exhibition was much less successful than his expectations. In 1865 he traveled to Spain for two weeks. Of the Spanish Masters that he saw at the Prado, he took little interest in Goya, but he found Velasquez's pictures closest to pure painting.

In 1867, he painted several versions of *The Execution of Emperor Maximilian*. This painting reminds one of the subject of Goya's *The Shooting of May Third*, a picture that is a cry against tyranny. Whereas for Manet, who considered that the message loses its meaning through time, like *Olympia*, the subject was used as a mere pretext for the permanent values of painting that reside in its color and form, its variations of light and dark, its tone, and its brush-strokes, not the message attached to the image. Malraux, in his "Les Voix du Silence," pointed out that Manet's deliberate indifference to death in this picture destroyed the subject matter. The orientation that Manet gave to his picture is what we rediscover in modern painting

The feminine grace, delicate color, and firm structure of Berthe Morisot's paintings exhibited at the Salon of 1867 attracted Manet. The following year, Morisot, an advocate of painting en plein air, became Manet's pupil and companion, and she introduced him to her preimpressionist friends. Before meeting Morisot, Manet worked only inside the studio. In 1874, watching Monet paint converted him to outdoor painting; but, not interested in pure landscape painting, he painted people in the open. He got rid of black to give luminosity to his pictures, but he was opposed to complete dissolution of lines, which define planes, and he kept his black contour lines and did not use the "comma" brushwork of the impressionists because this would lead to painting human figures with numbers of spots of color. Manet, a cultivated and mundane Parisian, with a technique emancipated from the bondage of the academy and a choice of modern subjects, assumed leadership of the innovative painters of his generation. But eager to display his work at the salon, he did not follow the impressionists in withdrawing from the salon competition, and he refused to participate in the first group exhibition of the impressionists in 1874.

Similar to the composition of musical sounds that are meant to create a harmonic piece or to seek inner expression, Manet's pictures are pretexts for the play of form and color, and his portraits have nothing of the personality of the sitter. The only exception is the *Portrait of Mallarmé*, which is all Mallarme, a poet of musical symbolic verses.

Despite signs of paralysis in 1880, he continued to paint and exhibit. At the Salon of 1882, he exhibited his last work, *Un Bar aux Floies-Bergere*, a picture of a handsome young woman standing motionless behind a bar, facing the crowd. The real subject of the picture are the reflections of dazzling light in the music hall onto the bottles and still life on the counter, and the reflections in the large mirror behind the barmaid. After the closing of the salon, he was nominated Chevalier de la Legion d'Honneur. On his death Degas admitted that "Manet was greater than we thought."

EDGAR DEGAS (1834–1917)

Degas was born in Paris to a prosperous family. In 1845 he was enrolled in the Lycée Louis-le-Grand, where the emphasis was on Latin, Greek, and rhetoric. After his schooling, he studied painting with Louis Lamothe, a follower of Ingres's style, with sessions of copying at the Louvre. In 1855, admitted to the École des Beaux-Arts, his professor was Hippolyte Flandrin, a student and friend of Ingres.

Valpincon, a collector and the father of his schoolmate, in the course of conversation revealed to Degas that he had refused Ingres's request to lend Ingres's *Bather* to be exhibited at the Universal Exposition of 1855. Pressured by Degas, he reversed his decision, so the next day the two men informed Ingres of his change of mind. On the recovery of the canvas after the exhibition, Degas informed Ingres that he too painted. Ingres advised him, "Draw lines, many lines from memory or from nature." This advice had a lasting effect on Degas's art.

Although the decline of neoclassicism had eclipsed the magnetism of Italy, still some believed a visit to Rome and Florence was indispensable for a serious artist. In 1856 he went to Rome to study painting and sculpture. In Italy, he executed in Ingres's linear style a series of portraits of his relatives living there. Whereas Ingres told his sitter how to pose, Degas's portraits show sitters in their typical attitude, which was far from Ingres's approval.

Degas's work could be divided into three phases:

- In the first phase, from about 1855 to 1865, he studied masters of the Renaissance and romantic paintings. He selected his subjects from mythology and history, and he painted portraits. Instead of more lively compositions, he grouped his figures horizontally. Painting horse racing in early 1960s provided him an opportunity to move into contemporary life. As time passed, to avoid facileness, Degas got rid of the earlier rigidity of his figures; several portraits of his transitional period, between 1865 to 1867, show interest in the personality of his subjects.

- Being introduced through Manet to the circle of naturalist writers and impressionist painters at the Café Guerbois turned him toward contemporary urban scenes, such as café-concerts, laundresses, and milliner's shops. He lightened his palette, and Japanese prints influenced his compositions. This second phase lasted until 1885.

- In the last phase, the most creative period of his art, he abandoned many of the topical themes of his previous phase, along with many stylistic preoccupations implicit in them. He concentrated on generating variations of two subjects: ballet and female bathers.

Around 1860, Degas began to use the style of Ingres's drawing, employing a finely pointed pencil on a smooth surface; however, comparison of his drawings with Ingres reveals a difference in temperament. Degas's drawings are more inward-looking and lack the energy of Ingres's. Degas, who revered Ingres and was an open-minded artist, after his return from Italy began to study the dramatic compositions of Delacroix and his use of color, and he made copies of Delacroix's pictures. Unlike the lasting influence of Ingres, that of Delacroix declined when he was introduced through Manet to the circle of naturalist writers and impressionist painters at Café Guerbois.

Degas met Manet around 1862. Two years younger than Manet, well dressed, with elegant manners, and highly intelligent and intellectual, he was the perfect companion for Manet. Friendship with Manet gradually changed the course of Degas's art. Through Manet he met naturalist writers and painters at Café Guerbois, and he became engaged in modernity, abandoned historical subjects, and shared Manet's oppositional stance to the artistic establishment.

In the 1870s Daumier's lithographs attracted him. Between 1870 and 1885, the influence of Daumier's scenes of closed entertainment is apparent in Degas's pictures of cafés, café-concerts, ballets, and theaters. He said, "There have been three great draftsmen in the nineteenth century: Ingres, Delacroix, and Daumier." Thus Degas synthesized the three artistic trends of his time: the harmonious forms of Ingres, the poetical conception and colors of Delacroix, and the realism of Daumier.

He met future impressionist painters at the Café Guerbois, but Degas, a Parisian molded by the art of museums and faithful to his respect for Ingres and Delacroix, who worked indoors, did not adopt painting en plein air, a practice that required a painter bound by his/her sensations to finish the painting on the spot. Race courses painted in the 1860s are his only pictures made en plein air. Degas participated in the impressionists' exhibitions and was one of the leading organizers of the first impressionist exhibition, but believing that solitude of mind is needed to be creative, he distanced himself from the group.

Degas was basically a conservative and complex person. Despite his deep respect for old masters and his admiration for Ingres and Delacroix, he was always an innovator. He approached with audacity and experimented with diverse materials and methods to create his intellectually sophisticated art, and he drew lessons from the decorative qualities, the subtle lines, the off-center placement of the principal subject, and the asymmetry of the compositions of Japanese prints. His practice of cutting the foreground makes his objects appear closer to the observer. Fascinated by the novelty and authenticity of photography, he drew lessons from its contribution to the study of movement.

Technically Degas's art had little in common with the outdoor paintings of the impressionist group. Nonetheless, his choice of scenes of Parisian life, his reduced emphasis on line, his experiments with color and form, his study of indoor artificial light, and his exquisite scale of colors relate him to the impressionist movement. While landscapes of the impressionist painters unfold sceneries of Paris at the end of the nineteenth century, Degas, of all the impressionist painters, was the one who explored the indoor activities of Paris: theaters, operas, café-concerts, and circuses.

In 1872 he went to New Orleans, where his brothers were in the cotton business. Although the city and the life of New Orleans attracted him, he limited his paintings to a few family portraits. In 1876 one of his brothers lost his fortune by imprudent speculation in American securities. By giving up great part of his fortune to help his brothers, Degas became dependent on occasional sales of his work.

Fascinated by movement submitted to rigorous discipline, as early as 1870, he launched into painting ballet rehearsals and performance scenes, a subject that would constitute the major part of his art during the rest of his career. For these paintings, in a sequential process, he began by sketching the dancers in attitudes approximating each other and then making a synthesis of those sketches. To structure these pictures of lessons, practice sessions, or rehearsals, he used special devices. To emphasize the flatness of his composition while preserving the plasticity of his forms, he used a high horizon line or asymmetrical placement of figures. To depict the speed of ballerinas, he fused line and color, a process in which his drawings lost Ingres's refinement. The selection of sophisticated and subtle hues gave a dreamlike atmosphere to his ballet scenes, which were an expression of a very refined poetry.

In parallel with ballet subjects, images of female bathers are the major theme of the third phase of Degas's art. Through dramatic contortions of the bodies of bathers, he explored the rotation of masses in space. Some of Degas's bathers twist the full expanse of their backs toward the viewer. The nudity of a woman in an austere composition devoid of furniture and an absence of narrative increase the solitude and self-absorption of the women in these pictures.

The sequential procedure of the Renaissance in building up a picture, which Degas followed in his early oil painting, persisted as a model in all his oil paintings, and in all his works in other media. Degas, who had experimented with a vast array of media, in the last phase of his art, abandoned oil painting, adopting charcoal as the preferred medium for his drawings, a choice related to his failing eyesight because it allowed him to make bolder lines. Pastel, which enabled him to reconcile line with sensuous colors, became his selected medium. For his late pastels, Degas drew first in charcoal over a tracing paper that was more resilient to the absorption of color particles than soft or textured papers. He applied an underlying tone to establish the dominant lights and shadows, and then he added colors, preserving the charcoal drawing beneath.

At the 1881 impressionist exhibition, Degas unveiled the wax sculpture of *Little Dancer of Fourteen Years*. Despite high esteem expressed for this creation by visiting artists and critics to his studio, he chose not to exhibit his sculptures to the public or sell them. Complaining about his failing eyesight, he chose a self-imposed solitude. After 1886, he participated only once at an exhibition, and he spent much of his time in sculpture and in pastel.

EUGÈNE BOUDIN (1824–1898)

Boudin, born at Honfleur on the bank of the estuary of the Seine, across from Le Havre, was the son of a sailor. In 1835 his family moved to Le Havre, where his father opened a framing shop. Eugène worked at his father's shop and later continued the same business. While operating his business, he began painting the sea and the shore of Le Havre, and became one of the first French landscape painters to paint en plein air.

One day, Millet walked into his shop. Boudin showed the painter his own studies, which Millet corrected. This meeting resolved him to follow an art career. He left the business to his associate and went to Paris, where he made copies in the Louvre. A three-year scholarship from the city enabled him to study in Paris. Undistinguished as an art student in Paris, and a modest man loyal to his birthplace, he returned to Le Havre. A painter with genuine feeling and a sensitive eye, who believed in the importance and power of touch in reflecting the first impression that cannot be recreated in studio, he went back to painting landscapes en plein air.

He met Courbet and Baudelaire in Le Havre. Courbet admired Boudin's skies, and Baudelaire praised Boudin's art in one of his reviews of the salon. The bright hues of his beach scenes and marine paintings link him to the impressionists. In 1874 he exhibited with the impressionists, but from 1875 on, he exhibited in the salon.

CLAUDE MONET (1840–1926)

Monet was born in Paris and passed his youth in Le Havre, where his father and uncles were wholesale grocers. He was a tough-minded and persistent person, not asking for social approval. At the school, where he hated to remain, he passed his time in making caricatures of his teachers. At the age of fifteen, he was famous in Le Havre as a skilled caricaturist.

Boudin displayed Monet's caricatures in his shop windows, which led to their friendship. Monet watched Boudin paint outdoors. The devotion of the simple and humble man to nature and to his art became a guiding light for Monet, who announced to his father that he wished to go to Paris to study painting.

In 1859 his father consented to his short visit to Paris to ask the guidance of Parisian artists and see the salon. In Paris, he decided to stay and study painting. As he refused to enter the École des Beaux-Arts, his father cut his allowance, and he had to live on his savings. He went to the Académie Suisse, where artists could work from live models.

When he arrived in Paris, classicism and romanticism were under the attack of realism. At the Brasserie des Martyrs, he had the opportunity to listen to the arguments that painting should represent contemporary life without idealization. At the studio, exchange of ideas with other artists expanded his knowledge of art.

In those days, it was possible to buy a substitute for the seven years of military service. Monet's father intended to use this advantage for his son, but Monet refused and chose to be sent to Algeria. After two years, seriously ill, he was sent back to France, and his father bought him out of the service. While in Le Havre to recuperate from his illness, he met Jonkind, a painter, who, faithful to his impressions, had made atmospheric conditions the real subject of his paintings. Jonkind's audacity of mind, freshness of vision, and marvelous watercolors of varying aspects of nature impressed Monet. He introduced Jonkind to Boudin, and a close friendship bound the three together.

In 1862 his father consented to sending him back to Paris, on the condition that he work under the supervision of a master. In Paris, Monet entered l'Atelier Gleyre, whose academic teachings contradicted the realism of Courbet and the opinion of Boudin and Jongkind that a painter had to be faithful to his observations. But in order not to exasperate his family, he continued to attend Gleyre's classes and occasionally participated in gatherings at the Café Guerbois. A close friendship bound him to Renoir, Bazille, and Sisley, his fellow students at L'Atelier Gleyre. He took the lead over his friends, who lacked his experience of working with Boudin and Jonkind and listening to the discussions at the Brasserie des Martyrs and at the Café Guerbois. He told his friends about the viewpoints of realism, the concept of naturalism, and the art life beyond the teachings of the École des Beaux-Arts. After the closing of Gleyre's studio, Monet took his friends to Chantilly, a village on the edge of the Fontainebleau forest, to do some studies en plein air.

In 1864 Monet joined Boudin and Jongkind at Honfleur to paint together. Inspired by Jongkind's vibrant watercolor landscapes, Monet painted seascapes that he submitted to the Salon of 1865. Monet's works, accepted and hung in the same room with Manet's works, received more favorable comments than Manet's pictures.

To paint large-sized figures immersed in outdoor light was not an easy problem to solve. Monet ventured to be the first painter to paint a vast composition with large figures en plein air. Familiar with Fontainebleau, he chose the inside of the forest for the location of his *Le Dejeuner sur l'Herbe*. To complete the picture in the forest was out of the question; it had to be finished indoors. In 1866, while putting his last touches on the painting, Courbet, who was fond of

Monet to the extent of helping him financially, paid him a visit and suggested some modifications. Following the advice, Monet was no longer satisfied with the canvas. He rolled it and left it with the land-lord. Unable to present this canvas to the jury of the salon, he rapidly painted the portrait of *Camille*—his future wife—wearing a green-and-black-striped skirt. The half turning of Camille's head while she stepped forward gracefully provoked the admiration of viewers of the salon. Zola praised its vitality and realism. Even the detractors praised the rendering of the skirt.

Monet's *Les Femmes aux Jardin*, entirely painted en plein air in the garden of a house he rented in 1867, was a new approach to paint-ing. To reach the upper section of the large canvas, he dug a trench into which he lowered it. Immersed in light, the picture created an enchanting world of light and color. To spatter warm sunlight and cool shadow on leaves, the play of the shade of trees and reflections of the colors of flowers on his figures, he used bright hues and a flat handling. However, there is a lack of atmospheric unity, figures are not incorporated in the landscape, and the picture shows signs of studio painting. Academicians hostile to any originality rejected Monet's canvas.

The rejection of this canvas by the jury while Camille was ex-pecting a child aggravated Monet's financial situation. To help him Bazille bought *Les Femmes aux Jardin* for the price of 2500 francs, to be paid in monthly installments of fifty francs. Yet this goodwill was far from Monet's need. Bazille took it upon himself to write a letter to Monet's father to explain the difficulties in which the son found himself. The answer was that Claude alone would find a room and meal in the house of his aunt. Obliged, Monet left Camille in Paris, and went to stay with his aunt.

The year 1868 was a painful one for Monet and Camille. Penniless, he left his aunt to search for a temporary shelter for his wife and his one-year-old son. He was so desperate that he thought of suicide.

Painting outdoors and avoiding picturesque traditions, Monet and his friends had to solve various problems of visualization and interpretation. In 1868, he found the Seine near Paris an appropriate subject for painting. While painting on the bank of the river vibrations of light over the water attracted his attention, and to study and to paint reflexons of light over the waves of water became one of his primary subjects.

In 1869 Monet lived at Bougival, where he was often joined by Renoir to paint together side by side from the same motif. Both used dotted and commalike brushstrokes to capture the movement of water, yet each painted according to his own vision. Renoir's touches envelop his pictures in tender light and give them luminous unity, while Monet studied the reflections of light, and learned to adopt the rhythms of his brushstrokes to the reflexions of light on the changing waves. Although both were under extreme financial stress, they worked eagerly, and their paintings have no sign of pessimism. Renoir said, "Without my dear Monet, who gave courage to all of us, we would have given up." Their common efforts found expression in the pictures of the famous bathing place of La Grenouillère (*Bathers at La Grenouillère*). The crowd of people on the bank and the glistening surface of the water with its colorful reflections had all been captured with sketchlike strokes of the brush.

With the outbreak of the Franco-Prussian War in 1870, the painters in the Batignolles group reacted to the war in a variety of ways. As a republican, Monet had no taste for defending the imperialistic dreams of Napoleon III. He left his wife and child in France and took refuge in England. In London, Daubigny, moved by Monet's distress, introduced him to his art dealer, Paul Durand-Ruel, who had also escaped the war and had opened a gallery in London. Through

Durand-Ruel, who henceforth became a defender of impressionist art, Monet got in touch with Pissarro, who was likewise in London. They worked in concert with each other and studied works of the English painters. At this time Monet had not yet established a wholly personal style. Constable's art based on visual sensation, Turner's art subjected to the sensation of light and color, also the pecular light and the quality of the London atmosphere that soften outlines, affected the course of evolution of Monet's art. After the war, he returned to Paris via Holland, where he came upon a print of Hokusai used as a wrapping paper in a spice shop.

After returning to Paris, Monet and Pissarro again became the head of the two impressionist tendencies. Monet rented a little house close to the water in Argenteuil, a village with vibrant light on the banks of the Seine near Paris, and he lived there from 1872 to 1878. As before the war, Renoir often paid a visit to Argenteuil to paint with Monet on the same theme. Through their close relationship, they found and applied the technical principles of impressionism, based on observation of nature and the vibration of light. This new concept of picture making based on ephemeral manifestations of nature was against the traditional wishful thinking that we live in an unchanging world. They discovered that the old notion of local color[11] is a pure convention, that color of every object derives from its proper hue, its surroundings, and from atmospheric conditions. They did not insist on details but reduced everything they saw to sensations of color, expressed in juxtaposed dabs of pigment. Their palettes grew more brilliant, with the commalike brushstrokes giving a vibrant tissue to the surface of their pictures. As this gradual stylistic change was not programmed, the Argenteuil pictures have the appearance of spontaneity. The balance between subject, vision, and technique of the pictures of Monet and Renoir was so complete

---

11   - Local color = In painting, the actual color of an object.

that it captivated other avant-garde painters. Manet, who was converted to plein-air painting, began to join Monet and Renoir to paint in Argenteuil.

The year 1873 marks the passage from the preparatory phase of preimpressionism to the mature impressionism. Technique and vision became united, and sensation was detached from any intervention such as reverie, the literary suggestions of romanticism, or the social concerns of the realism. Monet's landscapes of the Argenteuil period excel in their transparency of space and are a marvelous world that appears to be the emanation of light and atmosphere.

Besides river scenes Monet painted a few studies of figures in a landscape. In the delicately brushed *Wild Poppies*, the silhouetted Camille and her son strolling in the field are parts of nature. The shape and color of the flowers are poppy, but the treatment is abstract.

Snow in the winter of 1874 provided an opportunity for Monet, Pissarro, and Sisley, who used to choose their subjects in accordance with the search for a pictorial solution, to paint a group of snow scenes. While painting, they observed that, similar to the reflections of light over water, shadows over snow are colored. At the same time, they noticed that small touches of pure color next to each other have more luminous intensity than white. Consequently, they abandoned the contrast of black and white, and used intermediate tones of gray and brown.

During these years, landscapes of populated quarters of Paris with their moving forms and vibrant colors and the dynamics of the modern city offered appropriate themes to the personal inclination and style of each impressionist painter. These paintings give us an authentic view of life in nineteenth-century Paris.

Upon growing of hostility of the salon, Monet took up his old idea of a group exhibition free of the judgment of a jury. Monet's idea was well received, La Societe Anonyme Cooperative was found-ed, and the vacant studio of photographer Nadar was rented for the exhibition. The exhibition opened on April 1874 and lasted for one month. The public, still unable to accept an art different from the system of the salon, made their visits to the exhibition motivated by curiosity, not a desire to enjoy art. After the closing of the exhibition, the financial statement showed that the majority of the participants did not even earn enough to pay for their annual dues. An article in the satirical journal *Le Charivari* derisively used the name of one of Manet's pictures, *Impression, Soleil Levant*, for their article, entitled "The Exhibition of the Impressionists." The term *impressionism* was soon adopted by the public and the artists themselves to designate the group.

After his return to Paris, Durand-Ruel showed interest in the works of the members of the Batignolles group. His purchases brought financial and moral support to these young painters. But the crush of 1882, following the prosperity of 1880, put Durand-Ruel under obligation to return money advanced by a bankrupt friend. Durand-Ruel himself, encountering serious financial difficulties, could not sustain his assistance to these painters for a few years.

The years 1878 and 1879 were beyond the endurance of any head of a family. Camille was pregnant and ill. Monet, without funds to pay the rent, the family had to leave the house at Argenteuil and jointly rent a house farther from Paris at Vétheuil with Mme. Alice Hoschede, whose husband, bankrupt, had left for Belgium, leaving behind his wife and his six children. After the birth of their second son, Camille's health continued to deteriorate, and she died in 1879. The death of Camille marked the loss of cheerfulness of Monet's earlier works. Mme. Hoschede, who had taken care of Camille, re-mained with Monet afterward and helped him to raise his two sons. They continued to live at Vétheuil until 1881, then spent a year at

Poissy before moving to Giverny, halfway down the Seine to Rouen. After the death of Mme Hoschede's husband, they married in 1892.

Following of the acceptance of Renoir's paintings at the salon, Monet, who had been the one to suggest a group exposition, decided to submit two pictures for the Salon of 1880. His pictures were accepted, but his decision met with the disapproval of Degas.

In 1883 and 1885, he painted landscapes of the beach and of the spectacular rock formations of Étretat. His paintings of the cliffs are impressionistic, but some of the pictures of the rocks indicating movement express nature's power. In the asymmetrical composition of *La Manneporte*, the texture and colors of the cliff and the waves around the cliff separate them from the distant horizon.

An established life at Giverny gave Monet some relief. In 1886, for the third time, he returned to figure painting. The light brushstrokes conformed to the summer breeze, and the luminous shadows of *Lady with a Parasol* create an image of an enchanting summer day.

That he joined an exhibition with Auguste Rodin in 1889 is an indication that he was an established master. In 1891, to capture the transient effects of light, he painted fifteen pictures of haystacks at various times of day. In these pictures, the first set of serial paintings, he was more interested in capturing the ephemeral light than in rendering the intrinsic value of objects, and they represent his move toward a lyrical handling of color. The canvases, presented next to each other, had an impressive impact on viewers. Four years later Wassily Kandinsky, impressed by the exhibition of one of the *Haystacks* at Moscow, wrote, "The unsuspected power of the palette, previously hidden from me, surpassed all my dreams."

The geometric skeleton of the facade of the Rouen Cathedral offered an appropriate field for the play of light and shadow. By eliminating the environment of the cathedral, he brought forward the facade. To paint the *Rouen Cathedral* series, he changed canvas with the changing of light in the day, from the misty blue shadows of early morning to the golden light of sunset.

As he grew older, Monet's art mirrored the evolution of his internal logic and his continuous discovery of new variety in the infinite changes of the natural world. In *Branch of the Seine near Giverny*, painted in 1897, the reflections on the water have the same quality as nature.

During the winters of 1899 to 1901, Monet made three trips to London and painted close to a hundred pictures of the Thames. *The Houses of Parliament*, painted in 1903, with its architecture dissolved by fog, looks like a vision. His many touches of pigments give depth to the picture. In his last canvas, a rapprochement to Turner's vision of art is noticeable.

More interested in the architectural lines and patterns of the palaces than the romantic appeal of Venice, he made two trips to Venice in 1908 and 1909. The illness and death of his second wife prevented him from returning to Venice. Consequently, he had to work from memory on many unfinished pictures of Venice at Giverny. As he had finished these from memory, he was dissatisfied with the paintings, but critics liked the horizontal and vertical rhythms of these painting. To leave unfinished his painting of Venice shows that his concern was not rapid notation of a transient effect of light.

In 1891, for a place for relaxation, by diverting a tributary of the Epte River, he made a pond with a Japanese footbridge over it. Lonely and discouraged by the death of his second wife, and with cataracts beginning to form over his eyes, Monet was reluctant to start another large task. Persuaded by his closest friend, George Clemenceau, who used to meet Monet regularly, in 1899 he began painting water lilies, which occupied him until his death. The first small pictures were followed by large murals with an unprecedented open composition. These murals, installed in two rooms of the Orangeries of the Tuileries, were called by André Masson "the Sistine Chapel of Impressionism."

After Monet's death, Seurat's constructive lay-out of pictorial space obscured impressionism as a formless style. Critics, forgetting that postimpressionism had its origin in the art of Monet and his friends, and ignoring the fact that Monet's marvelous colors had motivated us to look with more care at nature. Cezanne once exclaimed, "Monet is only an eye—but what an eye."

CAMILLE PISSARRO (1830–1903)

Born on an island of the Danish West Indies, Pissarro was the son of a French Jewish merchant. At the age of twelve, he was sent to Paris for high school. In Paris, he began drawing and visiting the Louvre. At the age of seventeen, he returned home and worked in his father's general store. As he could not obtain his father's permission to devote himself to painting, in 1852 he ran away to Caracas. Reconciled with his father he returned home, and in 1855 he left for Paris to study painting. His arrival in Paris coincided with the Universal Exposition of 1855, where he saw paintings by Ingres, Delacroix, and Courbet, but it was Corot's soft harmonies, firm structure, and organized planes that impressed this humble man with intimate feelings for nature. He went to see the master; Corot urged him to paint from nature and to study form and value. He began to work in different studios and paint at the Louvre. At the Académie Suisse, he met Monet, Cezanne, and Guillaumin. Later, through Monet, he met Renoir, Sisley, and Bazille.

Pissarro, by nature a poet of rustic landscapes, for his residence always chose rural areas outside of Paris. Deeply loving nature, he did not follow Monet to dissect some aspects of the visible world. Always respecting the lessons of Corot and the Barbizon tradition, he gave solid construction to his pictures. But whereas the Barbizon painters, and Corot in his final period, used the receding perspective of a road into the heart of the landscape, to encompass a wider block of space into the pictorial space, Pissarro substituted the turning perspective of a road instead of the receding perspective.

Finding out that placing color on the canvas creates an edge that gives color its own contour, Pissarro refused to take a position on either of the two opposing views about the superior merits of either line or color. The Salon of 1868, which had included Daubigny in its jury, became more relaxed in its selections and accepted two of Pissarro's pictures.

With the advance of the Prussian army on Paris, Pissarro took refuge in London, where he met Monet, and they worked together. Returning to France after the war, he found out that Prussian soldiers had destroyed most of his paintings.

In 1872 Pontoise's unspoiled countryside with cultivated fields and woods appealed to Pissarro. He settled at Pontoise and lived there until 1874. The poetic qualities of his Pontoise works, and at the same time the use of different painterly techniques for the treatment of the same motif, reveal the extent of his research in those years. He shared with the impressionists the quest to convey impressions of light and color through loose brushwork, but his part in the impressionist movement was more as a fatherly figure than a man of ideas like Monet. He was the only one who participated in all impressionist exhibitions.

He was a good artistic guide, generous in sharing his experiences, and always a loyal friend. In Pontoise, a few young painters gathered around him. Cezanne, a friend and admirer of Pissarro's personality and art, bought a house in the neighboring village of Auvers to work with Pissarro. They discussed matters of art and painted from the same motifs together; while each one kept to his own method, they influenced each other. The poetic values of Pissarro's style attained the monumentality of Cezanne, and Cezanne's colors grew lighter. Later, Pissarro said, "We were always together, but what is certain is that each of us kept the only thing that matters: one own's sensation." Artistic interchange was not limited to collaboration with Cezanne. In 1879 to 1880, he engaged in shared research with Degas. Degas believed that there is always a gap between an immediate perception of a motif and its representation and that in a picture memory and reflection are factors. Pissarro also ascribed to this opinion, which contradicted the impressionist notion of the direct recording of sensation.

Pissarro was disappointed with public and critical response to the first impressionist exhibition. Nonetheless, considering independent exhibition a correct path for the group and assisted by a painter named Alfred Meyer, he formed L'Union, supposedly to replace the syndicate of 1874. But the intrigues of Meyer against the impressionists, particularly Monet, threatened the unity of the group. Impressionists were planning for a new exhibition in 1877. To get a step ahead of the impressionists, Meyer opened the first manifestation of L'Union at the Grand Hotel, but Pissarro, Cezanne, and Guillaumin resigned from L'Union and did not participate in its exhibition.

An arduous financial situation obliged Pissarro to accept the offer of a friend to go to live at his farm at Montfoucault. Montfoucault, a tiny hamlet with a few houses enclosed by trees and rocks, lacked the broad vistas of Pontoise. His pictures of Montfoucault evoke a sense of isolation. Interested in studying the interiors of farm and peasant life, his work included genre subjects. His genre painting was short-lived, but it was important for his exploration of figure painting. After a year the family returned to Pontoise, to live there until 1882.

At the end of Pontoise period, he demonstrated interest in figures. The critics of the time compared his figures to those of Millet, but Pissarro's figures—sitting or working in their habitual surroundings or when alone absorbed by their reveries—do not convey any sociological message. His market scenes are pictures of the intermingling of vendors and buyers from all ages and classes.

His final settlement was in the tiny village of Éragny. Despite the confined area of the village, its gardens, pastures, and cultivated land offered him enough variety of visual material to paint hundreds of paintings and watercolors. The varieties of research that he did throughout the last twenty years of his life make his time in Éragny a significant period.

Dissatisfied for some time with his own work, Pissarro became receptive to Seurat's innovation and decided to follow the scientifically minded execution of neoimpressionism. As the paintings were mainly executed at the studio, for Pissarro, not enjoying being confined indoors and losing direct contact with nature, this conversion became short-lived. He returned to impressionism, and divisionist experiments gave his art a greater purity of color.

PIERRE-AUGUSTE RENOIR (1841–1919)

The son of a poor tailor, Renoir was born in Limoges. Four years after the birth of Pierre, the family moved to Paris. When he reached the age of thirteen, his parents hoped that with his gift for drawing he would have an opportunity to be admitted to the state-owned porcelain factory at Sèvres, and they found him a job with a porcelain decorator. He spent four years in this job. After the invention of a machine for printing pictures on china made porcelain painters redundant, he turned to painting ladies' fans and then church banners for missionaries.

In 1862, he attended evening classes at the École des Beaux-Arts. To make up for inconsistency of method caused by the rotation of the teaching by different masters at the école, some of the teachers opened their own private studio. Renoir continued his study at L'Atelier Gleyre, indirectly connected to the école. Gleyre was a modest man and rather indulgent. Having no preference in subject matter, he let his students paint what they wanted. There, Renoir became a friend of Monet, Bazille, and Sisley. During the first week, there was a clash between Gleyre and Renoir. Gleyre looked at Renoir's work and said, "You obviously paint to amuse yourself, don't you?" Renoir replied, "But of course. You can be sure that I would not do it if it didn't amuse me." Despite this conversation, Renoir showed a true respect for their teacher.

He was turned down at the Salon of 1864, but he accepted in 1865. At the Salon of 1868, Renoir's full-length portrait, *Lise*, painted entirely en plein air in the forest of Fontainebleau, stood out among the official entries. The natural grace of the portrait attracted the attention of the critics. Softer in line and color than Monet's *Camille*, and contrary to the indifference of Monet to volume, Renoir showed his admiration for the sensual plenitude of the woman's body.

Renoir and his friends, deeply impressed by Manet's daring pictures, looked at him as a standard bearer, but they followed their own temperaments. Renoir's treatment of his landscapes of 1868, painted in La Grenouillère, already showed signs of his move toward impressionism.

Renoir was penniless. For a while, he lived in Bazille's studio, and in the summer of 1869, he lived with Lise, his model and mistress, and her parents; and he occasionally would take some food to Monet, who was living in total destitution. But Renoir by nature was a happy guy who enjoyed his work and being alive. He wrote to Bazille, "Although we don't eat every day, I'm still quite cheerful." His art, which is a feast for the eye, contains no sign of the difficulties of his life or the frustrations caused by rejection of his art.

After the Franco-Prussian War, the friends were together again except for Bazille, who was killed. When Monet moved to Argenteuil in 1872, Renoir joined him to paint together. Their joint efforts matured the works of the impressionists. Throughout his impressionist period, Renoir used a variety of brushstrokes in the same picture. He used thick strokes of color in the foreground and flat patches in the background, while the middle ground glides away.

The subjects of Renoir's pictures that celebrate the joy of life were portraits, genre pictures, theater and dance scenes, the hustle and bustle of the crowds of Paris, and landscapes. Some of these works are among the great pictures of impressionism. In the works of this period, he placed his models under trees, so that spots of lights create light and shadow on their faces and dresses. The patches of light and subtle reflections of the foliage on the half-length portrait of *Nude in the Sunlight* (1875) merge the woman with her surroundings.

Montmartre, a hill in the northeast of Paris, has a magnificent view of the city. At the beginning of the nineteenth century, the hill was covered by vegetation and towered with windmills. As its rural simplicity attracted people for excursions, soon open-air restaurants and night bars opened their doors there, and one of the mills was converted to the Moulin de la Galette as a dance hall.

Renoir painted the relaxation of the populace in open-air cafés and bars. His *Le Moulin de la Galette* (1876), which has been referred to as the most beautiful picture of the nineteenth century, is a celebration of life. Its composition is of a compact, casual gathering of a group around a table and a wider group of dancing couples. Despite an apparently chaotic composition, which is due to its subject of a gathering of unrelated people trying to have the best of times, the composition is well conceived. The verticality of dancing figures, lampposts, and lighting fixtures give stability to the picture.

Renoir did not love nature the way Pissarro loved it. His preferred subject was always the human figure. Through his apprenticeship in porcelain painting, he had acquired a pearly, brilliant color and a delicate touch that served him well, especially in his portraits of women. His pictures of women, with gentle contours bathed in light, bought forth a totally new type of feminine beauty that was fresh, with delicately warm and pearly skin. Proust wrote, "Women pass in the street, different now from those of another time…from now on we see them not as women but as Renoirs." In 1878, Charpentier, a publisher, asked Renoir to paint a portrait of his wife and children. Although the portrait of *Mme. Charpentier and Her Children*, painted indoors, lacked his usual outdoor abandon to sensibilities, it opened the door of high society to Renoir, and famous people asked him to paint their portraits.

In 1878, the impressionists met in Paris to decide about a group exhibition. Renoir, Cezanne, Sisley, and Berthe Morrisot disengaged themselves from the impressionists and returned to exhibit at the salon. In spite of their absence, the impressionists opened their fourth exhibition.

In 1881 Renoir traveled to Algeria. Renoir, whose feeling for form had never been repressed by impressionism, confronted for the first time by the Greco-Roman civilization, decided to visit Italy. He had already been fascinated by Ingres's *Madame Riviere* at the Louvre, and he believed that a painter learns more by looking at masterpieces than nature. In Italy while studying the art of Raphael and Pompeian frescoes, he realized that, becoming too preoccupied with light, he had neglected the line. Trying to capture the purity of form, he concentrated on the study of rhythm and linear balance. His gradual transition to the new style led to his break with impressionism.

The years between 1884 and 1887, known as his Ingresque Period, marked a turning point in Renoir's art. Although he had already painted numbers of nude pictures, it was after the second half of the 1880s that the subject acquired a major position in his art. For his large composition of *Les Grandes Baigneuses*, from 1884 to 1887, he painted a number of studies. He applied his thin and smooth colors with great care and no longer tried to render patches of sunlight and spots of shadow on a figure's body. Rather, he concentrated on drawing clear and accurate lines. Limiting this rigid style to the treatment of nude subjects shows that he was struggling to change his whole concept of art.

As the cold manner of painting he had adopted in his Ingresque period was ill-suited to his temperament, he changed direction. His thinly brushed colors dissolved lines, and his art recovered its earlier freshness. Now he emphasized modeling, his color became more sumptuous than before, and free-flowing brushstrokes gave his pictures a flowerlike quality. He painted figures in a luxuriant landscape, and his light brushwork fused figures and their environment together. In this sensual art, the colors of nudes acquired the substance of flesh.

Serious illness overshadowed the end of his life. In 1888, he developed facial paralysis. After an attack in 1913, it became necessary to attach the paintbrush to his hand. Gauguin said of him that he was "a man who does not know how to draw but draws well."

AFRED SISLEY (1839–1899)

Sisley, a Parisian by birth, was the son of a wealthy British businessman. His father sent his eighteen-year-old son to London for a commercial apprenticeship. There, Alfred devoted more time to studying Turner and Constable than trade. Upon his return to Paris in 1862, he enrolled at Gleyre's studio, where he made the acquaintance of future impressionists. Despite the difference in their social origins and their economic statuses, a close friendship bound them together.

Monet, who had experience of outdoor painting, took his friends to the forest of Fontainebleau. The effect of this contact with nature made Sisley choose his objective. Although he painted a few still lifes and indoor scenes, he remained exclusively devoted to landscape painting.

From the beginning, the study of shimmering reflections of light on water and on snow were Sisley's two favorite themes. In his landscapes of the Canal Saint Marin, painted in 1870, his colors became lighter and his brushstrokes shorter to suggest reflections of light on water. The same year he also painted *Early Snow at Louveciennes*.

His father, ruined by the Franco-Prussian war, died after an illness. Faced with an unforeseen situation, he had to fend for himself, his wife, and his children. Consequently, Sisley, who was an amateur painter before the war, dedicated all his time to painting, which became his only source of income. He often joined Monet at Argenteuil and painted landscapes exclusively. But not accustomed to financial hardship, he began to isolate himself.

Sisley, under the influence of the solid and precise forms of Corot, was concerned about the structure of the space of his pictures, while a pure light enveloped his composition. Close communication with nature gave him the confidence for a new approach to painting. He studied the changes of the same motif in different hours and seasons. To indicate the individual texture of each element of his picture, while careful not to damage the pictorial unity, he used a variety of brushwork on the same canvas. The heavy floods of Marley provided him with a subject for a series of paintings, and their reflection of light over water and delicately chosen colors remain among the best that he ever did.

Durand-Ruel's own financial problems, which deprived the impressionist group from the financial assistance of the one dealer who believed in them, aggravated Sisley's situation. In 1880, Durand-Ruel began to buy again, and in 1883, he arranged a retrospective of Sisley's work, which was not very successful.

In a general way, Sisley's work is divided into three periods. The first is the brief period distinguished by the influence of Corot, which lasted until 1870. The second period, between 1870 to 1880, includes his most luminous paintings. In the third period, which co-incided with the aggravation of his financial situation, he attained technical perfection.

Although his friends began to break with the impressionist con-cept of painting, Sisley always remained loyal to the creed of impres-sionism. A few months after the death of his wife, Sisley died as well, in 1899. An auction of twenty-seven of his pictures in 1900, to raise money for his two children, was unexpectedly successful.

BERTHE MORISOT (1841-1895)

Berthe Morisot, the intelligent, and talented daughter of a rich magis-trate took painting more seriously than did most women of her stand-ing in the nineteenth century. Berthe and he sister Edma started to study painting under Josph Guichard. As their stuy was limited to copy masters, they told their teacher that they wished to paint en plein air. Guichard introduced them to Corot, who accepted them as pupils.

In 1868, Berthe Morisot met Edourad Manet; they formed a lasting friendship and influenced art of each other. In 1874, she participated at te first impressionist exhibition. She experiencd with numerous media, including oil, watercolor, and pastel. She was con-siderd a painter who represents Impressionism with talent.

*   *   *

In 1880, disagreements and the increased pursuit by each impres-sionist painter of his own aesthetic interest divided the group;

nevertheless, they remained friends. In 1881, the state finally abandoned its supervision of the exhibitions of the salon, and an artists' association assumed the task of the organization of the show. In 1885, the American Art Association invited Durand-Ruel to organize an exhibition of impressionist paintings in New York. The exhibition had limited success, but the future looked bright. Berthe Morisot organized the eighth and last impressionist exhibition in 1886, in which Monet, Renoir, and Sisley refused to participate. After 1886, each impressionist painter chose the path of independence from the others.

Despite all the misery they endured, the impressionist painters stood fast in defending their art against critics and the restrictions imposed on progressive art. Their research and their struggle against academism paved the way for new generations of painters with new ideas. The effect of their bright colors on the following movements is undeniable. But similar to other art movements, impressionism had reached a point where research could not move further. Their aesthetic of replacing local color with vibrations of waves of light volatilized the forms of their subjects, which instigated the reaction of postimpressionist painters.

Section 7

Paul Cezanne (1838–1906)

Cezanne was born at Aix-en-Provence in southern France, close to the Mediterranean Sea and plentiful sunshine. He was a shy, unsociable, persistent, and hardworking boy. His father, a hat maker, in the process of the liquidation of a bank took over it and then with a partner cofounded a new bank. In 1852 Paul entered at the College Bourbon, where he met Emile Zola, and they became intimate friends. Artistic questions absorbed them, and they wrote poetry.

From 1858 to 1860, Cezanne attended the School of Drawing in Aix, where he won a second prize. Encouraged by Zola, Cezanne decided against the wishes of his father to become a painter. With the help of his mother, he succeeded in persuading his father to let him devote his life to painting.

In 1861, he went to Paris. The next ten years were a period of uncertainty for Cezanne. Disgusted with the life of the large city, he returned to Aix, took a job in his father's office, and enrolled at the art school. In 1862, he went back to Paris, and at the insistence of his father, he tried for admittance of the École des Beax-Arts. Unsuccessful in going to the école, he attended the Académie Suisse, where he became acquainted with Guillaumin, and Pissarro a painter ten years older than him. Guillaumin brought him into contact with Monet, Renoir, and Sisley, the future impressionist painters studying at L'Atelier Gleyre. But Cezanne, living a solitary life, did not participate in the activities of the preimpressionists.

Those years were of crucial importance in the history of modern art. Courbet's realism had lost its earlier political suggestiveness but was still order of the day. In 1863 following the strong protests of angry artists, by the command of Napoleon III, the Salon des Refusés was established for those works rejected by the jury of the official salon. Among thepictures exhibited in this new salon was Manet's *Le Dejeuner sur l'Herbe*, painted on the concept of pure painting. But at that time, Cezanne, believing himself to be a visionary, and considering painting as an instrument to release passions, found that the realism of Courbet and the purely visual representations of Manet could not serve his needs. Within the next ten years, to give form to his inner vision, he painted without reference to models.

In Paris, he was an assiduous visitor of the Louvre. The swirling compositions of Delacroix and the baroque masters, and the richness of the colors of the Venetians, particularly Veronese, intensely appealed to the romantic exaltation and inner agitations of the ambitious young man, who lacked the science of picture making of those masters. Confident of himself and believing himself to be a visionary, he gave form to his imagination and his stormy nature without referring to the outside world. These pictures, despite their immaturity, anticipate the expressionist style of the following century.

The deformed and out-of-proportion figures of Cezanne's romantic period, of orgy, rape, and murder, with a narrative content more literary than plastic, were a product of a restless mind. With planes not sufficiently distinct, and extreme contrasts of dark color against lighter tones and white, these pictures were executed with expressive brushwork or influenced by Courbet's application of a thick layer of pigment with a palette knife. Little by little, Cezanne admitted to himself that he lacked the knowledge of how to transmute his vision into plastic images, and he needed to reference the outside world. The decisive change came through working side by side with Pissarro in 1972.

Essentially, Cezanne was a self-taught painter, who, against the advice of Pissarro and Renoir, received no other art instruction. All his life, he struggled with the problems of picture making, and with himself. He underwent many influences of the masters during his long hours of study at the Louvre, but he lacked the details of their methods. His constant struggle for discovery and innovation was an impediment to painting with the same ease with which Monet or Renoir painted. Despite the deformed figures of his romantic period, his pencil drawings of baroque sculptures prove that he knew how to draw, and the portrait of his father painted in 1863 shows his knowledge of establishing volumes. He was a gifted colorist under all conditions and was concerned with composition.

Despite the expressive helix form of a shellfish, *Black Clock* (1870) is a well-composed still life built on verticals and horizontals that give monumentality to the picture. This picture shows that beyond the emotional fervor of the painter of violent scenes of his romantic period existed a logical mind that in the end subdued emotion and shifted the emphasis to artistic sensibility. Possibly a relationship with Hortense Fiquet, a young model whom Cezanne met in 1869 and eventually lived with, had brought him emotional stability.

Pissarro, a kind person and an excellent guide for painters, gathered a small group of painters around him in Pontoise. Cezanne, who knew Pissarro since L'Atelier Suisse and had great respect for him, accepted his suggestion of taking his family to Pontoise. They painted frequently together from the same motif. Pissarro's companionship and guidance were a salutary influence on him. Painting next to Pissarro en plein air developed Cezanne's knowledge of the art of painting. Pissarro's humble approach to nature, which helped Cezanne to discover nature, turned him away from inner visions to a more visual approach to painting. He got rid of heavy material, replaced the sweeping brushstrokes with cautious brushwork. He learned the impressionists' method of breaking up a color by small juxtaposed touches of pure color, and he realized that there is no line in nature, only a contrast of tones. Perhaps the most important effect of his relationship with Pissarro was to learn to be patient and control his emotions. Still far from the maturity that revolutionized the art of painting, for a few more years, he continued the impressionist method.

In 1873, Cezanne left Pontoise and settled in Auvers, but he walked to Pontoise to work with Pissarro. In Auvers, a place that was little more than a village, Cezanne could work without being disturbed by the curiosity of passersby. The other motivation was the presence of Dr. Gachet in Auvers, who was a friend of Pissarro and interested in art. In 1874 and 1877, Cezanne exhibited with the impressionists. In 1882, he was accepted at the salon as "Guillemet's pupil."

Although he never rejected sensation, a characteristic of the aesthetic of impressionism, and he always retained the use of pure colors, he was a deeply intellectual person in search of the reality hidden beneath appearances. He could not content himself with the analytical methods of the impressionists at the cost of the form of objects. Looking at nature for more than an impression, his interest in picture making differed from that of the impressionists. Cezanne, whose sensation was within the context of his logic of picture making, sought to solve the problems of space, color, and rhythm in order to lay out the elements of a picture in a new order.

By watching nature beyond its diversity, he saw stability and permanence made of geometric shapes. Consequently, his pictures, rather than imitating nature, became representations of a deeply cerebral creation and an intellectual search to solve the problems of painting. Stripping natural forms of the accidental variations of their individual appearances gave monumentality to his pictures. Photographs taken from the sites he painted show his attachment to his subjects, and that instead of copying nature through his compositional rearrangements, he created a harmonic, colorful, and monumental world of solid forms. He said that a painter should treat nature in terms of cylinder, sphere, and cone—a remark that meant a platonic representation of the world, rather than reducing a picture to abstract forms. His research for timelessness led him back to the local color, which he had rejected while working with Pissarro; and instead of the impressionists' touches of color that dissolved objects into the atmosphere, Cezanne's method of the application of color built solid forms.

In the Renaissance system of perspective, objects in the distance become smaller, with fewer details, and in the Impressinism distant elements of the picture are dissolved in atmosphere and painted with different brushstrokes. With a vision of the world more intellectual than what the eyes perceive, Cezanne realized these systems limited his ability to create harmony between distant and near objects. To give depth to his picture, he replaced the Renaissance perspective with a succession of two-dimensional planes. In his systen, parallels suggested distance, diagonals defined spatial depth; and reduction of the scale of pictorial elements depended on the requirements of the composition.

In a traditional style, a suggestion of volume is achieved through linear perspective and modeling. As Cezanne had rejected linear perspective, color was his only means of defining volume. He discovered that through modeling with color he could give solid structure to objects. Through his method, which he called "modulation," with an accurate selection of tone, he gave volume, mass, and precision of contour to the objects of his pictures. By maintaining a uniform direction of short, rectangular brushstrokes, he built a world of solid forms. His watercolors and unfinished oil paintings show that he started his pictures with the main contours to establish relationships and planes, and then during the process of painting, he had to go over the contours to reestablish a meeting place of different colors. To modulate volume, he would start from the dark, cool side of an object, going to the light, warm side of it. Emile Bernard, one of the few to be allowed to stand by while Cezanne was painting, described the process. "He started with the shadow, with a brushstroke, then covered it with another larger one, then a third." In his early work, he had a sweeping brushstroke. After working with Pissarro, he used uniform, rectangular brushstrokes in a parallel direction, but in his later phase he used larger strokes and with more freedom.

For Cezanne, each picture was an investigation into solving a problem of picture making. In contrast to his earlier paintings, his approach to his subject was humble, and he kept the same attitude toward still life, landscape, and portraiture. He devoted much of his time to painting still lives. His forms are compact, and his beautiful colors appeal to the touch. In his landscapes he avoided accidentals, thus creating timeless landscapes that the spectator is mainly invited to look at it, but not, as in traditional landscapes, invited to enter. In an often-quoted phrase, "to do Poussin over again after nature," Cezanne expressed his admiration for the logical order of Poussin's work.

His approach to painting portraits, far from the overly expressive forms of his romantic period, become similar to his still life pictures. In the portrait of *Gustave Geffroy*, with the masklike features of the writer, he shows no interest in the character of the model or an intimacy between painter and sitter. This portrait, one of Cezanne's masterpieces, is constructed with infinite complexity. Different tilting of books from shelf to shelf, and books on the desk opened in various directions, create a balance to the pyramidal posture of the writer, treated as a still life.

In 1872 Hortense Fiquet, the model living with Cezanne, gave birth to a child. Cezanne, who had always lived in fear of his father, kept this relationship a secret from his father. In 1886 Cezanne's sister obtained their father's consent to the marriage of Cezanne and Hortense. A few months after the marriage, his father died, and Cezanne came into a large inheritance.

The relationship between painting and literature had been one interesting intellectual feature of the second half of the nineteenth century. Painters chose themes from literary sources, and writers extensively expressed their opinions of particular pictures or the general trends of art. In 1886, in his novel *L'Oeuvre*, Zola modeled an unsuccessful painter on Cezanne. Degas, despite his solid classical education and his attraction to literature, criticized writers who meddled in art. He considered Zola's *L'Oeuvre* "simply to prove the immense superiority of the writer over the painter." The novel caused the break of the old relationship of Cezanne and Zola. Despite this the death of Zola was a great blow to Cezanne. When he learned of Zola's death, he burst into tears and locked himself in his studio.

He painted watercolors from 1875 onward. In the early watercolors, baroque movements of pencil are mixed with watercolors. In the later oil paintings, he progressively developed two specific qualities of watercolor: lightness and transparency. His impasto became thinner to the point of transparency; thus, when he applied a color over another, the underlying color remained visible.

The year 1889 was a turnaround in his life. He settled peacefully for five years in Aix. His art received the acceptance of enlightened critics, and several of his pictures were accepted by the Musée du

Luxembourg. In 1895 the art dealer Vollard organized a large one-man show of Cezanne's paintings at his gallery. The critical discussions that followed the exhibition of Cezanne's pictures established his reputation.

Cezanne belonged to the bourgeoisie, but he did not care for the sophistication of city life. The simplicity of peasantry was closer to his soul, and he felt more at ease with them. He painted five versions of *The Card Players*, of peasants absorbed in their game. The postures that he selected for these peasants point to his respect for them. In his portraits, Cezanne showed no interest in the sitter's character but treated him or her as a still life motif. But *The Card Players* reflects a moment of pure meditation.

The exceptional range of versatility of handling in his work shows that Cezanne was never content with his progress. Each picture was painted as a response to the process of his perpetual redefining and reevaluation. The struggle to find answers for the problems of painting aged him prematurely. Aware of his failing health, and deeply upset by his mother's death in 1897, he withdrew gradually from his wife and friends, sold his house, and rented a cottage in Bibémus Quarry, outside Aix.

The forms of trees in the landscape of *The House with the Cracked Wall* (1892–1894), repeating the cracks of the house, and the window as an opening to the dark empty house, hint at his solitude and morbid mood. The chaotic nature, and the solitary corners of woods appealed to his contemplative mood. He painted the wild vegetation and the powerful shapes of cut stones of the abandoned Bibémus Quarry at the clearing of the Fontainebleau forest, and of the Chateau Noir.

The great turbulence of his inner life led to a change in his vision of art. The years from 1890 to his death in 1906 are the period in which he synthesized his experiences. In control and at ease with his motives, trusting his sensibilities more than ever, he set aside visual enchantment and began to see with his mind's eye. The most important characteristic of this period is the restless treatment of brushwork that replaced his constructive brushwork, emphasizing the unity of each object in his pictures. Now, by breaking up their volumes, he let his objects breathe and move in space. Similar to watercolor technique, the transparency of a thin layer of subtle and somber tones allowed the underlying color to be visible. These changes, the effects of pathos, were a return of the emotionality of his romantic period in a new way.

The wavy forms of onion tails and tablecloth—and the less voluminous shapes of vegetables within a subdued atmosphere of *Still Life with Onions and Bottle*—show the deviation from his previous approach to still life subjects, reflecting his change of mood.

La Montagne Sainte-Victoire had a special attraction for Cezanne. He painted over sixty views from the site. In his version of 1885–1886, the lines and planes give a panoramic illusion of the site. In the last version, built of marvelous subtleties, which was painted in 1904–1906, dynamism of emotion has replaced the compositional complexities, and the restless brushstrokes of rich tones unite land, mountain, and sky.

In his last period, realizing that his obsession with emphasizing the contours of human forms strangled his figures, he chose short-line brushwork to overflow the contour line. Now the figure, free from the austerity of Gustave Geffroy's portrait, was breathing and moving in its environment. In the *Portrait of Vallier*, painted in 1906 of his gardener, multiple short lines around the body of Vallier correlate man and space. The noble and tranquil posture of the man, the compactness of the body, the wonderful luminosity emanating from the figure, and the freedom of a sure brush in this portrait are the climax of his lifelong research.

From midseventies on, Cezanne began painting a series of iso-lated nude figures. Compositions of bathers merged with natural elements give monumentality to these pictures. *Bather* (1885) is a strange picture, echoing the forms and colors of the earth, sea, and sky on the body of the man, connecting him to nature. But the man is so absorbed in thoughts that he pays no attention to his sur-roundings. From 1895 he began three large compositions of female *Bathers*, but their chronological order of painting is not clear. Based on the reports of Cezanne's visitors and compositional progress, the unfinished *Bathers* in the Philadelphia Museum of Art, named *Les Grandes Baigneuses*, is the last version. He worked for several years over this version, which is composed of repeated pyramids of fig-ures under soaring trees as in a Gothic cathedral vault. His palette is reduced to two colors: blue and orange-ochre. The dominant cool color of blue, delicately applied, is spread through the whole picture.

At last his genius had been recognized. The Salon d'Automne of 1904 set aside an entire room for his works, and his house became a pilgrimage place for the younger generation of painters. His letter to a young friend reflects the sadness of old age. "Perhaps I have come too soon...I was the painter of your generation more than myself." In 1906, while painting in the field, he was caught in a rainstorm. He collapsed on the roadside and was taken home by a passing cart driver. He died a few days later. As an incomparable colorist and the inventor of new rhythms in his compositions, Cezanne had an enor-mous influence on modern painting.

Section 8

Neoimpressionism

The breakup of impressionism coincided with two fundamentally opposing artistic perceptions: neoimpressionism, an attempt to retrieve a scientific system from impressionism; and symbolism, a movement developed in art and literature to give sensible form to ideas in lieu of objective representation of the world.

GEORGES SEURAT (1859–1891)

Seurat was born in Paris into a modestly well-off family. He began the study of art at a municipal school of drawing. At the age of eighteen, he was admitted to the École des Beaux-Arts. His teacher, Henri Lehman, who was one of the best pupils of Ingres, taught him to turn perception into line. He studied and made copies of the old masters at the Louvre—particularly of Raphael, Poussin, and Ingres. Copies of the Piero della Francesca frescoes at Arezzo had been placed in the chapel of the École des Beaux-Arts. The monumentality and the motionless groups of the art of this master left a lasting effect on the mind of Seurat. He visited the fourth exhibition of the impressionists, but he had no interest in open-air painting or capturing the fleeting moment. However, in the course of research, he benefited from the large body of the impressionists' technical discoveries.

Seurat was a gentle, withdrawn person with the delicate feelings of a poet. An intellectual, he was an avid reader of technical treatises. Among the books that influenced Seurat were Charles Blanc's *Grammaire des Arts et du Dessin*, Chevreul's *De la Loi du Contraste Simultané des Couleurs*, Charles Henry's *Introduction à une Esthétique Scientifique*, and Humbert de Suerville's *Essai sur les Signes Inconditionnels dans l'Art*, which emphasized the expressive value of the general orientation of dominant lines in a drawing.

In 1879, he went for one year of military service. During that year he made sketches of the motionless attitudes of people, such as when reading a book or dozing on a bench. While in military service, he read David Sutter's article on "The Phenomena of Sight." Sutter's idea that there is a hidden harmony in the world that artists, musicians, and poets have to find and that there is no opposition between art and science pleased Seurat.

In 1881, in a series of notes on Delacroix's painting, Seurat analyzed the harmonious color combinations of the master. He also studied the art of his predecessors, without succumbing to their influence. These studies helped him to give form to his scientific method. His landscapes of the environs of Paris and the edge of the Fontainebleau forest show no sign of Corot's lyricism or the objective observations of the Barbizon school.

From Lehman, he had learned to turn perception into line, but his pictures of 1882, painted with thick brushstrokes emphasizing areas of tone and reducing his figures to their essential elements, reveal his own approach to painting. At the Salon of 1883, he exhibited portraits of his mother and his friend Aman-Jean, drawn with the medium of Conté crayon. Through this medium, he found an appropriate language to give monumental stillness to his subjects.

Seurat, for his first large canvas, *Une Baignade à Asnières*, made many prepatory outdoor studies and drawings of models posed in studio. Immobility of figures had given a monumental character to the picture that recalls Piero della Francesca. The torpor of a hot summer that gives stillness to everything has stopped the time of the picture. He reconciled optical sensation and abstract forms and gave monumentality to the simple and carefully arranged masses of the large forms of his motionless figures, all of which seems to be an assimilation of the influence of Piero della Francesca's frescoes to a contemporary landscape. The canvas was painted in broad, smooth brushstrokes, but in 1886 he added dots of pure color to the picture. The *Baignade*, rejected by the jury of the salon, was exhibited in the first Salon des Artistes Indépendants, which was organized by the artists rejected by the jury of the Salon of 1884. There, the *Baignade* drew the attention of a few critics.

As drawing and shading on rough-grained textured paper preserves the vibrancy of light next to the dark areas, it is possible that preparatory drawings for *Une Baignade* gave him the idea for his chromo-luminarism. Less concerned with recording his immediate color sensations than with making his picture a vibrant source of light, Seurat worked out a system based on scientific color theory to substitute an optical mixture for the mixture of pigments. In this system colors not blended together were dots or patches of color placed closely next to each other, with their size according to where they occur. Seen at the appropriate distance, they achieved maximum luminosity, and obtained subtle gradations. He called this system, which revolutionized the treatment of color, chromo-luminarism. This system, better known as divisionism, developed into pointillism, the application of tiny daubs of colors, which was not necessarily focused on the separation of colors.

In the summer of 1885, he went for a few weeks to Grandcamp on the Normandy coast and painted landscapes that reflect a delicate feeling for the luminous space of the fishing village. The following summer he went to Honfleur. The complex composition of masts, ropes, and geometric forms of ship and yard in *Honfleur Harbour* show that his passion for intellectual construction had gotten the upper hand over his delicate sensibilities of the previous summer.

After *Une Baignade*, he devoted two continuous years to outdoor and indoor studies and made more than sixty preparatory drawings and paintings for the large canvas *A Sunday Afternoon on the Island of la Grande Jatte*. In this picture, which is a dream of a platonic world, he has frozen the movement and has perfectly integrated his figures into the landscape. For the first time, he applied his color technique of chromo-luminarism in this painting. With little care about the subject, Seurat's intention was to create a harmonious picture of luminous colors and a well-balanced composition of verticals of figures and trees, the horizontal of the distant embankment, and the diagonals of shadows and shoreline. When this painting—with its bold and unprecedented concept of meticulously chosen values and forms that have fixed light, people, and landscape in an abstract design—was exhibited, it aroused public indignation, but art critics recognized its revolutionary character.

In 1887 he began *Models*, his third major composition. For this seemingly simple painting of three different poses of the same model in back, front, and side views, he studied for one whole year. Each pose was the subject of an individual study and several oil paintings. The canvas of *La Grande Jatte*, hung on the wall to divide the composition into two parts. The upright form of the back of the seated nude is prolonged into the two upright figures of *La Grande Jatte*. The standing nude divides the composition into two halves. With the relationship of the legs of the seated model in side view to the clothing and an umbrella, he formed the sides of a pyramid. *Models* is the only work between Seurat's major paintings that is enriched by a naturalistic view. By posing his models next to the figures of *La*

Grande Jatte, he contrasts reality with a world on the verge of pure abstraction.

The year of 1887 marked a turnaround in Seurat's career. Besides Signac and Pissarro, his ideas attracted other painters and gained the interest of important art critics. He went to Brussels to exhibit at the fourth Salon des Vingt, a group of Belgian artists against academic painting, who every year invited foreign artists to participate in their annual exhibition.

La Parade, painted in 1888, marks the beginning of new research by Seurat. The light of previous paintings was natural daylight, whereas in *La Parade* he used the artificial light of gas lamps, which augmented the dreamlike quality of the picture. The composition of the picture is a collection of verticals, horizontals, rectangles, and ovals.

Beyond the solid forms of his visual impressions was a sensible poet. In 1887 to 1888, Seurat drew scenes of café-concerts. The actresses were always in white dress in the brightly lit background, while in the foreground spectators in the shadow give a poetic vision to these drawings.

In 1888 he painted six pictures directly, without drawings or preliminary paintings, of the landscapes of the Port-en-Bassin. One of the major differences of some of the beautiful landscapes of the *Port-en-Bessin* paintings is the prominence of buildings over the sea.

He met Madeleine Knoblock, a young model who became his companion and the model for *Young Woman Powdering Herself.* In 1889 the organizer of the exhibition of Les Vingt, by inviting Seurat as well as Gauguin, who strongly disapproved of divisionism, to their exhibition, brought under the same roof two opposing art view of the heirs of impressionism.

In 1889, he painted *Le Chahut.* The diagonals of the lifted legs of dancers and the neck of the double bass, which provide the dynamics to the composition, show his interest in the expressive value of line. Due to his formulas, the ascending lines and warm hue create gaiety, while the horizontals create calmness, and descending lines and cold hues create sadness.

In the summer of 1890, he painted four landscapes of the small seaport of Gravelines. Their flat areas of unbroken forms followed the same concept of picture making as *La Grande Jatte*. The precious atmosphere and subtle chromatic variations make this series the best thought-out of his landscapes.

In 1891, at the eight Salon des Indépendants, he exhibited his uncompleted *The Circus*, which shows the influence of poster art. Its subject of an animated spectacle in the arena, similar to *Le Chahut*, is composed of spirals. His death left *The Circus* unfinished.

While supervising the hanging of pictures at the Salon des Indépendants, he caught a chill that developed into an infection that confined him to bed, and he died at the age of thirty-one.

Seurat considered art as the harmony of value, hue, and line. Beyond his scientifically organized figures and space, which antici-pate cubism, one senses the feelings of a poet. A lover of modern subject matter, he painted people relaxing in the open air and spec-tacles of circuses and music halls. He was not always praised during his lifetime, and he sold few paintings. Roger Fry defined his art as "alive, but not with the life of nature."

PAUL SIGNAC (1863–1935)

Signac was born in Paris. His father was a prosperous luxury saddler and harness maker. At the age of fourteen, Paul was listed as a board-er at the College Rollin in Montmartre. After the death of his father in 1880, he continued his study as a day boarder, but he left school prior to taking his baccalaureate and began painting. Attracted by impressionist painting, in their exhibition of 1880, Signac began to sketch after a Degas, but Gauguin showed him the door, saying, "One does not copy here, sir."

Fond of literature, he came into contact with naturalist writers, who later became supporters of neoimpressionism. Except for studying the works of Manet, Monet, and Degas, he had no formal art instruction. His first paintings date from 1881.

In 1884 he participated in the first exposition of the Salon des Indépedants. There he met Seurat, and he became one of the few friends of Seurat. He recalled their visit to Chevreul, the old color theoretician, as "our introduction to the science of color," and he read scientific art treatises.

The friendship of Seurat and discussions of various art theories did not lead to an immediate change in Signac's manner of painting. It was after seeing Seurat's *La Grande Jatte* that he reworked his first major work, *The Milliners*, and became an advocate of pointillism.

Signac's initial interest in color contrasts was due to his concern with luminosity in painting. Then his friendship with Charles Henry, who speculated about the expressive power of colors and the effect of various directions of line, moved his interest to explore the abstract expressive power of color and line. The figure of his *Portrait of Félix Fénéon*, set against color contrasts of a background of spiraling lines, inspired from a Japanese woodblock print, is a demonstration of Henry's theories. Yet being an intellectual interested in the literary works of symbolists, he emphasized that the painter is a poet, not a scientist.

In a series of coastal landscapes, he applied Henry's theories and Chevreul's principles. To give musical harmony to his work, he simplified the composition and eliminated anecdotal details; he even added opus numbers to the titles of his works. At the end of 1880, inclined to left-wing movements, he painted politically engaged pictures, but since art at the service of a political movement was at odds with his concept of art, his new trend faded away.

The death of Seurat in 1891 was a setback for neoimpressionism. Signac, deeply affected by the death of his friend, withdrew to Saint-Tropez. His technique became looser, he simplified the structure of his pictures, and he laid colors not as dots but as tessera blocks.

In 1899, attracted by the works of Delacroix, whom he considered the precursor of optical color mixture, Signac published *D'Eugène Delacroix au Neo-Impressionism*, a treatise that Apollinaire considered a book marking an important date in the history of contemporary art. By the turn of century, Signac provided a transition between neoimpressionism and fauvism.

Section 9

Charles Baudelaire was the first to point to the symbolic values of line and color. At the end of the nineteenth century, the symbolist movement, a reaction to the naturalist movement in literature and art and expanding materialism, was a revival of some tendencies in the romantic tradition. The movement was more concerned with spiritual forces and imagination than external reality. In painting ideas are suggested through color, line, and form. Emile Bernard wrote, "Since the idea is the form of things collected by the imagination, one ought to paint no more in front of the thing, but by taking it from the imagination."

VINCENT VAN GOGH (1852–1890)

Vincent was born in the town of Grootzundert in Northern Brabant, in the Netherlands. His father was a pastor in the Dutch Reformed community. Born into a Protestant family, he was subject to individualism with its inner conflicts. After attending the local school, he went to a boarding school. There he learned English, French, and German. Of his three uncles, two were art dealers. One of his uncles sold his gallery in The Hague to the art firm of Goupil. In 1869 Goupil Gallery in The Hague hired Vincent as a salesman, and three years later his brother, Theo, became an apprentice at the

Brussels branch of Goupil. In 1873 Vincent was transferred to the London branch, and there he fell deeply in love with the daughter of his landlady. Rejected, he became depressed and withdrawn. His uncle managed to have Vincent transferred to Paris. In Paris, he read a lot. He was first gripped by Dostoevsky and Tolstoy, but the Bible became his final choice. Having spent the Christmas holiday of 1876 with his family without the firm's permission, Goupil dismissed him. He went to England, where he obtained a job as assistant teacher with a minister. But he accomplished his task of collecting the pupils' boarding fees so poorly that he was dismissed.

Already a religious person, Vincent was reading of John Bunyan's *The Pilgrim's Progress*, a spiritual allegorical work of Christian litera-ture composed in the seventeenth century, which deeply impacted him. Returning home for Christmas, he decided to study theology. While preparing himself for the entrance exam of the university, he found the emphasis on the study of Greek, Latin, and mathematics irrelevant to theology. He failed the exam, lost faith in conventional religion, and opted for a more practical program to accomplish his aim of giving himself to others. He went to Brussels and enrolled in a short course to become an evangelical missionary. After a few months, he was found unsuited for the job. In December 1878, he went to the village of Wasmes to work without compensation as an evangelist among poor miners. In January 1879, he received a tem-porary paid position, but his superiors, displeased with his fanatical behavior of dressing like a miner and sleeping on a pile of straw, terminated his appointment.

While living among miners and drawing aspects of their miser-able lives, suddenly he realized that art could be the appropriate vessel to portray the sad life of the poor, stand against the miseries and vulgarities of life, and express his emotional experiences. This discovery changed the course of his life. Seven years later, he wrote to Theo, "I can very well do without God, both in my life and my painting, but I cannot, ill as I am, do without something which is greater than I, which is my whole life: the power to create." He started by going to Brussels to study anatomy and perspective in Van Rappard's studio.

Despite his brief career as an artist, from 1880 to 1890, he became the first great Dutch master since the seventeenth century and a leading modern painter. During these ten years, he lived in The Hague, Paris, Arles. The art that he produced in each of these places has particularities that could be produced only in that place. But his preoccupation with the purpose of life and his deep humanism bound all these periods together.

Theo transferred to Paris to manage the branch of Goupil and Company, and he decided to send a share of his monthly salary to his brother so that Vincent, with no concern about an income, could concentrate on his art.

In January 1882, Vincent went to The Hague. There, he received some lessons for drawing and painting in watercolor and in oil from Anton Mauve, and he also experimented with lithography. His early works reveal his Dutch roots.

In the seventeenth century, Rembrandt and other Dutch painters started a type of painting of the entire head, bust, or occasionally of the whole body of a single figure, called *tronie*—meaning "face" in Dutch. These pictures, not intended to be portraits, exaggerated the facial expression or showed an interesting character. A particularity of these paintings was the use of proper costumes for expressive purposes.

Van Gogh made several *tronies* of poor old men and fishermen. For drawing he used black lithographic crayon, graphite, or chalk on thick watercolor paper. The sitters for these drawings were pensioners of the Dutch Reformed old people's home. His drawings of these old pensioners show the sitters in the clothes of the home. But for the drawings of fishermen, in order to be true to his representation, Van Gogh had to acquire a sou'wester and the standard headgear of fishermen for the sitter. His *Beardless Fisherman Wearing a Sou'wester* is a powerful image of the face of an old fisherman.

The realism, a characteristic of the art of The Hague schoo[12], suited well to his inclination. Subjects of his works in The Hague are old, destitute people resigned to their fates. Even for still lives, he chose old worn-out shoes. His first great painting, *The Potato Eaters* (1885), is of worn-out peasants eating a humble food after a day of toil. In search of greater expression, he did not mind exaggerating the essentials. Exposed to the art of the masters while working for Goupil and then to the art of The Hague school, he became an admirer of Millet, and he appreciated Rembrandt's handling of light and Hals's bold brushwork.

While living in The Hague, following his personal convictions, he sheltered in his house an unfortunate woman forced into prostitution. After a few months, he was forced by his father to abandon her. Before leaving, he made a drawing of the poor woman. The drawing, named *Sorrow*, shows her naked body with signs of decrepitude, and her head on her knees is covered by her arms, possibly to hide her weeping.

A three-month sojourn in Drenthe at the end of 1883 was a turning point in his art. Seeing the peasants working the land turned his attention from portraiture to rural landscapes; a vacillation between portraiture and landscape painting remained a characteristic of his art. In Antwerp he discovered Japanese prints, which transformed his exaggerations to distortions of form.

---

12 - "The Hague school" is a term used for Dutch realist painters, active in Hague between 1860 and 1900. They painted ladscapes and activities of fishermen and farmers. Initialy their colors were somber colors, consisting of mostly greish tints.

In February 1886, he went to Paris and enrolled at the studio of Fernand Cormon, where he met Emile Bernard and Toulouse-Lautrec. Theo introduced Vincent to Gauguin, Seurat, and other avant-garde painters, but Vincent did not adhere to the doctrine of any of them. Exposure to the world of light and color of the impressionists and postimpressionists changed the gloomy manner of his paintings. He began a scientific investigation of the expressive value of color, and he experimented with a variety of brushstrokes, such as the impressionists' comma strokes or small dots of color in imitation of pointillism. The symbolism of color in the service of emotions and the thickness, shape, and direction of his hatchlike brushstrokes became the hallmarks of Van Gogh's style. He painted landscapes en plein air, views of the interior of restaurants, and for lack of a model, two dozen self-portraits. Believing that portraits have a life of their own, he did not seek a likeness in his portraits. The *Self-Portrait as an Artist*, painted before leaving for Arles, is the culmination of his intensive experiments in Paris.

In Paris, he lived in Theo's apartment. Theo, in his letters to their sister, complained of Vincent's violent mood swings and disorderliness, similar to the problems he had later, while living with Gauguin. To get away from the tension of life in Paris, in February 1888 he boarded a train for Arles. In a letter to their sister, Theo mentioned, "Vincent left for the South…Years of worry and adversity have not made him any stronger."

In Arles, he found the light of the sun as intense as his inner flame. The solar blaze of Arles brought to eruption the dormant volcano inside of this most lyrical painter of his time. Exhilarated, he turned this light into colors, his *Sunflowers* became like a "beautiful bouquet of yellow flame," and his art broke loose of constraints.

To reproduce the blazing light of Arles was only one problem. He wanted the symbolic use of color. He wrote to Theo that he wanted to "express the love of two lovers by a marriage between two complementary colors, their mixture, their oppositions, the mysterious vibrations of close tints." Of *Night Café* he said, "I have tried to express the terrible passions of humanity by means of red and greens." In Arles, he painted many portraits of people and of himself. He said, "It lets me cultivate what is the best and deepest in me."

The group painting of impressionists, where each painter shared his gift with others, gave him the idea of sharing his studio with other painters. Gauguin accepted his proposal but did not move to Arles until the end of October 1888. The contact between these two painter-poets was beneficial for both painters, but two opposite personalities living together under the same roof could not last for long.

On December 17, after a visit to the Musée Fabre of Montpellier, a strain in their relation surfaced. On December 24, Van Gogh threw his glass into Gauguin's face. The next day, Gauguin heard rapid footsteps behind him and turned around to find Van Gogh holding a razor, approaching him. Gauguin stared him to a halt, and to be safe, he passed that night in a hotel. The same night Van Gogh cut off his ear, wrapped it in a handkerchief, went to a brothel, handed his ear to a girl, and told her to keep it as if it were a treasure. In the fall of 1889, he expressed his hope that he would work again with Gauguin.

On February of 1889, he had a breakdown involving hallucinations, and he was hospitalized for a few days in Arles. Following intermittent attacks of his illness, as suggested by Reverend Salle, in May he left Arles to go to the asylum of Saint Paul de Mausole in Saint Remy de Provence. In the asylum, he was given a second room as a studio, and he was also allowed to paint outside in the confines of the asylum. His doctors considered his illness a form of epilepsy.

(There is speculation that his epilepsy was possibly caused by excessive consumption of absinthe as well as the effects of syphilis.) In July, he went to Arles to collect his paintings and store his furniture. Following this trip, disabled by a serious attack, he could not paint for five weeks. Until early October, his work was confined to indoors, and he painted portraits and copied the art of Millet and Delacroix. In March of 1890, Theo exhibited Vincent's paintings at the exhibition of the Artistes Indépendants.

Expressing his desire to leave the asylum, in May 1890, Vincent went to Auvers-sur-Oise and stayed in a hotel under the supervision of Dr. Gachet, who was also a painter. The picturesque nature of Auvers stimulated Vincent to paint en plein air. In early summer, he was averaging a painting per day.

At the asylum and Auvers, Vincent painted portraits, self-portraits, landscapes, and a few copies. In these pictures, the color intensity of Arles shifted to expressive movements of form. His powerful brushstrokes created an explosive world that was unprecedented in Western art. His self-portraits seemed like a means of pondering his own self. His portrait of *Doctor Gachet*, painted a few weeks before his death, rather than rendering a likeness or depicting character, is more a self-projection. His landscapes took on a hallucinatory nature. *The Starry Night* depicts a view of the sky just before sunrise from the window of his asylum room in Saint-Rémy-de-Provence. Since from the window he had no view of the surrounding landscape, he idealized the landscape of the village under a cascade of swirling lights of the moon and stars and convulsive spirals of the Milky Way. At the base of the mountains, in front of he coils of an orchard are the geometric shapes of the village's houses. The tiny yellow light emanating from some of the windows, compared to the magnificence of light above, emphasizes the insignificance of the humble lives of humans. At the left side of the picture, an enormous cypress like a flame leaps up toward the whirling and exploding stars. The vision stated in this landscape is beyond any mystical attempt in the art of any time.

A few days before his suicide, he painted *Wheatfield with Crows*, in which he inverted the perspective. Converging three paths of the field toward the forground seems as if the world was moving toward Van Gogh.

On July 27, 1890, he shot himself in the chest with a revolver. Dr. Gachet and Theo were called. To Theo, who tried to persuade him that they would save him, Vincent replied, "The sadness will always last." Two days later, with Theo at his side, he passed away. In October Theo suffered a breakdown, and in the clinic he was diagnosed with the terminal stage of syphilis. He died on January 25, 1891, and his wife buried him next to Vincent.

The sudden madness and subsequent attacks of illness should not affect the merit of Van Gogh's art. His work is exempt of his illness. His letters to Theo reveal a highly sensitive person. While Cezanne and Seurat investigated architectural stability and permanence and new rules for color, Van Gogh exploited color to express his emotional experiances. Van Gogh's works were not products of transitory impressions. They arose from the deep layers of his soul to represent the lamentable situation of the human condition. He remained always committed to the visible world, and he avoided dreams. In a letter, he wrote, "To think, not to dream, is our duty." His highly emotional drawings and paintings were based on intellect. On the occasion of the exhibition of Van Gogh's pictures at the Salon des Indépendants in 1890, Gauguin said, "In things painted after nature, you are the only one who thinks." Van Gogh belonged to the family of great artists of the end of nineteenth century who considered originality to be the requisite for the culture of individuality. The intensity of Van Gogh's colors, and his sharp brushstrokes and varied textures, influenced the fauves and the German expressionists.

PAUL GAUGUIN (1848–1903)

Gauguin's father was a Breton, and his mother's family were Peruvian. His father, Clovis Gauguin, impelled by republican sentiment, was an anti-Napoleon political reporter for *Le National*, founded by Thiers, and his mother, Aline, was the daughter of Flora Tristan, a bluestocking socialist anarchist and a writer of book and articles. His father, foreseeing the coup d'etat of 1852, decided to emigrate to Peru to found a newspaper in Lima. On their way to Peru, Gauguin's father, already suffering from a heart ailment died in Port-Famine. In Peru Aline's old and very rich uncle who had been a viceroy of Peru accorded an affectionate welcome to his niece and her two children, Paul and Marie. Gauguin always had a vivid memory of that period—living in a residence as large as a castle, with luxury and comfort. After four years, Aline had to go back to France to settle the senior Gauguin's estates. The following year, the uncle died. He had settled on Aline an annuity, but on his deathbed, the family made the old man change his will.

Gauguin began his study in a boarding school in Orleans. Then, at age eleven, he moved to a Catholic secondary school. His goal was to attend the naval academy, but when the hour of the exam arrived, he was not ready. At the age of seventeen, as an apprentice, he entered the merchant marine and saw remote places. At the age of nineteen, for his military service he chose the Imperial Navy.

Aline, who had retired to Saint-Cloud, established a close relationship with the Arosa family, who had a country house neighboring Aline's house. Obsessed by the idea of death, Aline appointed Gustave Arosa as the guardian of her children.

While Gauguin was at sea, his mother died. After his service, with the recommendation of Gustave Arosa, Gauguin became employed at the stock brokerage of Bertin, where he stayed for eleven years. In 1873, he married Mette-Sophie Gaad, a very conventional woman from an honorable Copenhagen family. They had five children in ten years.

Arosa was an art collector. At his house Gauguin met artists, became an art lover, and collected impressionist paintings. While he was at Bertin, he started painting in his spare time. Of great significance was his friendship with Schuffenecker, a colleague at Bertin, who dreamed of becoming a great painter. They discussed art, went together to the Louvre, and on Sundays painted together. Gauguin was not a spontaneous painter. It was through will and laborious work that he gradually discovered his ability.

He submitted a painting to the salon of 1876, and it was accepted by the jury. Pissarro, who was often a guest at Arosa's home, introduced him to his impressionist friends. Gauguin adopted their new vision, and Pissarro included Gauguin in the impressionist exhibition of 1879, without putting his name in the catalog. In the summers of 1879 to 1882, he joined Pissarro at Pontoise, and from painting at Pissarro's side, he adopted Pissarro's technique of rendering objects with short brushstrokes as well as his preference for light colors.

In 1883, he dedicated all of his time to painting. It is not quite clear whether he left his job or lost it due to the market crash of 1882. In 1884, to reduce expenses, the family first moved to Rouen and then to Copenhagen, where he became a salesman for a French manufacturer of tarpaulin, but as there were no buyers for the product, he tried to sell his paintings, also without any success. His relationship with Mette grew worse. As his later correspondences with Mette indicate, pressure from Mette's family was one of the reason to leave Copenhagen.

Both Gauguin and Cezanne were self-taught artists and anti-academics. Their close relationship with Pissarro, an impressionist painter, familiarized them with impressionism and helped the development of their painting, but neither approved the transitory form of impressionist painting, and each of them in his own way searched for the essence of the motif. While Cezanne, in search of the spatial relations of fundamental forms, never abandoned the depiction of the visible world, Gauguin was concerned with the mysterious complexity of an inner response to the visible world, and he broke off from the objectivity of impressionism to explore the capacity of painting to represent his inner life. He said, "They sought around with the eye and not in the mysterious depth of the mind." The patterns of wallpaper of *Child Sleeping* (1884), suggesting the fairy world of the child's dream, signal Gauguin's deviation from the naturalistic view of impressionism.

In July 1885, with his son Clovis, he returned to Paris. That was the beginning of a miserable life of poverty and wandering. For a while, he worked as a bill poster. Selling a painting at the impressionist exhibition made it possible for him to place Clovis in a boarding school, and in search of seclusion, to leave Paris for Pont-Aven, a village at the mouth of the River Aven in Brittany. The landscape and stillness of the village, the traditional way of life of its inhabitants that was untouched by the progress of Paris, the traditional Breton local garb, and the sharp outlines of the white headdresses of Breton women, captivated Gauguin. In Pont-Aven, young artists, looking at him as a revolutionary painter, gathered around him.

Back in Paris he began working for Ernest Chaplet, a ceramist. At the time of making ceramics, he found that to create by hand rather than with a potter's wheel gave new impetus to the art of ceramics. Theo, Vincent van Gogh's brother and the manager of the art dealership on the Boulevard Montmartre, organized an exhibition of Gauguin's paintings and ceramics. In the discussions that followed the exhibition was the evidence that Gauguin's art had attracted the attention of art critics. His meeting with Degas bound them together. Mette came to Paris, visited Paul, and took their son back to Copenhagen.

In April 1887, longing for exotic subjects, Gauguin and Charles Laval, a young artist he had met in Pont-Aven, left Paris for Panama. In Panama, Laval became ill, and Gauguin worked as a labror at the Panama Canal. After two weeks, they decided to leave for Martinique. In Martinique, Gauguin fell seriously ill, but despite his fever, he made sketches of the natives and the nature of the island, and he painted several canvases. Affected by the intense light of the blue sky of Martinique, his colors became brighter. Being short of money, he left Laval in Martinique and signed on as a sailor on a ship for Europe.

In the summer of 1888, Gauguin went back to Pont-Aven, where a group of young painters—and Emil Bernard, a young painter who had an intellectual approach to painting—joined him. The group worked together, exchanged ideas, and influenced each other. Gauguin and Emil Bernard talked extensively about painting, particularly the cloisonnism style[13] of painting in which forms, in contrast to the delimitation of impressionism, are separated by dark contours. These discussions paved his way toward a new concept of art. Later, Bernard never ceased to resent assumptions that Gauguin had influenced him, rather than vice versa.

The same year he painted *Vision after the Sermon*, one of the most discussed pieces of Gauguin's art. In a letter to Van Gogh, he gave some explanation of this picture of groups of Brittany women who pray after the sermon: " The landscape and the fight exist only in the imagination of the people who pray after the sermon— that's why there is a contrast between the life-sized people and the

---

13   - Cloisonne, a technique that combines transparency and intensity, is used in the stained-glass windows of French Cathedrals. To ensure stability, pieces of stained-glass are joined together by metal stripes, which as a part of visual elements heightens the effect of colors.

unnatural and disproportionate fight in the landscape." By using a dark purple tree that crosses through the painting, he separated the women from their vision; and by two perspectives—from the side for people, and from above for the battle scene—Gauguin fused reality and vision.

Already past the stage of passive observation, the decorative effects of flat areas of color in Japanese prints, unbroken by modeling, deeply impressed Gauguin. The sinuous cut-out pattern of *Over the Abyss* (1888), and the overlapping networks of arabesques of *Womann the Waves* (1889), are careful arrangements of line and color. His interest in decoration influenced young painters he met in Pont-Aven. Maurice Denis acknowledged that in Ponte-Aven, Gauguin initiated a modern aesthetic movement, which released him and his friends from the idea of copying from nature. Paul Serusier was painting a little landscape near Pont-Aven. Gauguin advised him, "How do you see those trees? Good, paint them yellow. That shadow is rather blue; paint it with pure ultramarine. For those red leaves use vermillion." Later, Serusier's friends at the Academie Julien enchanted by that little landscape called it *The Talisman*.

On August 1888, Van Gogh—who had met Gauguin in the art dealership of his brother, Theo—in a letter to Gauguin proposed the establishment of an art studio. After several postponements, in October, Gauguin left Pont-Aven for Arles. They worked together and influenced each other. But clash between two different temperament was inevitable. In December, a dispute brought on a profound emotional crisis, Vincent cut off part of his own ear, and Gauguin returned to Paris.

The Paris World's Fair of 1889, organized for the centenary of the French Revolution, was to emphasize the progress of France and its colonial power. The Eiffel Tower, as the symbol of the fair, was erected at the entrance arch to the fair. There were palaces for industry and galleries for machines. Officially recognized painting and a few impressionist paintings were presented at the Palais des Beaux-Arts. Gauguin, whose work was not admitted to the fair, arranged "The Exhibition of Paintings of the Impressionist and Synthetist Group" at the Café Volpini, just outside the grounds of the fair, to display his recent synthetic and symbolic paintings and the works of young painters gathered around him in Brittany. A special section of the fair was dedicated to the Exposition Colonial. This section, with the art of colonies entirely different from Europe and the participation of the natives, attracted Gauguin's attention.

He returned to Brittany in 1889, but crowded by tourists, Pont-Aven was transformed. Revolted by the touristic atmosphere, he left for Le Pouldu, where he lived in an extremely humble hotel. In August, because he had no more money, he returned to Pont-Aven, where he could obtain credit. In this period of his intense productivity, the ancient Breton calveries that gave life to the presence of the sacred and mysterious, drifted him away from the pitfalls of a purely decorative style of careful arrangements of line and color. He learned to use figures and nature as motifs to represent the mysterious relationship between the world of the mind and line and color. The religious solemnity of *The Yellow Christ* and *The Calvary*, the strange figures around *Nirvana* (portrait of Meyer de Haan), and the mysterious idol in *Belle Angèle* show his move toward unseen powers. *The Yellow Christ* summarizes all Gaugin's research before leaving for Tahiti. Elimination of all but essentials augmented the effect of the sharp contrast of the elongated body of Christ with the curves of the landscape. Along with its flat colors, its clean-cut outlines showing the effects of the study of Japanese prints, and a perspective close to primitive painting makes the picture a "synthesis".

At the end of the nineteenth century, there was an extensive exchange of ideas among poets, writers, and artists. The quest for appropriate forms to express the world of the mind was the matter of discussion for the symbolist poets, to whom poetry consisted of bringing to light the human soul. Every Monday in the Café Voltaire, there was a gathering of whoever was interested in this intellectual movement. In 1889 Gauguin began to participate in these discussions.

Mallarmé was a poet who used objects of the real world allegorically to evoke an immaterial world. While there was a concordance of mind between the poet and the painter, Gauguin, at the heart of appearances of the outside world, discovered an unexpected phenomenon: the suggestive power of line and color. His pictures submitted to the symbolic values of color and line and became a complex fusion of plastic forms, an expression of his inner life, and his profound sensation of nature. Thus Gauguin, by associating painting with music, an art that directly affects the mind, sought to suggest rather than to describe, and opened the door into a world of mystery.

In 1891 Albert Aurier, a critic close to the symbolists, defined the principles of symbolism in painting as follows: *ideaistic*, to explore ideas; *symbolist*, to express ideas through forms; *synthetist*, to synthesize forms and symbols in such a way as to be understood; *subjective*, to express an idea perceived by the subject; and *decorative*, to create harmony through line and color.

Cities and the standardized way of life of Western civilization provoked a need for silence and isolation in Gauguin, and he saw the journey as an escape from external constraints that would allow him to maximize his creativity. He wrote to his wife, "Beethoven was blind and deaf, he was isolated from everything, so his works are redolent of the artist living in a world of his own." In the course of a search for an aesthetic by which he could find the essence of man, he realized that individuality and the logic of modern man had severed him from his community. As he perceived that man needs to return to a more normal social structure, he became attracted to primitive art. He said, "Primitive art comes from the spirit and uses nature."

In Brittany, he had found only traces of primitive life, so he decided to go farther away from the civilized world. First, he thought of Madagascar, where he hoped to have the necessary calm environment in which to work. Emile Bernard, who had read Pierre Loti's novel, *Le Mariage de Loti*, suggested Tahiti as a possible alternative. Gauguin modified his plan, and Tahiti became his desired destination.

He confided to Charles Morice his need of money for his plan to go to Tahiti. Morice, a student of Mallarmé, went to see Mallarmé to ask his advise. On February 16, 1891, Octave Mirbeau, an art critic and a friend of Mallarmé, wrote a glowing article in *L'Echo de Paris* describing Gauguin as an exceptional artist who was planning to go to Tahiti. And on February 18, in an article in *Le Figaro*, he announced the sale of Gauguin's paintings and pottery at the Hotel Drouot. The articles produced the desired effect. With the sale at the Hotel Drouot, Gauguin was able to leave for Tahiti. He went to visit his family in Copenhagen. Back in Paris, his friends and the intellectual elite of Paris held a farewell banquet at the Café Voltaire.

After two months sailing, he reached Tahiti on June 1891. Soon he found that Papeete, the capital of Tahiti, had become an imitation of the civilization from which he had run away. Suddenly reality obliterated the dream that had brought him to Tahiti. In order to live among the natives, he went to live in a hut in the wilderness between the mountains and the sea. Once beyond the city limits, the problem was that he had to turn to nature for his survival, but he did not know how to catch a fish or to climb tall trees.

One day a woman, one of the neighbors, entered Gauguin's hut to look at photographs of paintings hung on the wall of the hut. Gauguin hastened to sketch her portrait. In *Noa Noa*, a kind of diary that he wrote later of his life in Tahiti, he describes his first Tahitian model as a beautiful woman and that her traits in combination had a Raphaelesque harmony.

During his sojourn in Tahiti, he became aware of the extent of cultural loss that had taken place under the influence of the mission. The mission, by eliminating the Tahitian priest cast and banning the old dances, songs, and images of divinities, had destroyed the identity of the people. In Papeete, a resident of Tahiti since 1867 gave Gauguin a book entitled *Voyages aux Iles du Grand Ocean*, a work published in 1837 by Jacques-Antoine Moerenhout, who had lived in Tahiti as a consul of the United States. Through this book Gauguin acquired knowledge of the customs, mores, and various religions of Mahori, slumbering beneath an imitation of Western civilization.

Long before the Tahitian trip, he had formulated his concept of painting. He had rebelled against the Greece-Rome tradition, and had distanced himself from passive observation of nature. He studied stylistic principals of variety of art traditions, and used nature as a pretext to reveal the charm of the mystery. Expressive lines, suggestive colors that make viewer think as music does, became essential elements of Gauguin's celebral art. He said that every feature in a painting has to be considered and completed in the mind of the artist before he or she begins a canvas.

In Tahiti, carved wood offered him a well-suited medium for an unpolished, expressive art. Eager to study the landscape of Tahiti and the intimate lives of natives, he made many sketches of nature and the natives of the island. In his early paintings of Tahiti that represent the compilation of various sketches in the studio, he gave anecdotal and narrative context to his first Tahitian pictures. But in his paintings of 1892, he abandoned the realistic approach of anecdotal depiction, and his art acquired a spiritual dimension full of symbolic motifs.

The book of Moerenhout opened the door to a fantastic legend of gods, in which, as he mentioned in *Noa Noa*, "spirit and matter are a twofold manifestation of a single substance." In this view of the world, every element of nature is part of the greater whole.

A few months after his arrival, he decided to make an excursion to the interior of the island. While traveling, he was asked the purpose of his travel, and he replied, "To find a wife." A woman offered him her thirteen-year-old daughter, named Tehura. The little girl changed the quality of Gauguin's life; she gathered food, fished, cooked, and served as his model. About that time Gauguin began writing *Noa Noa* (meaning "fragrance"), a kind of diary of his life in Tahiti, and a summary of Tahitian theology. In his notes, he refers to Tehura as his teacher of Tahitian morals and customs. He wrote, "Now that I can understand Tehura, in whom her ancestors sleep and sometimes dream, I strive to see and think through this child."

One night he returned late at home. He saw Tahura immobile, naked, lying facedown, flat on the bed, with eyes inordinately large with fear. He painted *Manao Tupapau* ("The Spirit of Death is Watching"), an image of the intensity of the world of superstition, which dominated Tahura's mind and her race. The frightening background of the picture suggest the mysterious world that caused Tahura's terror.

In September 1893, Gauguin was called to Orleans for the settlement of the will of his uncle. During his eighteen-month stay in Tahiti, he worked on more than one hundred paintings, twenty sculptures, numerous sketches and watercolors, and to describe his life among the natives he wrote *Noa Noa* and provided a summary of Tahitian theology. He also compiled notes for his manuscript, entitled *Ancien Cult Mahorie*.

With this unexpected heritage, Gauguin was in a position to rent an inexpensive apartment, where many painters and writers went to visit him. Galerie Durand-Ruel organized an exhibition of his works—mostly paintings done in Tahiti. The brilliance of the pure colors and simplified drawing of his Tahitian paintings, expressing states of mind, profoundly impressed Mallarmé, Degas, and the Nabis. But as his former colleagues and the public did not understand him, that was the final break between Gauguin and the Western world.

Accompanied by Armond Seguin and Annah, a Javanese woman, Gauguin went to Brittany. As they were walking through the port, some children threw stones at them, which led to a fight between Seguin and the father of one of the children. Gauguin intervened to defend his friend, and a few fishermen came to the aid of the child's father. In the stupid fight that ensued, Gauguin broke his ankle, which never healed properly, and its pain lasted until the end of his life.

In Paris, he completed the woodcuts for *Noa Noa*. But as a painter, he was not as productive as in Tahiti. He complained to Durand-Ruel that he could not work with the same intensity in Paris. He left France in July 1895. His first trip to Tahiti was a part of his search for an artistic concept, the second was a good-bye to the Western world.

Back in Tahiti, he decided to go to the Marquesas Islands, which were more primitive than Tahiti. In the village of Atuona, in the county of Hiva-Oa, he learned that there was no land for sale or rent except from the mission. The bishop was away for a month. Waiting for his return, he attended Sunday Mass, so, to this good Catholic, the bishop sold a small lot. He did not go back to church anymore, and he carved two statues, one that portrayed the bishop as a horned devil, the other a charming woman that he called Sainte Thérèse. Since the bishop's maid was named Thérèse, he was alluding to their love affair. Gauguin lived in a wooden hut. In his neighborhood, within a few hundred meters, were living two or three simple French colonists and several native families. In 1896 Vollard, possibly under the advice of Degas, made a contract with Gauguin to buy his entire output.

The administration had put moral pressure on the parents to send their little girls to the nuns. Gauguin discovered that natives residing farther than three kilometers away were under no obligation to send their children to nuns. Gauguin, who had a true worship for the country and its beautiful and savage nature, and wanting to bring natives back to their primitive way of life, explained to the parents that they need not fear any penalty if they withdrew their children from the nuns' school. Next, he took on the civil authorities, especially the police, who from his point of view harassed the natives, and he advised the natives to stop paying personal taxes. He helped to edit the opposition newspaper, *Les Guepes*, and founded a satirical monthly review, called *Le Souire*, in which he induced the natives to reject the imposed Western discipline.

In 1897, Mette informed him of the death of their oldest daughter by pernicious pneumonia. Deeply depressed by the death of Aline, he ceased writing to Mette. Three years later his son Clovis, died. His friends, who knew of his depression after the death of Aline, refrained from informing him of the death of Clovis.

Depressed by the death of Aline, betrayed by his wife who sold his paintings without considering his financial needs, and sick and exhausted, in December 1879, he decided to commit suicide. So, he worked day and night to finish a canvas that is considered his pictorial testament: *Where Do We Come From? What Are We? Where Are We Going?* After he finished the picture, he went to the mountains—he later wrote, "where my body would have been devoured by ants," but the dose of arsenic was too much, and vomiting saved him.

On this painting he had given a summary explanation: "On the right, a newborn baby; on the left, an old woman. Between these extremes of life is mankind, loving and active. And in this terrestrial space, a statue symbolizing the Divinity that is inherent in humanity." André Breton called this picture an "unwinding of the human condition."

In 1901, Gaugin settled in a remote village in the Marquesas Islands, where he painted his last masterpieces. Three months before his death, his conflicts with police and the bishop led to his being sentenced to fifteen days in jail and fined five hundred francs for supposedly insulting the police. But he was sure he would be acquitted.

On the morning of May 8, a servant came to inform the pastor Vernier of Gauguin's death. A vial of morphine was found beside him. Vernier wrote to Rotonchamp, Gauguin's friend, that Gauguin was a very likable man, perfectly sweet and natural with the natives. He heard several natives cry something like, "Gauguin is dead. We are lost." The next day, the bishop who had been ridiculed by Gauguin, decided to have his revenge on Gauguin's body, and buried him with a full Catholic ceremony in the Catholic cemetery.

Despite the suffering from his ankle, he did an enormous amount of work in the Marquesas. His art of this period provides evidence of the development of more monumentality. An unprecedented melancholy, a sacred sense derived from the Mahories' cult, and the mystery of natural forces envelop his art. The extensive variation of the delicately chosen, luminous colors of Gauguin's landscapes of sumptuous Tahitian nature, and the natural forms of its mysterious, graceful figures, captivate the eye and the deep layers of the mind.

Of all the European artists and poets who traveled to exotic lands, Gauguin was the first to break from the logic of Western civilization.

His rebellion was against organized thought, which enslaves the mind by its limitations. He believed that primitive art would lead us toward the origins of thought and would help us find the truth about the human condition. Gauguin's search to synthesize subject and idea, form and color, gave mystery and a visionary quality to his art, which during his lifetime was not fully appreciated by the public and critics, but his influence upon the art of the twentieth century, along with the art of Cezanne and Van Gogh, is undeniable.

Section 10

Henri de Toulouse-Lautrec (1864–1901)

Henri was the son of the Count of Toulouse. His stunted growth and fragile body were caused by generations of inbreeding. After breaking his legs, incapacitated and unable to participate in many activities of an aristocrat such as hunting and sports, he devoted his time to art and began painting with a painter who was a friend of the family. After studying at the Lycée Fontanese in Paris and passing his baccalaureate, in 1882, he entered the studio of Leon Bonnat to study painting. After a few months, Bonnat closed his studio, and Lautrec and other students resumed their studies at the Cormon studio in Montmartre. He studied for two years with Cormon, whose easygoing style of teaching, more relaxed than at the École des Beaux-Arts, developed Toulouse-Lautrec's personal style.

In Paris, Toulouse-Lautrec lived with his father at the Hotel Perey, off the Rue de Saint-Honore. In 1884, he rented his own studio in Montmartre, fascinated by the bohemian life of this district of Paris, and he made contacts with the heterogeneous groups of Montmartre. Friendship with artists, writers, and performers connected him to the life of Montmartre, and his art focused on the subculture of the hill. Participation in discussions at Le Chat Noir, a center for avant-guarde artistic and literary activity in Paris, helped him to get rid of aristocratic prejudices and get close to the margins of society. Toulouse-Lautrec's participation in the Salon des Indépendants, and in the exhibitions of Les Vingt in Brussels expanded his circle of friends and brought him in contact with young painters, such as members of the Nabis, who by their poster-making, printmaking, and book and journal illustration sought to describe modern life in a style reflecting the dynamism of their time.

The economic prosperity, flourishing of visual art and literature, and optimism that characterized the period of peace from the end of the Franco-Prussian War in 1871 to the outbreak of World War I around 1914, made the period a time to enjoy life. In those years, called in retrospect La Belle Epoque, all forms of entertainment, such as café-concerts, cabarets, dance halls, and brothels, became aspects of modern life in Paris. In 1881 the impresario Rodolphe Salis and the poet Emile Goudeau founded Le Chat Noir, the first of numbers of artistic cabarets in Montmartre. In 1886, the cabaret offered *Shadow Theater*, created by Henri Riviere and Henri Somm. The two artists, who had transformed the traditional Asian shadow theater into a proto-cinematic form of entertainment, performed their sophisticated production, which included movement, color, music, and voice, for ten years at Le Chat Noir. The two-dimensional silhouette and flat colors of the show had the same aesthetic that concerned modern artists, especially Toulouse-Lautrec and the Nabis.

In 1889 the Moulin Rouge opened its doors at the foot of the Montmartre hill. Toulouse-Lautrec, who had a predilection for decoration, was attracted by large surfaces of posters and began to make a series of posters for the Moulin Rouge in 1891. His first poster was *Moulin Rouge: La Goulue*, an advertisement for a dancer who created the French can-can dance. Toulouse-Lautrec's assymetrical composition, his dissonant colors, and his free drawing, expressing the movement of flat figures in the foreground of the poster with a few lines, were derived from Japanese prints, whereas the silhouetted figures in the background were derived from the Chat Noir shadow theater. But Toulouse-Lautrec gave each of these elements a new tone that became an innovation. Toulouse-Lautrec's innovative style, and his long and keen observation of his subjects, which gave him psychological insight into his subjects, were well beyond the demands of the advertising medium. The poster, pasted on the walls of Paris, brought Toulouse-Lautrec's art to a massive public—and his first great success. This success convinced him to become more active in lithography.

Montmartre, overlooking Paris, was an ideal site for landscape painters. But Toulouse-Lautrec's interest was in exploring the behavior of Montmartre's populace. He used his marvelous powers of observation to capture essentials. Without being a caricaturist, he used exaggeration and rapid execution, two features of caricature, to express his grim satire of facial expression and explore the body language of his subjects.

Paintings he made of entertainers show interest in their private personalities. In *Jane Avril Leaving the Moulin Rouge*, we see the dancer deep in her thoughts. He was a great painter of portraits. He represents alcoholic working women with some bitterness but with no judgment. Dance halls—with their public composed of families, artists, the working class, and prostitutes—and concert halls with their wide spectrum of people were well-suited subjects to Toulouse-Lautrec's desire to depict the behavior of diverse classes of people.

Prostitutes and their work had always been a subject of interest for painters; the most famous recent picture of a prostitute was Manet's *Olympia*. His many paintings representing the lives of prostitutes and the attitudes of their clientele, and his *Elles*, an album of eleven colored lithographs of brothel life, show that Toulouse-Lautrec, always focused on representing a deeper reality than the outward appearances. His interest in this subject went beyond a simple attraction to another aspect of the pleasures of Paris.

Drinking heavily led to his mental collapse in 1899. He was committed to a sanatorium for three months. While in the sanatorium, he produced from memory a group of drawings from the circus. After his release, he continued to live in Montmartre. He died in 1901 from complications of alcoholism and syphilis. A few days before his death, he murmured, "And life is a fine thing, they say."

In 1888 Paul Serusier, back in Paris at the beginning of a new term at the Académie Julien, showed the Pont-Aven landscape he had painted under the guidance of Gauguin to his friends Maurice Denis, Pierre Bonnard, Paul Ranon, Gabriel Ibels, Edouard Vuillar, Ker-Xavier Roosel, and René Piot, at the Académie Julian. Impressed by the little landscape, they called it *The Talisman*, and each of the young painters interpreted it according to his own temperament. In an article, Maurice Denis acknowledged that Gauguin had freed them from the chains of copying nature.

These young painters, avid to absorb all forms of intellectual expression—music, poetry, art criticism, and philosophy—went to the Louvre and visited art exhibitions of modern painters. They admired Cezanne, were particularly attracted to Gauguin's teachings, and were influenced by Japanese prints. This vast knowledge developed their sense of judgment. Gathered around Serusier, they named their group the Nabis, a name from a Hebrew word meaning "prophets." Later, a few foreign artists, Jan Verkade, Mogens Ballin, and Jozsef Rippl, joined the group. The first exhibition of the group took place in 1891. Maurice Denis, one of the most receptive of the group to new ideas, and as the theoretician of the group, defined the philosophy of the movement, which from Gauguin's guidance to

Serusier and the influence of Japanese prints had grown to a new art of half painting and half decoration.

Despite their closeness, from the beginning different tendencies existed within the group. Serusier and Denis had mystical tendencies, while the friendship of Vuillard with Bonnard was different. Of all the Nabis, those two were the closest and the least interested in theories.

The Nabis considered painting to be a mental creation, not a demonstration of sensibility, and the power of the lines, flat colors, and decorative elements of Japanese prints influenced them. Flat colors, stylized contour lines, and no depth gave a decorative impression to their work and were a move toward abstraction. As they wanted art to be a part of life, they were against the confines of easel painting and tried to reestablish decorative arts. They designed wallpaper, textiles, and furniture, and they worked in the media of poster-making, printmaking, painting stage sets, illustrating theater programs, and book and journal illustration, but painting remained their main interest.

In 1895 Siegfried Bing, the art dealer and an exponent of art nouveau, asked the Nabis to create various interior designs for his gallery. After their last exhibition in 1899, as members of the group turned toward becoming more conservative, and each of them followed his own inclination, the group disintegrated. The Nabis, despite their brief existence as a group, by their theories and by transmitting the revolutionary ideas of Seurat, Cezanne, Van Gogh, and Gauguin to the twentieth century, paved the path for the development of nonrepresentational art.

PAUL SERUSIER (1864–1927)

Born in Paris, Serusier joined the Académie Julian in 1885. His first exhibition was at the Salon of 1888, the same year he painted the *The*

Talisman, under Gauguin's guidance. Serusier's early paintings of the landscapes and people of Brittany followed Gauguin's guidance. The contemplative mood of Breton peasants is a characteristic of these pictures. Like the other Nabis, he participated in scene decoration and costume design for theaters. Serusier tendency to various mystical philosophies brought him close to Denis.

MAURICE DENIS (1870–1943)

Born in Granville, in 1888 he began to study art at the Académie Julian, where he met Serusier. The same year he was accepted at the École des Beaux-Arts. Extremely intelligent, he had a well-developed opinion of art. He became the chief theoretician of the Nabis and wrote extensively on theories of modern art. Faced with the nature of painting, he defined it this way: "A picture, before being a war horse, a naked woman, or some anecdote, is essentially a flat surface covered by colors assembled in a particular order."

In 1892 he painted *The Ladder in the Foliage*, a ceiling decoration for his friend. The sinuous lines of this picture, and particularly the edges of the women's dresses, belong to the art nouveau style. He visited Italy for the first time with Seusier in 1895, and again in 1889 with his wife. Study of the art of Fra Angelico lightened his palette and enlarged his compositions.

Denis was a devoted Catholic with mystical tendencies, and his subjects were often religious or drawn from poems. The tranquility of the attitudes of his figures transports the viewer into a dream world. He decorated churches, illustrated Mallarmé's poems, and executed lithographs for André Gide's book. His art was characterized by sinuous lines, delicate color, and space suggested by gradations of color.

EDOUARD VUILLARD (1868–1940)

At the art school, Vuillard was friend of the future Nabis. After he lost his father, he lived with his mother, a dressmaker. A reticent person with no mystical inclination, such as characterized the art of some of his friends in the Nabis group, Vuillard preferred intimate scenes for his pictures. The happy intimacy of Vuillard's art reflects the atmosphere of serenity that his mother had created at home. The countless dots and small flowers that decorate wallpapers and women's dresses were inspired by his mother's dressmaking. Similar to his friends of the Nabis group, he followed the idea of art as decoration, and his interior decoration work links him to the art nouveau movement that was intended to unify society. His colors were rich, and he applied his pigments thinly and flatly, avoiding modeling. With his painting *The Path in Front of the House*, Vuillard's work from 1898 on, reveals a change of direction. Despite decorative elements, the picture shows a renewed interest in capturing immediate impressions.

PIERRE BONNARD (1867–1947)

Bonnard was the son of a high-ranking civil servant in the War Ministry. After completion of his law study, he enrolled in the École des Beaux-Arts. Then he went to the Académie Julian, where he became one of the founding members of the Nabis group.

The pure colors of Gauguin's works exhibited at the Café Volpini and the flat colors of Japanese woodblock prints with their expression of everything through color alone—and all with a decorative effect—mark the characteristics of his art during the Nabis period.

His real interest was in interpreting his visual impressions, and his love for pure color moved him toward impressionism at a time that the movement was under criticism. From 1895, his work is of large outdoor landscapes and of intimate scenes of Marthe, the young woman he met in 1893 and who later became his wife.

Despite his interest in impressionism, his pictures were reconstructed in the studio, rather than painted from life. He used to draw the layout of his subject, make notes on color, and then paint from memory. From the complex inventiveness of arbitrary colors and from constant alteration and retouching, which gave a dreamlike quality to his paintings, the subject emerged in a created space.

Between 1906 and 1910, he painted four murals for Misia Sert, a cultured collector, that fancifully represented fables and allegories of East and West in a decorative spirit. The four panels were painted with broad strokes of thinly applied color related to the dining room for which they were intended.

In *Dining Room in the Country* (1913), the color of the door being the same as landscape unifies the picture and moves the eye between interior and exterior. The verticals of the door and window frames are structural devices of the picture. He used different vantage points for his compositions; the very long landscape of *Woman in a Landscape* (1914) is constructed around three perspective lines. Forms dissolved by colors and the absence of perspective in *The Artist's Garden at Le Cannet,* painted two years before his death, recall the increasing abstraction of Monet's late works.

Section 12

Pre-Raphaelism

The social and artistic revolution of the realist movement in France assumed a rebellious zeal against the teachings at the Royal Academy. The writings of John Ruskin, the influential art critic, about medieval painting and insisting on "truth" as a criterion of painting, incited three young painters, Hunt, Rossetti, and Millais, to create an art fresh, sincere, and free of the artificial manner of the academy's teachings. Soon after, they formed the Pre-Raphaelite Brotherhood, later known as pre-Raphaelism. In 1848 they were joined by four more painters.

The group considered the influence of the late Raphael and the heritage of mannerism and baroque artifice as a corruption of painting, and their intention was to return to the complex compositions, intense colors, and ample details of the Quattrocento Italian painting. Although they considered imitation of nature the purpose of art, the ranges of their colors, unused since the Middle Ages, were chosen for their emotional effect and went far beyond natural colors.

Their paintings attracted the attention of the general public. To promote their ideas, they published the periodical *The Gem*. Within five years, although the group had started with common objectives, with the differences in development of each member of the group, pre-Raphaelism began to lose its original definition.

Part 4

The Twentieth Century

Modern Painting

We must learn to forget the past, to live our own lives in our own time.

—MARCEL DUCHAMP

I n the twentieth century, Einstein's theory of relativity, which replaced a closed and unchanging universe with an expanding one, changed human's picture of the world and of himself. Man, who had reduced the universe to his limited optical perception, suddenly found himself in a world with no absolute space or time, much more complex than his thousand-year-old belief. Certitudes reduced to hypotheses and skepticism about all answers previously taken for granted led to a confused sense of identity and the rejection of his past in terms of authority.

Psychology's statement that our actions are determined by motives operating in the subconscious was another blow to the old beliefs. Consequently, for the modern painter, the visible state of things became only a limited part of reality. To reach the unconscious become their obsession. To reveal the profound reality of things on earth and to penetrate into the domain of the subconscious, modern artists had to search for new forms.

Since the middle of the nineteenth century, a few avant-garde painters, to liberate painting from the shackles of strict representation, moved toward new concepts of painting that paved the way for the revolutionary picture making of the twentieth century. Manet was the first painter to assert color as the only reality of painting. For Monet, the great advocate of the decomposition of light, in his series of *Haystacks*, *Cathedrals*, and *Water Lilies*, color became the only element to make picture, a move that could not be defined as copying nature. Seurat fused optical reality with abstract forms. Cezanne searched for fundamental forms. Van Gogh said, "I am painting infinity." Gauguin wrote, "Painting should seek suggestion more than description, as does music." These new trends in pictorial vision gave rise to an art subject to its own laws, independent of objectivity.

Painters of the twentieth century, each responding differently to modern science, technology, economy, and social relationships, propounded new concepts of painting. The emergence of diverse approaches to painting brought forth extensive critical discussions about the nature of the aesthetics of painting. These discussions, emphasizing the concept of "pure art," promoted abstract painting.

Proponents of abstract painting consider the representation of natural forms to be a passive mirroring of things and therefore non-artistic, while abstract painting, unconditioned by the outside world and based on its own laws, is pure art. Advocates of natural forms argue that their pictures, selections from the material world and based on an artistic idea, are not passive representations. They remark that both abstract painting and the representation of natural forms are the products of artists' minds, and that abstract painters, by rejecting the external world, lose a whole range of values.

*　*　*

The carnage and destruction of World War I changed the world utterly. During the years of the war, art activity slowed down. With the end of the war, increased intellectual and artistic activity made Paris the meeting place of all painters of Europe. Montparnasse, with many of its cafés exhibiting paintings or organizing lectures, replaced Montmartre as the center of art activity. The opening of new art galleries, with some of them publishing their own bulletins, and the publication of new magazines that became the rallying point of avant-garde literary and artistic activity spread a taste for painting. Above all the desire to be informed reduced prejudices, and suddenly modern painting attracted the public.

For at least a century, Paris had attracted artists from all over the world and had nourished revolutionary movements in the visual arts. The Armory Show of 1913, the first large exhibition of works of modern European and American artists, and the opening of the Museum of Modern Art in New York in 1929, became landmarks in the development of modern art in America. During World War II, artistic activity ceased in Europe, and after the war, New York replaced Paris as the center of art activity.

As more of the art of the twentieth century has been based upon discoveries in science and intellectual doctrines, painting became so diverse that hardly any unifying characteristics exist between some of the movements. These modern painters, after taking over the discoveries of their predecessors, moved in a new direction. The diversity of goals and styles of artists make outlining modern painting in a single formula impossible; thus, to enjoy modern art, the viewer needs to understand the fundamental logic of each style.

Possibly the only straight development was a gradual movement away from the natural image to abstract creation. In the nineteenth century, the word *abstract* was employed to describe the aesthetic quality of one of the plastic elements of a painting, such as its line or its color. But during the early twentieth century, several painters, in search of a pure art and following the example of music and architecture by excluding reference to recognizable objects, derived their desired effects from color and unnatural forms.

Exhibitions of the art of other cultures, symbolism's promotion of psychological content, the rise of the art-dealer system replacing the old system of patronage, and the invention of photography changed the nature of portraiture more than other genres of painting. Consequently, the conceptual portrait replaced the sitter's appearan

Section 1

William Morris, the English artist and poet, was a friend of the pre-Raphaelites and a follower of John Ruskin's view that art should be beautiful and useful. To elevate the status of craft, which since the Renaissance had been replaced by the fine arts, in 1861 Morris founded his decorative art firm, which set in motion an arts and crafts movement that was against unnatural forms of artifacts and mass production by mechanization.

As opposed to the aesthetic and literary origin of the arts and crafts movement in England at end of the nineteenth century, in France a rational movement began in architecture and painting. Violet le Duc, the French architect and theorist of the nineteenth century, was an admirer of the structures of Gothic architecture. His logical consideration that architectural form develops from function and technique, not from aesthetic principles, led him to the use of iron, which allowed him the use of organic forms that were radically opposed to the past. On the other hand, Gauguin's rational approach to painting, before symbolism caused him to drift away from his decorative style, marked the end of obedience to optical reality and the beginning of a period of rational picture making in France, which opened the way to a style of painting whose decorative character became the essence of art nouveau.

Gauguin's guidance to Paul Serusier on how to paint a little landscape at Pont Aven became a basis for the theories of Maurice Denis, who defined painting this way: " A picture, before being a war horse, a naked woman, or some anecdote, is essentially a flat surface covered by colors assembled in a particular order." The Nabis, following Denis's theories, organized a new style in which their interest was decoration through harmony of shape and color. Denis said, "The depth of our emotions comes from the sufficient power of these lines and colors." The illustration of books, prints, posters, and stained glass became favorite areas for this decorative art, and its move into stained glass marked the renewal of interest in the applied arts.

At the end of nineteenth century, Brussels was a modest center for art innovation. In 1881 two art collectors started the magazine *L'Art Modern* in Brussels. From the magazine was derived the group "Les Vingt"—the name, better known as "Les XX," derived from the number of its founders. The group established an annual exhibition of the works of important European avant-garde artists. Despite hostile reactions of the public to new movements in painting, Belgian avant-garde artists, conscious of the decorative scope of these paintings, welcomed these exhibitions. The simultaneous presence on the one hand of products of the arts and crafts movement and on the other hand of the decorative tendencies of the French painters became decisive in the formation of art nouveau.

From the increased prosperity following annexation of the Congo in 1885 emerged a new upper class in Belgium. Their liberal views toward new ideas and art led to a burst of architectural commissions to Victor Horta, who, with the utilization of iron and modern materials, gave openness and spatial continuity to his constructions. But this architecture was not a true art nouveau, and without theoretical support, it was destined to a dead end.

Of the Belgian masters as founders of art nouveau, Van de Velde, a painter trained in Paris, gave the movement its theoretical foundation. To form a new style of art, by a sense of modernity and a logical approach, he synthesized Ruskin's and Morris's ideas of art, the sobriety of the disciples of the arts and crafts movement, and the decorative trend of French painting. He characterized his style by sinuous lines adapted from the organic world. Considering that art must surrender every form that would destine it for only one person, he abandoned painting to dedicate his art to decoration. In 1895 he sent his furniture and interior creations to Bing's Salon de l'Art Nouveau in Paris. In 1898 he opened his own arts workshop and exported its production beyond national boundaries. In 1902 he settled in Germany, where, as the artistic advisor to the Grand Duke of Saxe-Weimar, he organized the Weimar School of Decorative Arts, whose program, based on the promotion of the faculty of invention, prohibited the study of styles. This school was the first experiment in Europe that laid the foundation for the Bauhaus in 1919.

In 1895 Samuel Bing, a German man who became a naturalized Frenchman, opened the Salon de l'Art Nouveau in Paris. The name of this art gallery became that of the entire new movement that had taken shape in Belgium. Although in the face of violent reactions of the public and critics, who saw this new style as an attack of foreign arts against French tradition, Bing continued his sponsorship to create a typically French art nouveau, which led to Bing's Salon de l'Art Nouveau pavilion at the Paris World Fair of 1900. But as he turned his attention to Germany, in the context of art nouveau, painting and architecture lost ground in France. It was in 1901 that Gale, as head of the École de Nancy, gave rise to a real art nouveau movement in France, which triumphed in furniture and handicraft products. Gale's aesthetic, based on organic forms, resembled stems and blossoms of plants.

In Germany, in 1896 the first issue of *Die Jugend* ("Youth") was published in Munich. By its layout and its tendencies, it gave its name to the art movement of *jugendstil*, which roughly corresponded to art nouveau. Die jugendstil spread throughout Germany, Vienna, and Barcelona, and played a decisive role in the awakening of interest in the art nouveau movement. The settlement of Van de Velde in Germany brought to an end the jugendstil movement.

In Austria, a group of painters founded the Vienna Secession in 1897. They capitalized on the innovations made in other countries, and by their achievements, they contributed to the renewal of art nouveau.

In Spain, Gaudi, a visionary artist, followed a solitary path. He studied Gothic architecture in an analytical way, and from the beginning he used iron and unusual materials. At the turn of the century, he found his original organic form of architecture.

The International Exhibition of Modern Decorative Art of Turin in 1902 revealed distinct differences between the tendencies as well as a marked discord between architectural ensembles and individual objects. The movement, which began at the end of nineteenth century, ended in 1914.

GUSTAV KLIMT (1862–1918)

Klimt, born on the outskirts of Vienna, was the son of an unsuccessful gold engraver, whose children were raised in poverty. Klimt and his brother, Ernst, enrolled at the School of Applied Art. Both brothers, with the intention of becoming art teachers, enrolled in the Technical School for Drawing and Painting. After the completion of their studies, along with Franz Matsch, a painter, they formed the Kunstler-Compagnie for execution of mural paintings. For the mural of the Burgtheater theaters, their company received the Golden Order of Merit. With the death of Ernst, the two surviving partners gradually dissolved the Kunstler-Compagnie. In 1890 Gustav met Emilie Floge, the Austrian fashion designer, who was to be his companion until his death. In 1893 he was nominated for a professorship at the Academy of Fine Arts in Vienna.

Berta Zukerkandis, the daughter of Moritz Szeps, editor-in-chief of the *Neues Wiener Tagblatt*, married Emile Zukerkandi, a renowned anatomy professor at the Vienna University. Having grown up in the public sphere, Berta, with her liberal orientation, made her home a cultural center where scientists and artists gathered and discussed matters of culture and science, such as Darwin's ideas, which were a topic among the German-speaking nations. From these gatherings was generated the idea of the secession movement. In 1897 Klimt founded the Vienna Secession[14] as a revolt against academic art and in favor of a decorative style similar to art nouveau.

In 1896 the Ministry of Culture and Education commissioned Klimt for three allegorical painting called *Philosophy*, *Medicine*, and *Law* for the ceiling of the Vienna University's assembly hall. At the secessionist exhibition of 1900, Klimt presented his *Philosophy*. The allegorical program of the picture was given in an accompanying text: "On the left: genesis, reproduction, decay. On the right: the globe of the world, the riddle of the universe. Rising from below: the illuminated figure of knowledge." The concept of the painting, based on Darwin's scientific discovery of fundamental mechanisms

---

14 - Artistic secession, which refers to separation of modernist artists from institutions that dominated the visual art, was a feature of the art activity of nineteenth century.

- The Munich Secession, was a break away artists from conservative Munich Artist's Association in 1892.

- The Berlin Secession (1898), was an objection against rejection of a landscape by Walter Leistikow, who was among artists interested in modern art.

- The Vienna Secession (1897), was formed by artists objecting to the prevaing conservatism of the Association of Austrian Artists, the first president of the Vienna secession was Gustave klimt.

of biological change, was a blow to the manner of thinking of that institution and its metaphysical system of knowledge. The mural created a deep division within the university. The majority of professors, arguing that the overt nudity of the painting made it morally unacceptable, requested that it should not be installed at the university. A minority, led by Emil Zuckerkandi, defended Klimt. Finally, the installation of the mural was approved. But the depiction of a nude pregnant woman in *Medicine* and nude women in *Law* renewed protests. Ultimately, Klimt decided to refund advances he had received and withdraw his paintings. After he withdrew from government projects as the most prominent modern painter of Vienna at the turn of the century, he went on to paint portraits of many women of Vienna's cultural elite. In 1945 retreating SS forces destroyed Klimt's three allegorical paintings.

In 1902 the Vienna Secession decided for their fourteenth exhibition to honor Beethoven. The Viennese artists decorated the interior murals of the exhibition. Klimt, for his *Beethoven Frieze*, chose the theme of Schiller's "Ode to Joy," the closing chorus from the final movement of the *Ninth Symphony*.

Around the turn of the century, Beethoven realized with horror that he was losing his hearing. During these years his hearing deteriorated to the point of drifting him into a silent and solitary world. But as a man with an extremely strong personality, in his art he rose above suffering. He wrote, "I shall seize Fate by the throat." "Ode to Joy," the closing chorus of the final movement of his *Ninth Symphony*, is the embodiment of Beethoven's spiritual triumph.

For the symbolic evocation of the *Ninth Symphony*, leading from "aspiration to happiness," to "hostile powers," and finally to "happiness fulfilled in poetry," Klimt divided the imagery for *Beethoven Frieze* into seven compartments. Humanity, yearning for happiness, implores the strong hero to take up the struggle, and the hero, before reaching the kingdom of pure joy, passes through an army of sins and vices—Klimt symbolized these as a gruesome animal. His use of a decorative arrangement of flat patterns to express the content was a major achievement of art nouveau.

Klimt visited Ravenna in 1903 to see the sixteenth-century mosaics of the church of San Vitale. Deeply impressed by the richly decorated mosaics, in that same year, he returned to Ravenna to study them. The assimilation of many previous sources of inspiration with the Ravenna study, and the influence of Japanese art, transmuted his figure paintings.

Captivated by the image of Empress Theodora on a gold background, he painted the portrait of *Adele Bloch-Bauer I*, a centerpiece of his golden style. Through his training at the School of Applied Art, he applied semiprecious stones and layers of gold and silver to the picture, alternating the soft forms and colors of the sitter with hard, decorative elements.

Dialogues of Hetaerae ("Dialogues of Courtesans"), illustrated by Klimt, was published in Vienna in late 1905. The book was written by Lucian in the second century AD and consists of conversation among courtesans on subjects of their lives and profession. The eroticism that he developed in the drawings for this book and in his paintings is not to be approached as a product of the painter's fantasies. His intention was to put sexuality into the public sphere. Klimt, through his art, always stood for the denunciation of hypocrisy, the search for truth, and the celebration of life.

The high point of his golden style is *The Kiss* (1907); the man tenderly holds the woman, who allows him to do so with abandonment. The man wears an immense robe with rectangular designs, and the woman's sumptuous dress is covered with flowerlike designs.

In 1911 he painted *Death and Life*. On the left side of the picture stands the figure of Death, wrapped in a long robe in the cold color of blue. On the right is Life, full of motion and in bright vivid colors; on top a woman tenderly holds a child. His mosaic frieze for the Palais Stoclet in Brussels, completed in 1911, was his major commission in the golden style. He described it as "the final logical consequence of my ornamental development." The spatial complexity of the circular composition and the looser brushwork of *The Virgin* (1913) mark a change in style. After a stroke, which left him paralyzed on one side, he died in 1918.

Section 2

D iscoveries of the possibilities of color by Van Gogh and Gauguin inspired Matisse and a few young artists to explore possibilities of color in a new form of painting. In 1905, at the third Salon d'Automne, the group, under the leadership of Henri Matisse, exhibited paintings whose use of pure color to the point of harshness shocked viewers at a time dominated by niceties of the middle class. The critics called these artists the *Fauves* ("wild animals"). Among the characteristics of this movement were flat colors, a disregard of natural forms, the use of color as an end in itself, the use of color straight out of tube contrary to the sophisticated palette of the impressionists, and vehemently brushed colors. Opposed to impressionist naturalism, for the Fauves, color was more than a stimulus on the retina; it was a means of sensuous expression, as well as a way to construct space by intensity of tone. Matisse wrote, "When I use a green, it doesn't mean grass; when I use a blue, it doesn't mean the sky."

The Fauves, under guidance of Matisse, in revising the traditional way of picture making, applied logic by their handling of color:

- They replaced classical perspective and three-dimensional composition by building a picture with variations in the intensity of colors.
- They repudiated light as a source of illumination. Instead, to suggest light they transmuted it into color.

To construct with color did not mean an architectural construction of the picture. With a revival of interest in Cezanne's vision of structure, many fauvist painters rejected fauvism in favor of cubism. Only Matisse, who had pioneered fauvism, pursued the movement for some years more. Although the movement was short-lived, it liberated color from its age-old limitations as a descriptive function of local tone, and it prepared the move toward the use of color as a means of expression and a new kind of poetry in painting. Matisse, who had followed a logical course to build fauvism, by way of Braque and Derain, inspired cubism to an intellectual and logical approach to the art of painting.

HENRI-EMILE-BENOIS MATISSE (1869–1954)

Matisse was born into a middle-class family living in Bohain-en-Vermandois, a small town about twenty kilometers from Saint-Quentin. His father was a prosperous hardware and grain merchant. As young Henri suffered from chronic appendicitis that was not then operable, it was decided that he would have to follow an undemanding profession. He was sent to Paris to study law at the university. After he passed the law examinations, back at home he worked as a clerk in a law office. An attack of appendicitis forced him to stay home for several months. During his convalescence, it was suggested that he paint, and he was given a box of colors. Painting gave him an unprecedented feeling of contentment. When the convalescence was over, he went back to work, and before and after office hours, he also worked every day at a design school. After he had violent arguments with his father, it was agreed that he could go to Paris for a year to study painting.

In order to prepare for the École des Beaux-Arts admission examination, he enrolled at the Académie Julian, a private school taught by professors of the École des Beaux-Arts. The Académie Julian's instructions, consisting of drawing from plaster, disgusted him. In a trip to Lille with his father, he visited the Museum of Lille. The works of Chardin and Goya at this museum restored his enthusiasm. He said, "It was an open door. Académie Julian was a closed door." He failed the 1892 admission examination of the École des Beaux-Arts, but he did not give up.

Despite his skepticism about the value of teaching, he was aware of his need to learn the techniques of painting. In the large glass-enclosed courtyard of the école, he began to draw from plaster casts of antique sculptures. Gustave Moreau, one of the teachers, was generous and open-minded. One day, Matisse asked Moreau's criticism. Moreau invited Matisse to work at his studio. Moreau was a remarkable teacher, whose liberal teaching had attracted the most original students at the École des Beaux-Art to his classes. He encouraged students to their own originality and prepared them for an intellectual art. According to Moreau, the purpose of color was not limited to reproducing a reality that the eye sees; it also serves a reality that the mind perceives. He believed that a work of art should contain a harmony of the whole, in the eye of the viewer, superfluous details taking the place of essentials are a detriment to it. Moreau urged his students to copy the work of the masters, and he accompanied them on their visit to Louvre. He also advised his pupil to sketch in the streets. The importance that he gave to the physical application of paint and his ideas about imagination were valuable educations to Matisse. Later, several of his students formed the core of the group called the Fauves. Concerned about the future of his son, Matisse's father asked Moreau's opinion about the talent of his son. Moreau's response assured the continuation of Matisse's allowance.

Matisse spent some of his time copying in the Louvre. An attraction to copying at the Louvre was that the resulting artwork could be bought by the state for town halls or museum in the provinces. In 1894, he found out that Caroline Joblaud, with whom he was living, was pregnant. In September, he became the father of his first child. To appease his father, who was distressed by the birth of an illegitimate grandchild, he participated once more in the admission examinations of the École des Beaux-Arts. His admission to the école helped him sell his Louvre copies to the state.

The gradual unfolding of Matisse's art was due to his self-imposed and prolonged apprenticeship. As a young artist in the quest of his own style, he studied the masters and various art movements of nineteenth-century neoclassicism, realism, impressionism, and postimpressionism. For his earliest paintings, he selected still lives. Then he moved on to landscape, followed by figure painting. Before 1897, Matisse's paintings reflect the influence of Chardin and Corot and a palette that still retained dark tones.

Matisse's *The Dinner Table* (1897), a landmark because of its technical accomplishment, shows signs of his move to impressionism. When he met Pissarro, the kind old man left a profound impression on him. Through Pissarro he gained knowledge about impressionism and the art of Cezanne. With Pissarro's advice, his brushwork became freer and his colors brighter, and he showed more interest in modernism.

As his relationship with Caroline Joblaud had ended, in 1898 he married Amelie Parayre, who became a loyal wife. She also became a spiritual and material support for Matisse, and she adopted Marguerite, the child of Caroline, and treated her as her own child. For their honeymoon, they went to London, where, following Pissarro's advice, Matisse studied the vibrant colors and sense of light of Turner. After returning from London, the couple sojourned for several months in Corsica. The bright light of Corsica and the study of Turner influenced Matisse's choice of color. He chose pure tones for brightly lit interiors, reduced landscapes to their simplest elements, and loosened his brushwork. In Corsica, reading Paul Signac's *D'Eugene Delacroix au Neo-impressionisme*, a book that provided the history of modernism and explained pointillism in detail, was a revelation to him.

Back in Paris, Matisse saw the need for more study of painting. Moreau had died the year before, and he had been succeeded by Cormon, who did not like Matisse's work. Soon he was told that, as he was over thirty, he had to leave the class. To explore his knowledge of form, he went to work in the Académie Carriere, where he met André Derain.

His admiration for Cezanne's lesson that relationships between tones must be constructed and balanced became evident in his interest in the structure of his pictures. One day he noticed Cezanne's *Three Bathers* on the wall of Vollard's gallery, and despite his limited resources, he bought the picture and held on to it for thirty years. His move toward modern painting did not please buyers. Unable to sell any of his paintings, to provide some income besides his father's allowance, he worked as a laborer for a decorator shop. Interested in sculpture, he attended evening classes in sculpture.

In 1901 Matisse ran into André Derain in the company of Maurice de Vlaminck. He went to see them off and on at their studio. A few years later, the three began to work closely. Vollard's Gallery was rarely open to little-known painters. Aware of the growing reputation of Matisse among artists and encouraged by Roger Marx, a critic in touch with young artists, Vollard gave Matisse his first one-man show in 1904. In the preface of the catalog, Roger Marx wrote, "The art of Henri Matisse harmoniously reveals the synthesis of the combined teachings of Gustave Moreau and Cezanne."

At that time, there was the old Salon des Indépendants, of which Signac was the moving spirit, and the new Salon d'Automne, founded in 1903. Matisse, as an annual exhibitor at the Salon des Indépendants, attracted the notice of Paul Signac. At his suggestion, Matisse and his wife spent the summer of 1904 at Saint-Tropez, not far from Signac's villa. It was an opportunity to see Signac paint in his divisionist style. Despite agitated discussions between the two artists, Signac's tendency to overly systematic brushstrokes and color laid on in regular spots according to the logic of neoimpressionism affected Matisse, and the intellectual side of neoimpressionism changed the course of Matisse's art.

Lux, Calm, et Volupté is a landscape from nature combined with imagination, in which Matisse was concerned with contrasts of tone, color, and line. The technique is neoimpressionist, but the size of his brushstrokes and their direction around the forms differ from neoimpressionist painters. The picture, the center of attention at the Salon des Indépendants of 1905, was purchased by Signac. Although Matisse's neoimpressionism was short-lived, Signac had shown him the way toward the pure, high-keyed color that was to be of use in his fauvist period.

In the summer of 1905, Matisse and André Derain worked together in the fishing village of Collioure and painted their first characteristic fauvist pictures. While they were at Collioure, the sculptor Maillol took the two painters to see Daniel Monfreid, who owned some works of Gauguin. The supple curves and broad color planes of Gauguin, as well as the symbolic aspects of his art, were a revelation to Matisse. He broke away from pointillism and began to paint in flat areas of pure colors, and his paintings embodied a symbolic language.

Open Window, Coullioure, one of the central pieces of the short-lived fauvist movement, is one of Matisse's earliest paintings that contains his complex spacial structure and the range of his brushwork. The flat color of the space of the interior is thinly brushed, the transitional space of the window area is created with short strokes, and the space of harbor with its rocking boats is in linear strokes.

The intensity and discord of violent colors, held together by sweeping brushstrokes, of *Woman with a Hat,* one of the eight paintings that he sent to the Salon d'Automne of 1905, and the works of his friends, created a state of agitation among the public and critics that provoked a scandal. The purchase of *Woman with a Hat* by Leo Stein marked the beginning of a relationship between Matisse and the Stein family.

Leo Stein was one of the five children of a wealthy American family. After his studies at Harvard and at Johns Hopkins, he went to London. The guidance of art historian and collector Bernard Berenson introduced Leo to the world of modern art, and he became a discerning connoisseur and collector of paintings. In 1903 he settled in Paris, where he was joined by his sister, Gertrude. His elder brother, Michael, and his wife, Sarah, also began to acquire a large number of Matisse's paintings. The family became patrons of Matisse and Picasso. Another important modern art collector of that period was Sergi Shchukin, a successful Russian businessman who lived in Moscow in an eighteenth-century palace with sumptuous rococo decoration. He was a generous buyer of the paintings of the fauvists. He considered Matisse and Picasso to be two masters of the period.

After the Salon d'Automne of 1905, from his experiances Matisse retainend broad color planes, but his restrained brushwork of *The Green Line* (1905), a portrait of Matisse's wife, show the flexibility of his vision and his ability to explore different manners of painting. The divided face of this portrait into chromatically cooler and warmer sides was apparently inspired by the divided face of Manet's *Berthe Morisot with a Bunch of Violets* into a lighter and darker side.

Moved by Gauguin's symbolic and imaginative art, he painted *Le Bonheur de Vivre* (1906). The unprecedented looseness and simplicity of the dynamic and fluidly curved lines, and the broad, flat, brilliant colors of this large landscape point to a twentieth-century approach to painting. The trees in the upper part of the painting, forming a kind of Gothic arch as in Cezanne's late *Bathers*, rendered freely, show an abstract tendency; while in the lower part, despite its distortions, the figures, flowers, and grass have a naturalistic description. The curved lines of the forms of trees and figures link the two parts of the picture together. The two languid females in the center of picture, the meditating reclined flutist, the figure picking flowers, the pairs of lovers, and the ring of dancers all allude to the diversity of the aspects of human life and nature. The fluid organic forms and brilliant colors of this picture were a move away from sensation.

The twentieth century was reaching toward a global culture. Matisse, at the heart of the revitalization of art, and with the intention to investigate rather than imitate, studied Islamic art, French primitives, and African sculpture. Since romanticism, Algeria's intense light, colors, and primitivism had always attracted painters. As part of his broad study of the art of painting, Matisse made his first visit to North Africa in 1906.

He took a small African figurine that he had bought from a curio shop to Gertrude Stein's house, where he showed it to Picasso. The two painters had been introduced to each other by Gertrude Stein. Despite their difference in age and extreme personality differences, they judged each other as valued competitors for the primacy of the art of their time. An intense dialogue began and continued between the two painters. They traded pictures and influenced each other, and they even exhibited together in 1945. Matisse generously presented Sergi Shchuskin, his Russian patron, to Picasso. Matisse told Max Jacob that if he were not painting the way he was, he would like to paint like Picasso. Jacob replied, "Do you know that Picasso said the same thing about you?"

In 1906, African sculpture that represented human forms and had no similarities to ancient Greek sculpturehad worked on Matisse's imagination and provoked a departure from his earlier, more naturalistic sculptures. In 1907, he painted *Blue Nude* with heavy blue lines, rough modeling, and violent transitions. Both Matisse's *Blue Nude* and Picasso's *Les Demoiselles d'Avignon* rejected the the delicately painted art of that time and the notion of conventional beauty—and were more concerned with matters of concept than of sensation—are considered the departure points of the art of the twentieth century.

In 1907 Matisse made a journey to Italy. On his return, he painted *Le Luxe I* and *II*. These pictures, in which a modern image of Venus rises from the sea and is wiped dry by an attendant, and a bouquet-bearing figure hurries in from the right, synthesize diverse sources to create an original work. The style of *Le Luxe I* was fauvist without its brilliance, and due to a lack of vigorous drawing, it looks like a sketch. The thin line drawing of *Le Luxe II* and its large flat color areas, replacing brushed colors, herald a change in style. After years of absorption in the art of Cezanne, Matisse had finally chosen the fluidity of a dynamic style.

In 1908 Sara Stein and Hans Purmann had the idea of forming a painting school to be taught by Matisse. They organized the school and became its students. The program was traditional, yet Matisse did not impose an academic discipline or imitation of his style; instead, he taught students to see for themselves. As teaching required much time and energy, he closed the school in 1911. In these years Shchukin was the most important collector of Matisse's work; but

Gertrude Stein, considering him too persistent in tenaciously continuing his experiments lost interest in his work.

Matisse's tendency to arabesque culminated in *Harmony in Red* (1908). The picture, an essay in the contrast of curving and straight lines and warm and cool colors, is an ambiguous picture. The window could be read as a picture within a picture or an opening to the outside, and the floral motifs of the tablecloth are as real as the objects on the table. Despite the flattened space and decorative arrangement of objects, the setting is not imaginary. It synthesizes his earlier tendency toward depicting the world of reality and his later interest in conceptual image making.

In the world of ancient Greece, next to the rational, classical art, there existed scenes of ecstatic nude dancers performing Dionysian ritual dances that expressed abandon and spiritual exaltation, celebrating the seasonal emergence of a vital force that rejuvenates the earth.

At the end of 1909, Shchukin commissioned Matisse to paint two pictures for the stairwells of his palace. For the commissioned pictures, inspired by Dionysian art, Matisse chose the themes of *Dance* and *Music*. Both pictures were conceived in only three colors: the blue of sky, the green of grass, and the pink bodies of figures. Lack of a specific environment and the nudity of five women dancing vigorously on a hilltop make *Dance* an image of a cosmic dance. The vitality of the picture, reflecting the frenzy of the intoxicated dancers, make it a rare piece of art. The two pictures, *Dance* and *Music*, despite similarity in execution, coloring, nudity, and nonspecific space, represent two different moods. The image of dancers holding hands with each other, and the intensified gestures of each figure, are active, while the image of musicians separated from each other and the compact poses and complete stillness of the listeners are static. The two pictures, exhibited at the Salon d'Automne of

1910, impressed the public and other artists. But Shchukin, who had adopted two young girls, feared that the nude figures of the two pictures would be unsuitable in his house. After Matisse refused to make any changes, he accepted the canvases.

Matisse rented a villa with a large garden in Issy-les-Moulineaux, a suburb of Paris, away from the busy atmosphere of the city. There he began the *Back* series, large bas-reliefs of standing nude females seen from behind. *Back I* was a study of the relationship of masses to each other, the angular structure of *Back II* suggests the influence of cubism, and the simplified forms of *Back III* have turned the human form into a kind of column. He also sculpted *La Serpentine*, whose lyrical curves contradict the monumentality of the *Back* series.

In 1910 Matisse went to Munich to see a large exhibition of Islamic art. Impressed by the colored arabesques of Persian rugs and the color and composition of Persian miniatures, he stated, "Because of its dense details, this art suggests a larger space, a truly plastic space, and it helped me to go beyond intimate painting."

In *The Red Studio*, to return to the simplicity of motif, he abandoned ornamentation and reduced the volume to the level of the picture surface. The composition, without a symmetrical division of space, seems scattered. But the outline of the grandfather clock, not obvious at first glance, regulates the space of the picture.

From the end of 1910 to 1912, he made several trips to other countries. In Spain, flowered Spanish shawls attracted his attention. He painted *The Manila Shawl*, a full-length portrait of Mme. Matisse in Spanish costume. As Matisse's concern was to organize the space of the image, not to decorate it, he incorporated the floral element of the Spanish shawl as a constructive factor of the picture, not a decorative motif.

To renew his contact with nature, in the company of his wife he went to Morocco. The contrasts of curves of plants to the upright trees, and the rich colors of *Moroccan landscape* make this canvas his most beautiful painting of this trip. At the end of September 1912, he returned to Morocco. An article by Marcel Sembat described the process of painting of the *Moorish Café*: Matisse had his bowl of fish and pink flowers. The calmness of the Moroccans contemplating for hours a flower and some goldfish struck him. To reflect the calmness of men sitting in the café, he simplified, close to abstraction, the *Moorish Café*. A recumbent Moroccan reveals the relaxed atmosphere of the café.

Matisse's work between 1913 and 1916, under the influence of cubism, moved away from the bright colors that had characterized his paintings since 1905 and moved toward more somber colors and a more abstract style. *Blue Window* was the view to the garden from his bedroom in Issy. Instead of using outside space as a *trompe l'oeil* ("fool the eye ") to deepen the perspective, he brought the outside space forward to link inside with outside. The simplification and flattening of the forms of objects inside the room, and the reduction of outside trees to circular, flat, abstract forms emphasize the unity of space.

In *Portrait of Madame Matisse* (1913), the influence of Cezanne and cubism are evident, without losing the personal qualities of Matisse's art. The oval face is drawn like a mask. The orange scarf and the little pink flower in the hat balancing the cool colors, the solidity of curved and straight lines, and the overall austerity of the picture mark this canvas as one of his excellent works. The portrait, exhibited in the Salon d'Automne, aroused strong criticism both for and against it.

The Brazilian Landsberg family chose Matisse to make a portrait of Yvonne, their nineteen-year-old daughter. Matisse made several pen-and-ink drawings of Yvonne. Taken by the grace of the sensitive and shy young woman, he also made an oil painting of her. To convey Yvonne's personality, he progressively moved away from a naturalistic representation toward symbolic imagery. The face has a similarity to the masklike face in *Portrait of Madame Matisse*, and the symmetrical shoulders have heart-shaped contours. The arcing lines that he scratched in the *Portrait of Yvonne Landsberg* are like forces emanating from the body of the young woman.

In 1914 German forces crossed the French borders. Many of the French artists went into the army, but Matisse was rejected for military service. The family moved to Collioure, where he painted the ambiguous painting *Fench Window at Collioure*. The window opens onto a total darkness of night, possibly reflecting his pessimistic view of the future of Europe. Besides its emotional content, the simple composition of four colors and the varying width of verticals above an oblique edge make this picture an abstract painting. In Collioure he found Juan Gris, whose friendship stimulated Matisse's interest in cubism.

Matisse was a painter of his inner visions; thus, new sights were a pretext to go back to his private world. *Moroccans at Prayer* (1916), a picture composed from memories, evokes rather than describes. At the time of painting this picture, Matisse's mind was preoccupied with cubism. To build up its massive structure, he may have had Cezanne's advice regarding "building from cylinders, spheres, and cones" in mind, which carried his tendency toward abstract form to its highest pitch. The black ground of the picture separates its space into three areas of the architectural, the human, and the vegetal, each with its own view point. At the upper left, the view of a mosque is seen from a balcony. Below the balcony, a pile of melons are displayed on the pavement. At the right a few Moroccans, one seated and others crouching, are at prayers. The repetition of circular and curved forms in each area serves as the unifying compositional device of the picture.

The Piano Lesson (1916), is a complex painting, that synthesize imagination and reality. The room and the abstract view of the garden through the window have been flattened. When Matisse painted this image of his son Pierre, as a boy practicing at the piano, actually he was older then. At the bottom left corner, is representation of Matisse's sculpture *Decorative Figure*, a nude figure made in 1906. At the upper right, is aloof figure of Pierre's music teacher. But ambiguous space of the picture makes it hard to tell if the figure is really a teacher, or it is a painting by Matisse titled *Woman on a High Stool* (1914), that its rectangular form contrasts curve lines of the sculpture.

At a time when abstract forms attracted him, he turned to portraiture. The angular forms of the squeezed hands and the sharp features of the face of the wealthy manufacturer in *Portrait of Auguste Pellerin II* (1917), express the force and grim personality of the sitter. The straight lines of the frame of the picture behind the sharp curve of the head add to the image's rigidity.

The period between 1917 and 1925 was for Matisse a time to relax and move away from the constant endeavor to search for and create new, modern pictures. He began spending winters on the Mediterranean, and he then moved permanently to Nice.

Tired of the relaxed period, he produced the bronze sculpture *Seated nude* (1925). The discomfort and tension of the unbalanced pose and angular lines of this sculpture replaced the ease of the previous period. The problem of balance and harmony between figure and background came to a climax in *Decorative Figure on an Ornamental Background* (1927). The uniform tonality of the ochre, which represents the common denominator of all neighboring tones, links the figure to the profuse decor of the picture. But the rigid half-pyramidal form of the figure has given her back visual integrity.

To illustrate Albert Skira's new edition of the *Poesies de Stéphane Mallarmé* (1932), Matisse's problem was to balance the two pages of the poems—the black page of the text and the illustrated page. To balance the left-hand pages that carried the texts, the etchings on the right-hand side, done in even, very thin lines without shading, were spread out over a whole white page. For subject matter, which was as varied as the poems themselves, he chose nature rather than the imagination.

Dr. Barnes asked Matisse to decorate the lunettes over three tall French windows of a gallery at the Barnes Foundation, in Pennsylvania. After studying the location of the mural, Matisse was faced with serious problems. The lunettes were above three eighteen-foot-high windows. Through the windows one sees the trees. Between the windows and on the end walls were hung some of the best pictures of the collection. To overcome the handicap of nature seen through the windows, and the masterpieces below the lunettes, he later explained, "To treat my decoration like another picture would be out of place. My aim has been to translate paint into architecture, to make the fresco the equivalent of stone or cement." The subject he chose was *The Dance*, borrowed from Shchukin's canvas. While Shchukin's *Dance* had a circular movement, in the version in the mural, the movement of figures is from both sides toward the center, and in the middle lunette, the figures have a rotating movement. A major difference between *The Dance* of 1910 and *The Dance* of 1933 is the violent action of the mural figures.

Three decades after *Blue Nude*, he painted *Pink Nude* (1935). A comparison of these two pictures underlines the evolution of Matisse's style. Twenty-two photographs of work in progress of the *Pink Nude* represent a gradual simplification and at the same time an exaggeration of forms. The final picture displays a balancing of the organic form of a majestic nude figure against the geometric forms of flat planes, and the warm and cold tones.

With the outbreak of World War II, he secured a visa and steamer passage for Rio de Janeiro. While staying in Bordeaux, witnessing the scramble of refugees in the south, he changed his mind and decided not to leave France. In 1941, diagnosed with cancer, he underwent an operation with an uncertain outcome. After the operation, he considered his life to be an unexpected extension, and he determined to make the best use of it. As he could only spend two hours a day out of bed, he had to use a wheelchair.

Unable to stand for long, he created a new technique compatible with his disability. While seated on his bed, working on a table in front of him, he coated the surfaces of sheets of paper with gouache colors. Once dried, using scissors as a drawing tool, he would cut the colored paper into forms. Then an assistant would paste the shapes, according to his instructions, on a canvas. He called the process "painting with scissors." This "cutout medium" was different from the collage technique of the cubists, in which they pasted pieces of newspapers or materials in imitation of wood.

At the age of eighty, crippled by ailments, Matisse began his last work, the great ensemble project of *La Chapelle du Rosaire de Vence*, which was regarded by Matisse himself as his masterpiece. He spent more than four years on its architecture, murals, stained glass windows, interior furnishings, and the vestments of priests.

MURALS

For the three major and two minor murals, he drew heavy black lines on unglazed tiles that were sent to a kiln for glazing:

- *Stations of the Cross*—On the east wall of the chapel, he pictured all the traditional fourteen stations of the cross, which are usually depicted individually, as a continuous narrative in one composition.

- *The Virgin and Child*—Pendant in size to the calvary are the Virgin and Child on the north wall. He gave the image of the Virgin a frontal position as she supports the standing Child with spread arms to form a cross. To fill out the long rectangular panel, he drew rows of flowers and stars on both sides of the image.
- *Saint Dominic*—Behind the altar is the huge image of Saint Dominic. The flat figure, without any detailed features, the simple lines of the fall of the drapery, and the hand holding the book enhance the spiritual and monumental effects of the image.

WINDOWS

For the stained glass for the two rows of six narrow windows in the southern façade, he designed a series of *The Tree of Life*, with big leaves of three intense colors.

CHASUBLES

For the designs of the chasubles, Matisse used his "cutout medium," which, unlike cubist or surrealist collages, consisted of solid and fixed elements bound indissolubly.

On the opening day of the chapel, Matisse's physician forbade him from participating in the ceremonies. He died of a heart attack in 1954.

Matisse skillfully blended logic and sensitivity. His art was in continuous evolvement; the only static of his art was the tremendous power of color and light. Picasso said, "Matisse is…Matisse. It's because he has a sun in his belly."

Section 3

Taking into consideration the scientific discoveries of the century, the young painters of the twentieth century felt the need to direct their creativity away from the static experiences of traditional painting to a dynamic art. The plastic inventiveness of Negro and Iberian sculptures were among the factors that took part in the formation of cubism, a major art movement of the twentieth century.

A commemorative retrospective of Cezanne's works in 1908, and Cezanne's remark that the painter should treat nature in terms of the fundamental shapes of cylinder, sphere, and cone incited Picasso, who had always had a deep concern for formal organization, to some formal research. The collaborative experiments of Picasso and Braque went well beyond anything intended by Cezanne. The art that they created was an answer to the spiration of art of painting for a new poetic creation.

Cubism provoked many theories and forms; nevertheless, numbers of ideas were common to cubist painters:

- Considering canvas a flat plane of two dimensions, they refuted the classical way of picture making, for which spatial representation is an essential element.

- Although they looked at subject matter with their mind's eye and displayed a tendency toward abstraction, their conception of subject matter was never purely abstract, and there were always vestiges of a landscape, a figure, or a still life.
- The creation of light by the artist replaced a source of light.
- An object should be rendered from simutanneous viewpoints and from all dimentions.
- In the first phase of the movement's development, called analytical cubism, they began to break up their pictorial motifs into smaller parts and reassemble them in abstract forms. To represent the subject in its totality by depicting it from a multitude of viewpoints, they broke up the old fixed system of perspective; thus, they added the dimension of time to the spatial dimensions. The important part played in the development of this phase of cubism was the use of collage in the painting. As the development of cubism was leading toward the annihilation of visible reality, in 1911 Braque began to use letters and numerals to link his pictures to external reality. The idea was further developed when Picasso and Braque included pasted newspaper and printed papers in imitation of marble or wood grain into their compositions—a procedure called *papier collé*.

Breaking up the object reached its extreme logical conclusion around 1911. The transition from analytic to synthetic cubism passed through a form of cubism called hermetic cubism, in which the elimination of the subject was a move toward abstraction.

In the second phase, called *synthetic cubism*, which started around 1913, they realized that, in their concern with matters of form, they had neglected color and expression, so they began to create pictures less by breaking down the form of an object than by combining it with other objects or parts of other objects; thus, they built a new totality that looked like a symbol rather than a representation.

From 1910, a number of painters joined cubism, and the rapid spread of cubism led to variations of style that served to create new movements. The most significant contributions came from Juan Gris, Fernand Leger, and Marcel Duchamp. Picasso said, "Cubism is neither the grain nor the germination of a new art; it represents a stage of development of primordial pictorial forms."

Maurice Raynal compared contemplation of a cubist painting to looking at a landscape, in which the pleasure of gazing at a landscape comes from an interplay of colored forms imitating nothing. As a cubist painting is not alluding to something, it is an end in itself.

LA SECTION D'OR

La Section d'Or refers to a group of artists, poets, and critics associated with cubism but essentially influenced by Cezanne in different ways. Some admired Cezanne's Platonic construction; others followed his advice that "we must turn to the old masters via nature." The name of the group, referring to the ancient mathematical proportion between the diagonal and the side of the square, reflects the cubists' general interest in geometric forms. Apollinaire, in a speech, said, "Geometry is to the plastic arts what grammar is to the art of writers" As gatherings and discussions were held at the home of Jacques Villon in the suburb of Puteaux, the group was also known as the Puteaux group. In the first exhibition of the group, held at the Galerie La Boetie in 1912, the works of all painters associated with cubism except Picasso and Braque were exhibited. As time went on, the differences between painters of the group became more apparent. Of all the Section d'Or group, Gris and Villon were the only cubists who applied such scientific concepts to their works.

PURISM

A number of painters, critical of decorative trends in cubism and fascinated by clear and ordered forms of machinery, advocated a move toward pure form. The tendency to purism, notable in the works of Fernand Leger and the group known as De Stijl, was launched by two painters in 1917.

The French painter Amedée Ozenfant maintained that the decorative trend of cubism had sacrificed purity of form. After he met Edmond Jeanneret, the French-Swiss architect-painter known as le Corbusier, they jointly published a book as their manifesto.

In their book *Apres le Cubism* (1918), they set out the principles of purism, and from 1920 to 1925, through articles in *L'Esprit Nouveau*, their purist periodical, they promoted a well-ordered and precise form of painting.

In his pictures, Ozenfant rejected the complicated abstractions of cubism, and considering nonobjective art as a form of applied art, he did not push his pure forms as far as total abstraction. To preserve the clarity of his pictures, he reduced forms of everyday objects and human forms to flat planes. Jeanneret, who was inclined more toward nonobjective painting, based his art on horizontals and verticals, while by use of curves he broke down the rigidity of the picture.

PABLO RUIZ PICASSO (1881–1971)

Pablo Ruiz Picasso, the most extraordinary phenomenon in the art of the twentieth century, was born in Malaga. His father, Don Jose Liuz Blasco, was an artist and art teacher. Pablo began his first designs under the surveillance of his father. He attended drawing classes from 1891 to 1895, and he worked outside of the classroom to sketch everyone and everything around him. His later capability of a wide-ranging approach to figure drawings was due to this early drawing practice.

In 1891 his father was nominated to teach at l'École des Beaux-Arts de Barcelona. After the family settled in Barcelona, Pablo passed the entrance exam of l'Ecole des Beaux-Arts in one day, for which he was allowed one month, and he was admitted to the superior class of the school.

In 1895 all the family passed by Madrid on the way to Malaga for vacation. His father took him to the Prado to see the masters of Spanish art. His portraits from his blue period represent the realism of the Spanish masters, and his lengthening of forms is in the style of El Greco.

In 1898 he went to live for a few months in the village of Horta de Ebro, where he participated in the daily life of the simple and hardworking people of the village. Later he said, "Everything that I know I learned in the village of Horta."

At the end of century, Barcelona, a great modern seaport, was in touch with the art activity of major cities of Europe, and above all with Paris. After his Horta experience, Picasso went to Barcelona, a city that played a prominent part in the formation of his personality and his art. The gathering place of Picasso and his friends was Els Quatre Gats, a meeting place of intellectuals and artists, halfway between German brasseries and Parisian café-concerts. Picasso executed a poster in art nouveau style for Els Quatre Gats and designed portraits of his friends. An exhibition of his portraits in Els Quatre Gats showed his ability to succinctly characterize his subjects.

Through reproductions that reached Barcelona, Picasso came in contact with the works of other painters. Attracted by the art activities of Paris, in 1900, the year of L'Exposition Universelle, he left Barcelona for Paris.

In Paris, Manyac, a Catalan art collector and industrialist, offered him one hundred fifty francs per month for all of his works and introduced him to the art dealer Berthe Weill, who bought three of his sketches. After three months, he returned to Spain. In Madrid, Picasso and the writer Francisco Soler founded the ephemeral review *Arte Joven*. The first issue was entirely illustrated by Picasso. After participation in the second issue, he left for Barcelona, where his friends organized an exposition of his works. Then, in the spring of 1901, he again left Spain for Paris.

In Paris, he studied the works of the impressionists, avant-garde artists, and the art of the old masters at the Louvre. As the name of Ruiz was a current name, in Paris he started signing his works as "Picasso," the family name of his mother. Manyac, his patron put a studio at his disposal and presented him to Ambroise Vollard, who exposed Picasso's works in his art gallery. He was criticized that his works were only an imitation of contemporary art. He broke his contract with Manyac and returned to Barcelona. A self-portrait, painted toward the end of 1901 before returning to Spain, shows an prematurely aged young man.

Although he was drawn to Paris, it was in Barcelona, through understanding of the Spanish soul, that he pondered his own sensibilities and formed his aesthetic. To express the bitter sadness of the life of Spanish people, he painted exclusively in blue, a gloomy tone in harmony with his images of unfortunates living on the fringe of society. One of the touching pictures of this period, *Les Trois Pauvres au Bord de la Mer*, is a pathetic picture of a desperate and exhausted family. His pictures of mother and child—without any religious content—are images of a painful misery. *La Vie* (1901), the major painting of his blue period, represents a naked woman leaning on a naked young man and, on the other side, a mother dressed in long garment, holding her baby tightly and looking at them. Originally, the young man had Picasso's own features, but then he substituted it with the face of Carlos Casagemas, his friend who had committed suicide. The enigmatic gesture of the young man and the inclusion in the composition of two pictures of a squatting couple inspired by Gauguin—whose death coincided with the execution of this painting—have made this picture a subject of many iterpretations. Besides the sense of pathos, pictures of this early period already show Picasso's preoccupation with form and modeling considerations.

In October 1902, for the third time, he returned to Paris. Having no inome, he lived in poverty. Max Jacob took him into his room, where Picasso painted at night and slept by day while Jacob was out at work. After a few months, Picasso returned to Barcelona.

In 1904, for the fourth time he went to Paris to settle down permanently. He lived miserably, but he had his own studio in a building in Montmartre. As none of the ten studios of the building were rainproof, Max Jacob christened it the *Batteau-lavoir* ("wash house"). In the years after 1900, Montmartre was the meeting place of poets and artists from all over Europe. As Picasso was a poetry lover, his studio rapidly became a center of gatherings for poets and young artists. Friendships with Apollinaire, an avant-garde French poet, as well as with Max Jacob and André Salmon extended his world beyond the Spanish community and helped him to lay aside the gloomy blue period and move to more the affirming subjects of the rose period in 1905. At the *Batteau-lavoir*, Picasso met his neighbor, Fernande Oliver, who inspired him to depict more sensual images of women.

The more natural style of the rose period has better drawing, yet its deep view of the reality of life is a continuation of his previous period. Images of clowns and harlequins became central themes of this period. There is no sign of satire in the melancholy images of clowns, and he identified himself with the meditative harlequins.

Ricardo Canals, a Spanish friend, taught him the techniques of gravure, drypoint etching, and aqua fortis. These procedures allowed him to develop the precision and sureness of his drawing. The rounded and massive forms of portraits that he made during his short stay in Holland in the summer of 1905 display his interest in the problem of volume. After returning from Holland, meeting two American collectors—Leo and Gertrude Stein—and the Russian industrialist Shchukin solved his financial hardships.

Picasso was always interested in investigating the art of the past. In 1905 a sojourn in the village of Gosol in Spain, in the company of Fernande Oliver, produced profound changes in Picasso's art and moved his work from perceptual to conceptual. The solid modeling, with faces reduced to abstract oval shapes, and the tranquility of the poses of figures in the works done at Gosol made these images beyond time that had lost concern with likeness. The Gosol period marks the first major break in Picasso's art.

Picasso had a gift for creating likenesses, but he filtered the sitter's appearance through his own interpretation of the subject. Before leaving for Gosol, Picasso was painting the portrait of Gertrude Stein. Although he was satisfied with the monumental and intimate pose of the portrait, after eighty sessions he was still not content with the face he left for Gosol, in which he was influenced by the simplification of features in Iberian sculptures. After his return from Gosol, he painted the face of Gertrude Stein's portrait without referring to his model. The masklike face and oval eyes with heavy eyelids of this portrait represent the influence of Iberian sculpture and opened the door to more innovations.

Around the year 1905, the plastic freedom of the arts of Africa played the same part in the generation of fauvists and cubists as the art of Far East had played for the generation of impressionists and symbolists. The bold distortions, linear simplicity, and plastic poetry of Negro art inspired the young artists of Europe: Kirchner, a member of Die Brucke group in Germany; Vlaminck; Derain; Matisse; and particularly Picasso were the first to discover this art.

The hostility of the young artists to all methods of realism and their tendency toward esoteric arts were signs that a phase of Western culture was drawing to an end. Nourished by the arts of Seurat, Cezanne, and Iberian sculpture, and the discovery of the poetry of pure forms of the Negro art at the Musée du Trocadero, Picasso saw art in a revolutionary manner. *Les Demoiselles d'Avignon* was a move away from using bits and pieces of available vocabulary to an entirely coherent style. Picasso's thought that for creating art there is no need to follow the visible world, but one needs the imagination, led to the exceptional freedom of *Les Demoiselles d'Avignon*, a work that is considered to be the birth of cubism in 1907. He replaced the rounded forms of Iberian sculpture with the pure linear simplicity of geometric forms of Negro sculpture. He broke with the norms of the human body and suppressed individual identities. He made a considerable study of each of the five figures. The two figures at the right-hand side, and particularly their heads, differ from the others. The illusionistic perspective of the Renaissance makes the space of the picture a continuation of the real world; by thrusting the five women forward to the edge of his picture, Picasso separated their world from that of viewer. The geometrical nude women—and the heads of the two figures on the right side of the picture, influenced by Negro sculpture—shocked even Braque, who was introduced to Picasso by Apollinaire. Although Picasso considered the picture with its two rather different sides as incomplete, he made no change to it. The picture remained unexposed to the public for thirty years.

During 1908, Picasso's "Negro" period was characterized by flat, angular patterns and limited color. This period led to the first stage of cubism. At this stage, in which Picasso had opened a whole new area of artistic research, Braque joined him. It was a collaboration between two different lyrical temperaments, and two different approaches to art. Picasso's violent and expressive forms relied on his intuition, and Braque's Cartesian mind, taking a logical approach to the problems of painting, along with the experience from his fauvist period, shaped the aesthetic of cubism. A friendship bonded them together, and they collaborated intimately.

The improvement of Picasso's material conditions allowed him to rent an apartment with a studio and go to the Spanish village of Horta de Ebro. During a four-month stay in this village, he succeeded in synthesizing his research. At the same time, Braque painted a series of landscapes. From Braque's works and Picasso's research, crystallized the style that has been called analytical cubism. *Girl with a Mandolin* (1910) is an early example of analytical cubism, in which the figure of the girl and the shape of mandolin are still recognizable. The breast and arm still have sculptural roundness, but all forms are broken and flattened into rectangles and curves.

That same year, Picasso carried the abstraction of his figures to straight lines and segments of circles. He overlapped planes to suggest depth, restricted the picture to a few colors, and abandoned the old convention of a source of light. The efforts of Picasso and Braque led to a revolutionary art that represented human beings and objects in their manifold and successive aspects. Analytic cubism, which was a break with the traditional way of seeing the outside world, opened the door to the vast discoveries of modern painting.

At the end of 1910, Braque introduced letters or a real piece such as a nail into his pictures. Then, by pasting a piece of newspaper to their pictures, they announced the creation of *papiers-collés*. Picasso, by pasting a piece of oilcloth in *La Chaise Canée*, an oval-shaped picture, and partly painting cubist forms over it, brought reality and abstracted forms next to each other. The technique of collage balanced disregard of Analytical cubism of natural appearances.

Realizing that the fragmented natural forms of analytic cubism had exhausted their possibilities, Picasso and Braque began to develop cubism in new directions. The logic that had led them to break up objects, led also to elimination of subject and distortion of space, which meant moving toward the nonfigurative art of the hermetic[15] period in 1911. After this short interval period, they moved toward synthetic cubism, which became predominant around 1913 and reached its climax in 1921. In synthetic cubism, instead of breaking down forms, they built pictures of geometric patterns that are more a symbol than a visual representation. Planes became broader, completely flat, and more legible; bright colors replaced somber colors of the previous phase, and in the development synthetic cubism, the technique of collage played an importatant part.

Despite Picasso's fame, his works were rarely displayed in expositions. Apollinaire, the famous poet and brilliant art critic, and a close friend of Picasso who ardently defended his art since meeting him at the Batteau-Lavoir, published the theoretical work *Les Peintres Cubistes* and published Picasso's cubist drawings in the review *Les Soirées de Paris*, but under the threat of cancellation of subscriptions, he had to abandon his editorship of the review.

Picasso never limited his art to the aesthetic of a particular style. He would paint in parallel several works that had different directions. In an interview, he pointed out that his different manners should not be considered an evolution but an effort to rejuvenate his art through research into various styles. The two drawings that

---

15 - Hermetism is a mystical philosophy based upon hermetic principles attributed to the Greek god, Hermes. The word hermetic is often used to describe mystical or mysterious concepts. The term fitted this period of Cubism, because it was impossible to figure out the subject of the painting.

he showed to Kahnweiler in 1914 confirm his interest in classical design during his cubism phase. One of them, *The Artist and His Model*, is a combination of an oil painting of the model and a pencil drawing of the artist. The drawing of the artist lost in thought recalls Ingres's style. In 1915, along with painting synthetic cubist pictures, he made pencil drawings of Max Jacobs and Ambroise Vollard in the linear style of Ingres.

Although Spanish citizenship exempted Picasso from military service, World War I affected his life and art. The mobilization of Braque ended the joint collaboration of the two painters. Apollinaire's voluntary enlistment in the French army, followed by the forced return of Kahnweiler to Germany, deprived him of his close friend and his art dealer.

Deeply grieved and demoralized by the sudden death of Marcelle Humbert in 1916, a companion whom Picasso had met in 1911 and had named Eva, he moved to a new studio, a move that damaged many of his cubist works.

Toward the end of the war, he became a close friend of Jean Cocteau, who was planning a spectacle for the troupe of Serge Diaghilev's Ballets Russes. Cocteau asked Picasso's involvement for the famous spectacle of the *Parade*, a one-act scenario written by Cocteau, with music composed by Eric Satie. For *Parade*, a blend of dance, mime, and painting, Picasso painted the curtain with a certain degree of realism, contrasting with his cubist-designed sets, and cubist costumes in solid cardboard. In the notes for *Parade*, Apollinaire wrote, "from *Parade* arises a kind of Surrealism, where I see the starting point of a series of manifestations of this New Spirit..." Critics praised the *Parade*, but the public was shocked and turned the first representation into a scandal.

During his trip to Italy, to prepare for *Parade*, Picasso met Olga Koklova, one of the ballerinas of Diaghilev's troupe, and they married in 1918. Picasso made many drawings and oil paintings of Olga. His *Olga in an Armchair* is a harmonious combination of Ingres's linear style with experiments from cubism. The face and upper body of Olga are seen frontally, but the viewpoint of her left arm and the fan she is holding are from above, and the notion of single source of light is rejected.

After the war, the possibilities of the cubist aesthetic began to dry up. Picasso's love for life and nature turned him to the possibilities of the human figure to express his emotions. Three of his drawings listed in the catalog of Paul Rosenberg's 1919 exhibition of his work were titled either *After Ingres* or *After Renoir*. In the works titled *After Renoir*, he expanded his art from the linear style of Ingres to the massive proportions of Renoir's late figure painting. His neoclassicism became host to a variety of representational styles. His pastels of close-up portraits of the head of Olga seem to be carved from tinted stone. That same year, he painted two compositions called *Les Trois Musicians*, in the cubist synthetic style. Three figures are a pierrot, a harlequin, and a monk, seated at a table.

Picasso's image of *Mother and Child* (1921), in his monumental neoclassical treatment, represent Olga holding Paulo, her one-year-old son. These pictures of a mother holding her baby are entirely different from the pictures of miserable mothers of the blue period, guarding the child in their embrace. From 1923, his paintings in a free style, which was a combination of curved lines, flat volumes, overlapping, and simultaneous viewpoints, represent Picasso's loss of interest in neoclassical style.

The birth of dadaism during the war and the appearance of new ideas and artistic activities after the war, among them new pictorial research toward abstraction; the founding of the Bauhaus in Germany; and the publication of the *Manifest du Surrealism* by André Breton overturned traditional concepts of painting. Surrealism, originally a literary movement, also became a pictorial movement in 1925. The charm of illogic and mystery attracted Picasso's attention, he became close to André Breton and Surrealism, and he illustrated Breton's *Le Surrealism et la Peinture*.

As Picasso's art took roots from his life experience, it is not surprising that women, who had always had an important place in Picasso's life, influenced his art and occupied the largest proportion of his work. The succession of Picasso's contradictory styles had been connected to the women who influenced his life. Although for pictures made at Gosol and thereafter, he treated Fernande more as a motif, she remained also a source of inspiration. Marie Thérèse's vitality and the forms of her body, and the intelligence and eccentricity of Dora Maar provoked different styles and techniques, each a vehicle for a different sensuality and plastic sensibility.

He met Marie-Thérèse Walter, a charming and sporty young girl in 1925. He did several paintings of her beginning in 1925, but his relationship remained secret until 1932. Marie-Thérèse's vitality and the roundness of the forms of her face and body motivated Picasso to paint her in harmonious supple lines, curving forms, and light colors that suggested her cheerful personality. Marie-Thérèse gave birth to Picasso's daughter Maya in 1935, which resulted in Olga's hysterical reaction and separation from Picasso. The pain of separation was so deep that he stopped painting for six months. After he went back to painting again, he executed *Minotauromachy*, which represents the opposing forces of kindness and brutality. The print is full of allegorical messages; on the left of the composition, a young girl holds flowers in one hand and a candle in the other, while the fabulous creature, half animal and half man, marches toward her. In 1930 Picasso purchased the Chateau de Boisgeloup near Paris. In his new residence, he allocated a vast studio for sculpture from wire and plaster.

In 1927 he made a set of echtings to illustrate *Le Chef-d'Oeuvre Inconnu* of Balzac. One of the themes was *The Painter and his Model.* Balzac's story concerns a deranged painter who spent ten years painting a portrait of a woman, and ended with a mass of incomprehensible scribbles. Picasso's choice of an absolute abstraction for the painting of the deranged painter possibly reveals his opinion of total abstraction.

Picasso had painted pictures of bullfights before, but the ferocity depicted in a series of bullfight pictures that he painted after a visit to Barcelona in the early 1930s is unprecedented. The fabulous creature of the minotaur that had appeared for the first time in his *Minotaure et la Femme Endormie* (1927) became one of Picasso's favorite themes, in which he depicted himself as a minotaur in erotic situations. A number of his designs and engravings fuse the theme of the minotaur and the corrida to express the violence and ferocity of combat. In 1933 Albert Skira published the avant-garde magazine *Minotaure*, which had a surrealist orientation. The cover of the first issue appeared with an artwork by Picasso. Vollard, the art dealer, commissioned him to produce more than three hundred etchings for the the *Vollard Suite*; for the theme of these etchings, Picasso developed the cycle of the minotaur.

Picasso met Dora Maar, a professional photographer, in 1936. For a few more years he divided his life between Marie-Thérèse and Dora Maar. During these years he continued to paint portraits of both of his lovers. At the outset, Dora's portraits are intimate and realistic representations. Soon followed surrealist representations and nonorganic portraits with strident colors, and her eyes, each looking at different direction, seem to reveal Dora's spiritual restlessness.

A great friendship bound Picasso and Paul Eluard. The poet was one of the first to support the surrealist movement. Eluard was married to Nusch, a young woman whose enigmatic and intriguing charm inspired Picasso to paint some of his most marvelous portraits.

The massacre and misery that brought the break-out of the Civil War in Spain in 1936 had deep effects on Picasso, who had always remained sensitive to the miseries of human life but had shown no interest in politics. He wrote the poem of *Songe et Mensonge de Franco*, and illustrated it in the form of American comic strips, in which he identified Franco with a horse and the Spanish people with a bull. He printed the pamphlet and sold it for the benefit of the Spanish government. He said, "Artists who live and work according to spiritual values cannot and should not remain indifferent to the conflict in which the highest values of humanity and civilization are at stake." The same year he promised the Republican government of Spain to participate in the decoration of the Spanish pavilion at the Universal Exposition of 1937. The bombardment without any justification of the small town of Guernica by Nazi Germany, killing two thousand people, became the theme of his black-and-white painting *Guernica*. Its expressionist distortions of desperate gestures and its angular cubist design reverberate with the horrors of the military action. At the right side of the picture, a woman, her clothes on fire, falls from a burning house, while another woman rushes toward the center. A lamp held out by a woman from a window and an electric lamp in the shape of an eye light the scene, so that everybody could witness the atrocities. In the center, a dying horse, his back pierced by a spear, screams in pain. Under the horse, a soldier lies dead, still holding his broken sword close to a flower. At the left a mother holds her dead child in her arms. A bird and a bull start to move out of the scene. In that same year, Picasso painted the *Weeping Woman*, a powerful expressionist picture done in broken lines and harsh colors.

During the occupation of France, Picasso, Matisse, and Braque, rather than making an exodus, preferred to stay in France. Except for portraits of Nusch and of Dora Marr, and images of Maya, his daughter—which are the bright side of Picasso's art during the period of World War II—his art reverberated with the horror and anguish of the events of Europe. Yet his *Chevre et la Femme Enceinte*, archetypes of fecundity, affirms the endurance of life.

Le Salon d'Automne of 1944, the first artistic manifestation after the liberation of Paris, invited Picasso. With works executed during the occupation of Paris, for the first time he exhibited at the salon. Just before the opening of the salon, the announcement in *L'Humanite* that Picasso had joined the French Communist Party triggered violent demonstrations in front of his works exhibited at the salon. In an interview, while explaining the logic of his adherence to the Communist Party, Picasso also explained his concept of art: "I have never considered painting as an art of simple pleasure, of amusement: I wanted, by drawing and by color, since there is my arms, to penetrate evermore further into the knowledge of the world and mankind, so that this knowledge liberates all of us more every day."[16]

To denounce the concentration camps, he painted the large canvas of *The Charnel House* in 1944–1945. As in *Guernica*, the palette is limited to black and white. In a vast composition, under a kitchen table lie dead a man, a woman, and a child.

Between 1945 and 1946, he made lithographs with an amazing audacity of technique and innovation, mostly of faces and silhouettes inspired by Francoise Gilot, a young woman he had met recently.

Before the war Vallauris had been one of the centers of ceramics. In the summer of 1947, Picasso visited the village and became passionately fond of this technique. The following year he returned to the village and stayed there the whole winter to make and paint

---

16 - Picasso Metamorphoses et Unite

ceramics. His first creations were in traditional means of making ceramics, and then he began to invent new processes.

In 1952 the municipality of Vallauris placed a secularized chapel at Picasso's disposal. With the intention of turning it into a temple of peace, Picasso painted more than two hundred fifty designs plus two large panels illustrating the theme of war and peace. Afterward the two panels were fixed to the walls of the chapel.

The death of Paul Eluard, Picasso's separation from Francoise Gilot, followed by the loss of Derain, Maurice Raynal, and Matisse, shook Picasso profoundly. His art, expressing his interior tension, became cruel and painful. The relationship with Jacqueline Roque, his future wife, changed Picasso's mood. Jacqueline's gentle personality, her love, and her unconditional commitment to Picasso, and loving surrounding that she provided him revived his creative impulse. They settled down in "La California," a large house on the flanks of a hillside in Cannes. The immense plastic lyric of his art of this time translates the happiness that Jacqueline brought to his life.

Throughout the twenty years living with Jacqueline he painted many pictures of her, mostly realistic and some expressionist. The erect carriage and the gaze of *Jacqueline with Flowers*, the first painting of his future wife, are of a proud woman. The colors, decorative patterning, and flowers in the background of this picture were influenced by Matisse. A few month later, he painted *Jacqueline in a Black Scarf*, an image of a tender woman. The brushwork and palette of *Nude in Armchair* (1969) convey once more the tenderness of Jacqeline.

Since his youth, without an attempt to improve upon works of earlier masters, Picasso associated his women with the paintings of those masters. In 1934 he made variations of Delacroix's *Les Femme d'Algiers*. In his first variations, Jacqueline is absent, then we notice

the resemblance of the crouching woman on the right of the picture to Jacqueline's figure in *Jacqueline with Flowers*, her presence
becomes visible in subsequent works.

To copy the great masters does not mean to paint better or to
surpass them in their domain. The intention is to challenge that domain. For a long time, the theme of *Las Meninas* of Velasquez had
interested Picasso. In 1957 he painted in his own way, forty-four
paintings of the Infanta and her maids of honor in *Las Meninas*. Two
years later he became attracted to the theme of *Dejeuner sur l'Herbe*
of Manet, a theme that, with its open space, was a contradiction to
the closed space of *Las Meninas*.

In 1958 he purchased the Chateau de Vauvenargues on the flank
of the mountain of Sainte-Victoire, and dedicated it to Jaqueline. In
1961 he abandoned the chateau and La California to settle down in
the farmhouse of Notre-Dame-de-Vie.

The deaths of friends and his old age limited his contacts with
the ongoing artistic activities of the world. For an artist for whom
social drama was always a source of inspiration, this isolation did
not serve him well. His response to this situation was to work more.
In the last ten years of his life, the calm environment created by
Jacqueline, turned him to a dialogue with his own past.

On the occasion of Picasso's eighty-fifth birthday, Jean Leymarie,
by gathering more than five hundred of Picasso's works, organized
an homage to Picasso in the Grand Palais and in Le Petit Palais.

Beneath the diversity of Picasso's work lay the unity of the personality and artistic experiments of a painter who had a constant
craving for new discoveries. Picasso remarked, "It is not after nature that I work, but in front of nature, and with it." The continuous transformation of his art was not related to evolution, but to his
temperament, to his life full of movement, and to his exposure to the
ideas of a world in continuous transformation.

GEORGES BRAQUE (1882–1963)

Georges Braque was born in Argenteuile-sur-Seine. His father was a house painter contractor and an amateur painter. In 1890 the family moved to Le Havre. At the age of fifteen, Georges, interested in studying the art of painting, attended evening classes at the École Municipale des Beaux-Arts. After two years, he decided to dedicate his time to learning his father's trade, and he gave up painting courses. For the final phase of his training as a house painter and decorator, he went to Paris. Benefiting from living in Montmartre, he continued the study of the art of painting in evening classes at the Batignolles. After completion of his military service in 1901, with his father's guarantee to support him for two years, he returned to Montmartre and went to the free Académie Humbert.

Besides the Louvre, with the art of entire world, there were exhibitions of the art of avant-garde painters at the Salon d'Automne, the Salon des Indépendants, and by art dealers. Impressed by the art of Matisse and Derain, he turned toward the intense colors of fauvism. He said, "They opened the way for me."

The landscapes he made in the summer of 1906 at Antwerp and in the fall of the same year at l'Estaque, were in the fauvist style, but the blocks of houses in the landscapes l'Estaque that recall Cezanne reveal his true tendency toward precision and order. Concentrated on developing his painting skill, he did not participate in any exhibition until 1906. Paintings that he exhibited at the Salon des Indépendants attracted the attention of Kahnweiler, the art dealer, who offered him a contract, and introduced him to Apollinaire. Through the poet, Braque met Picasso.

Following the logic of Matisse that painting is an intellectual creation, and the painter has no need to work outside, he began to work in the studio. The outline of *Bather* (1907), similar to Matisse's *Blue Nude*, expresses his interest in form and volume. Though Braque's fauvism was brief, his logical approach to painting made his mark on the movement.

Braque was a gifted colorist and a master of design. In 1907, Picasso's *Les Demoiselles d'Avignon* and a retrospective of Cezanne's works turned his attention from color to form. Despite differences in the temperament and artistic background of the two painters— Braque's limpid and precise temperament, Picasso's somber and revolutionary character, and Braque's being a landscape painter while Picasso hardly touched landscapes—a close friendship bound them together. Braque's *Still Life with Musical Instruments* (1908) followed Cezanne's rules of building forms. Encouraged by Picasso, the next step was to break old structures.

Braque was rejected by the jury of the Salon d'Automne of 1908, so Kahnweiler organized a one-man show of Braque's work in his gallery. This show gave rise to the term "cubism." The first phase of cubism, called analytical cubism, was constructed of closely packed volumes and included the use of letters and numbers, meaning that everything may serve as a sign. In the second phase of cubism, called synthetic cubism, both painters left behind excessive geometrization.

Married in 1912, Braque joined Picasso and Eva at Sorgues. At that time, the works of the two friends became very similar. But even in this common language of cubist forms, each of them remained faithful to his inner tendencies—Picasso to his expressionist touch and Braque to his lyrical feeling. To animate the picture with elements of the outside world, they began the collage of paper and real materials.

With the declaration of war in 1914, and the mobilization of Braque, the intimate collaboration of Barque and Picasso came to an end. Badly wounded, Braque was demobilized. Back in Paris he decided on a self-exploration free of any aesthetic formulas. His work of the postwar period, affected by the general feeling of a new epoch, moved toward real appearances. By diffusing the angular geometry of cubism into organic shapes, his work became less systematic than before. The reappearance of his former interest in fauvist color gave more freedom to his palette, but he backed away from pure tones.

The Salon d'Automn of 1922 invited him to participate and devoted a special room to his works. The purchase of a number of his paintings at high prices by Paul Rosenberg changed Braque's life. In 1923 he designed sets for the ballet of Diaghilev's *The Bores*, with music by Georges Auric. In the next two years, he designed sets for two more ballets.

The diversity of his work reveals his pleasure in painting without the restrictions of an orderly style of cubism. The rhythm and liberty of brushstrokes and white broken lines defined the forms of *Three Bathers* (1923). The flowers in *Basket of Flowers* (1924) have loose, circular shapes. The flowing organic forms of the nude figures of *Canephorae* became his manner of painting nudes, with massive bodies and broad shoulders. Arranging the subjects of some of his paintings in an elongated format allowed him to dispense with the need to center the composition. The completely flat colors and wavy lines of *Nude Reclining on a Gueridon* (1931) differ from the sensual nudes of *Canephorae*. To illustrate Hesiod's *Theogony*, influenced by Greek vase painting, he engraved continuous, interlacing, wavy lines on black plaster; this flat, linear style was also used for other paintings of the period.

At a time that it seemed that his art, with its rhythm and lightness that animated the large still lifes of the *Tablecloths* series of 1935, had attained its summit, the fifty-year-old Braque decided, by endowing ordinary objects with a lyrical mystery, to give a new dimension to his art. The powerful, elegant compositions and the ease of painting simple motifs with large brushwork of his works after 1940 point more to intensive contemplation than to immediate sensation.

With the invasion of France, Braque did not leave France, but he rejected the advances of the Vichy government. During the war, a retrospective of his work toured the United States. After the war, a surgery kept him from painting until 1946. At the Venice Biennale of 1948, leading French painters exhibited at the French Pavilion. Awarding Braque the grand prize demonstrated that his works were preferred to others.

From the beginning of 1950, a bird motif became an integral part of Braque's works. In his *Studio* series, the presence of a bird, or a flying bird in the heart of the studio, alludes to the poetic orientation of his creations. At the suggestion of George Salles, the director of the Musée de France, Braque painted three inlaid panels for the room of the Etruscan collection in the Louvre. Considering his interest in Etruscan art, it seems that with the choice of birds for the three vast panels, he alluded to the spirit of the present flying to meet the spirit of the past.

In his elongated landscapes painted in the 1950s, the seventy-year-old master, expressing himself only through color and free brushwork, searched to move beyond restrictions.

At the urging of André Malraux, the Musée National d'Art Moderne established an extension at the Galerie Mollien, where Jean Cassou presented a partial reconstruction of Braque's studio.

FERNAND LEGER (1881–1955)

Fernand Leger, born in Argenton in lower Normandy, was the son of a Norman cattle breeder. As he showed a talent for drawing, he was sent to serve an apprenticeship with an architect for two years. Then he went to Paris, where he worked as an architectural draftsman for two years. After finishing his military service, he entered the École des Arts Decoratifs. Failing the entrance examination at the École des Beaux-Arts, he attended the Académie Julian.

A few early paintings he did in Corsica are nondescript impressionist paintings. The sensation created by the Fauves in 1905 did not touch Leger, but the retrospective of Cezanne, who had spoken of cylinders, cones, and spheres, appealed to Leger's taste for architecture. Leger, a gifted painter, was not a follower of theories. By destroying the organic continuum of nature, he simplified his forms to the point of geometrical abstraction, and by integration of volumes with the flatness of the surface, he transformed the methods of Cezanne.

In 1908 he took a studio in Montparnasse, where he met leading avant-garde artists and poets. Through Apollinaire and Max Jacob, he met Picasso and Braque. Leger adopted their technique of breaking down forms, but he displayed a personal form of cubism in a dynamic manner that distanced his work from analytic cubism. *Nudes in the Forest* (1910), a picture in the cubist spirit, and evidence of his instinct for the monumental, demonstrates his principle of the play of forms. Leger was a great colorist, but being alien to the poetry of color, his colors have the function of defining objects and providing rhythm to the picture.

In 1912 Leger became one of the principal members of the group that founded the Section d'Or. The group organized an exhibition of the works of thirty-one painters. As many of the participants had in their own way tried or adopted the lessons of Cezanne rather than the research of Picasso and Braque, the exhibition was a sort of homage to Cezanne. As time went on, from the differences in the works of these artists emanated various important tendencies of the twentieth century. The World War I ended the activity of the group.

Between 1912 and the outbreak of World War I, in search of a personal cubism, to render his vast diversity of subjects, Leger adopted tube and pipe shapes for his cubist painting, which was termed "tubism" by his critics. To raise forms and colors to their highest power to express the dynamism and speed of new technology and machinery, he contrasted dissonant colors, lines, and forms placed side by side. These contrasts gave his art an enormous dynamism.

After years in the company of intellectual artists and poets, in the trenches of the World War I, Leger found himself shoulder to shoulder with simple people who became his new buddies, involved in the same tragedy as himself. The experience gave a more human atmosphere to his work and conditioned his art thematically and artistically.

After mustr gas attack by the German troops at the battle of Verdun, he was hospitalized for a long period. During his convalescence he painted *The Card Players* (1917). Leger, who had become committed to the social realities of modern life, and inspired by the product of factory workers whose task was to produce by machine objects with precise and polished forms, chose smooth and metallic cylindrical forms for his *The Card Players*. The precise and cold forms of this painting initiated Leger's mechanical period.

After 1920, people, nature, and objects in a stylized form, still marked by the form of machinery, replaced his mechanical period. In these works, the frontal presentation of masklike figures of women became dominant. In *Three Women (Le Grand Dejeuner)*, the expressionless faces of three colossal figures of women, reduced to elemental forms, face the spectator. After the polished figures of the women and their surroundings in this painting, Leger's art moved between abstraction and the actual appearance of things.

Cinema, as a mechanical art addressed to a vast audience, captivated him. In 1924, in collaboration with Dudley Murphy and Man Ray, he produced *Ballet Mécanique*, the first film made without a script. Through close-up shots, he discovered the value of objects as architectural elements, and he painted many still lifes until the end of his life.

Toward 1925 Leger adopted a more static conception to construct his paintings. Combinations of verticals and horizontals treated as elements of weight and solidity showed a tendency toward abstraction. In the mid-1920s, in association with the formalist movement called purism, which was an attempt by the painter Ozenfant and architect-painter Le Corbusier to strip cubism of its decorative aspects and return to precise and well-ordered forms of painting, Leger adopted flatter colors and black outlines for his work. Leger's first mural was for Le Corbusier's *Esprit Nouveau* pavilion.

During World War II, he lived in the United States and taught at Yale. Returned to France in 1945, he received great numbers of mural commissions; among them a mosaic for the facade of the church of Our Lady at Assy, stained-glass windows for the church of Courfaivre in Switzerland, and a pair of murals for the United Nations Assembly Building in New York.

Impressed by the progress of machines, and with his art far removed from intellectual and lyrical art of Picasso and Braque, Leger became limited to being an emblem of only one of the aspects of the modern civilization.

JUAN GRIS (1887–1927)

José Victoriano Carmelo Carlos González Pérez, later known as Juan Gris, was born in Madrid. He began to study engineering at the Escuela de Artes y Manufacturas. But after two years, he abandoned the escuela and began to study painting at the studio of Carbenero, whose traditional training pushed Gris toward avant-garde painting. Friendship with a German painter who was a contributor to the journal *Jugend* attracted him to art nouveau, and he became a contributor of satirical drawings to the German periodical.

In 1906 he left Spain for Paris. As his departure was prior to serving his mandatory military service, he was considered a fugitive and could not return to Spain. In Paris, a Spanish friend introduced him to Picasso, and he settled in Le Bateau Lavoir, where Picasso lived. There he became friends with avant-garde artists and poets, and he witnessed the birth and evolution of cubism. To support himself he did satirical drawings in the art nouveau style for French and Spanish publications.

Gris's first cubist works, produced in 1911, are contemporaneous with the end of analytic cubism. While cubism treated the canvas as a flat surface and had abandoned the source of light, in Gris's early works the foreground and background are still intact, and he used a single source of light.

In his first important work, *Portrait of Picasso*, a tribute to the founder of cubism, he fractured the face and the body into planes of geometric shapes. The motion emanating from the portrait reflect the personality of the sitter. In 1912 he became one of the participants in La Section d'Or gatherings and their exhibitions. In that same year, he signed a contract with the prominent art dealer Kahnweiler, giving him the right to purchase all his future works.

From 1913 on, he abandoned analytical cubism to convert to synthetic cubism, with more variety of bright, harmonious colors and extensive use of collage technique. To add to visual complexity, he painted areas in imitation of wallpaper or marble as part of a collage.

With World War I artists and poets entered military service. Spanish citizenship exempted Gris and Picasso from military service, but under the effects of war, both of them stopped their artistic activity for a year. Because of his German citizenship, Kahnweiler had to leave Paris. For several months he continued to send money to Gris, but as he could not continue his support, Gris's financial situation became desperate, and due to the terms of his contract with Kahnweiler, he had to refuse offers from other dealers. After Kahnweiler agreed to suspend the contract, Rosenberg signed a contract to purchase Gris's entire works from 1915 on.

Gris's imagination was always subject to the control of logic. To make pictures he used to start with a completely abstract structure, then he balanced and counterbalanced forms and colors. He said, "I start with a construction and end up with a real fact." His *Still Life before an Open Window, Place Ravignon*, is a good example of the utmost care he took to build a picture of antithesis—that is, the use of opposing forms, colors, and qualities playing against each other. He flattened individual elements, which gave surface unity to this picture. The objects on a table are lit by artificial light, contrasting with the outside scene under moonlight. Gris's attempt to bring interior and outdoor views to the same plane, and the choice of an open-window theme, were possibly influenced by his close relationship with Matisse during the preceding year at Coliliour.

After 1918 he began to consolidate his ideas and his technique, and he subjected his plastic poetry to the control of logic. He introduced new complexities in his art, and he made use of metaphor, using abbreviated forms for objects, such as a circular form to signify the mouth of a glass.

After the war, the movement toward a classical mode that he had started during the war became consolidated. Gris was a theoretical painter, and his version of cubism, closer to the clarity and order of the classical spirit than to spontaneity, moved him to the forefront of a movement that reached its peak in the movement called purism.

In the period between 1921 and 1927, his style, marked by health problems, became increasingly free and lyrical. He frequently designed sets and costumes for Diaghilev's ballets. His last painting, *Woman with a Basket*, is of a woman in Greek or Roman clothing carrying a basket of vegetables in front of a dark oval, possibly with some hidden message. After three attacks of uremia, he died in May of 1927.

Section 4

Solitary Concepts of Painting

GEORGE ROUAULT (1871-1953)

George Rouault was a solitary painter who became one of the pioneer of expressionist painting. He was born in Paris into an artisan family. At the age of fourteen, he apprenticed to a stained-glass artisan. After two years, he was employed by a stained-glass maker who did some restoration work on medieval windows. In his maturity, remembering the expressive power of the black strips of stained glass, Rouault applied heavy black lines to his pictorial art. During the years of apprenticeship and employment, he also participated in evening classes at the École des Arts Decorative. In 1890 he entered the École des Beaux-Arts and studied at the studio of Gustave Moreau.

Moreau was a leading symbolist painter who believed in modern movements but at the same time urged his students to study the great masters and the primitives. He helped each student acquire the technique that corresponded to his own temperament. Moreau appreciated Rouault's individuality, and soon he became Moreau's favorite pupil and close friend. In 1893 initiated by Moreau, Rouault participated in the competition for the Prix de Rome, but as he lacked overly precise craftmanship, the jury rejected him. In 1898 he tried once more for the Prix de Rome, but the jury again rejected him. In the same period that Rouault studied at Moreau's studio,

Matisse and other future members of the Fauve group were also Moreau's students.

After the death of Moreau in 1898, Rouault was named curator of the Moreau Museum. Although the art of Moreau and that of Rouault belong to two different views of world, he always cherished the memory of his master.

After leaving the École des Beaux-Arts, Rouault tried different styles. In the exhibition of the Salon d'Automne of 1905, although his works were exhibited in a different room than the works of the Fauve group, he was associated with that group.

Sacred subjects always existed in French painting, but since Daumier and Courbet, they had lost their power of inspiration. Reading two novels by Leon Bloy, a Catholic writer, inflamed Rouault's religious zeal and his concern for human misery. His art grew more individual and more revolutionary.

Having never considered painting a pleasure for the eyes, and expressing his disgust with the evils of bourgeois society, Rouault sought a new vision of art. He said, "So-called beauty quickly degenerates into Academism when we no longer observe life and the motion of human nature." Like Daumier, he recognized that a creator of art should have the courage to represent ugliness. His chosen subjects became ugly nude prostitutes as a symbol of a corrupt society, as well as tragic figures of clowns, and he revised his technique. He chose colors for their expressive values, used heavy black lines reminiscent of his stained-glass apprenticeship, and abandoned modulation and perspective. Some critics sensed his concern with the human condition, but in general, his art was not approved by the public and critics. The severest criticism came from Leon Bloy, whose judgment was not based on critical knowledge of the aesthetics of painting. In spite of Bloy's attacks, Rouault and his wife continued to go to see their friend on Sundays.

In 1907, to convey that judgment is a relative matter, hideous figures of judges, with somber colors to emphasis their abhorrence, became another theme for the early period of Rouault's art. He explained, "The reason I gave my judges such woeful faces was doubtless because I expressed the anguish I myself feel when I see one human obliged to judge another."

Rouault's first great exhibition of his art at the Galeries Druet in 1910 was followed by his second one-man show in 1911 and a third one in 1912. Moved by the horrors of World War I, he undertook two monumental volumes of the *Miserere*, accompanied by the text of the poet André Suares. These etchings, similar to Goya's *Caprices*, illustrate the sufferings of war and express the artist's disgust with the corrupt state of the world. Strong light, heavy black outlines, and expressive forms are characteristic of these etchings.

The art dealer Ambroise Vollard had the ambition of publishing limited editions of books. As his intention was to produce the editions of the century, he was looking for painters, not illustrators, to illustrate his books. He asked Rouault to make etchings for his books. Under Vollard's patronage, Rouault devoted his time to the production of graphic works and the illustration of books.

For the frontispiece of *Worker's Apprentice*, he executed his self-portrait. To identify himself with the working class, the portrait has sad eyes and tight lips. Rouault painted his self-portrait several times; in all of them, he saw his face as a personification of man in general.

After the long period devoted to etching, he returned to painting. Between 1930 and 1939, he painted a number of masterpiece from the Old Testament, the passion of Christ, clowns, and other figures from the circus. Besides its structure, the royal dignity and melancholy of *The Old King* (1937) makes the picture one of the best of Rouault's work. Another masterpiece of the same year is *Le*

Dernier Romantique; in this image of an intellectual person of bygone times, the contrasts of tone are the real motif of the picture.

With the advance of German forces, Rouault took refuge in Golfe-Juan. After the war, he received an order for five stained glass windows for the church Église Notre-Dame de Toute Grâce du Plateau d'Assy. For Rouault, who was not a believer in art for art's sake, the painting was a harmony between the visible world and his inner vision. His landscapes, not copies of nature, are means of self-expression through form and color. *Flight into Egypt* is a religious scene combined with landscape.

In 1947 Rouault brought a lawsuit against Vollard's heirs to get back his unfinished pictures. On the grounds of the moral right of the artist with respect to his work, the court decided in favor of Rouault. Out of concern that he would not have time to finish those pictures, in the presence of court officials, he threw some 315 canvases into the furnace.

Although the religious spirit of Rouault's art was a stranger to the secular climate of modern painting, he used it as a revolt against the vices of society. Thus, the works of this solitary painter who followed his own visions of art became another revolt against the social order.

ROBERT DELAUNAY (1885–1941)

Robert Delaunay was born in Paris, into a family that belonged to the French nobility. His parents divorced when Robert was four. As his mother traveled to faraway places after the divorce, the care of Robert was relegated to his aunt and uncle. Thus, Robert spent a large part of his childhood at his uncle's large estate, La Ronchere, near Bourges. His adult personality showed signs of his childhood contact with nature and country people, in contrast with the man of the world that he was. His affectionate relationship with Henri

Rousseau, a painter who combined a strange imagination with naivety, reveals his love and respect for simple people.

An undistinguished student, he did not pursue an education; instead, in 1902 he began a two-year apprenticeship in a studio of theatrical design. Unlike most painters, he received no formal art training. His early works passed through impressionism, neoimpressionism, fauvism, and a period influenced by the tonal relationships of Cezanne's art, and became interested in the possibilities of color discovered by neoimpressionism and the color research of Chevreul. He was drafted in 1907, but after six months of training, for health reasons he was assigned to work as a librarian; then he was excused from his second year of service.

Sonia Uhde-Terk, a young painter of Russian origin, after attending the Academy of Fine Arts in Karlsruhe in Germany, continued her study of painting in Paris. There she married Uhde, the owner of an art gallery. In 1908 Delaunay met Sonia at the Uhde's gallery, and soon their compatibility of ideas and interests attracted Robert and Sonia to each other. Sonia asked Uhde for a divorce, married Robert, and became Robert's partner in life and work. Their marriage became the basis of high artistic productivity, and gradually a circle of painters and poets formed around them.

The year 1909 saw the emergence of Delaunay's personal style, in which he replaced line with shafts of lights; light falling on objects and their reflections became the element to build up forms. For the series of *Saint-Severin* pictures, he drew a number of sketches of the inside of the church and then painted the pictures in the studio. Rays of light distort the massive columns of the church as if they were seen in a concave mirror, and the vibration of colors produces an impression of movement.

A painter who knew Kandinsky sent him photographs of Delaunay's work. Kandinsky invited Delaunay to participate in the first exhibition of the Blaue Reiter in Munich. One of the four pictures sent to the exhibition was the first version of *Saint-Severin*. The musical quality and lyrical effects of the picture deeply influenced Paul Klee and affected German expressionism.

Delaunay, a frequent visitor at Gertrude Stein's, knew Picasso and Braque but never became close with them. From 1907 to 1913, he was associated with cubism, but as the lyricism of his art was based on his passion for color, heightened by his love of light, and considering color alone as form and theme, his bond to cubism could not last long.

The Eiffel Tower series, one of his favorite subjects, occupied his time from 1909 to 1911. In his composition of the tower from many vantage points at once emerges the element of time. The light falling from circular forms of clouds, as the determining factor of the picture, swallows up the tower's physical reality and produces an impression of movement.

In 1910 he started *City* series, in which the motif remained the same, but the emergence of new methods prepared a later synthesis. In the beginning the composition was in line with analytic cubism, but then his love for pure color born of light ovecame the cubism.

Delaunay's combination of his previous themes of the Eiffel Tower and the city, with the ancient theme of the Three Graces, in *City of Paris* (1912), was a reconciliation of opposing themes. Although the whole picture is composed on the concept of a single plane, the landscape elements are not a mere background, and the three figures in the center connect both sides of the picture. The monumental cubist work, exhibited in 1912 at the Salon des Indépendants, was a triumph. He said he "wanted to create rhythmic relationships among the elements of the composition—city, women, tower—but the 'brisure' ("fragmentation") interrupts that very rhythm, that motion, that dynamism."

Delaunay's love of pure color, and his study of Chevreul's theory of simultaneous contrasts, led him to break with the forms of material representation in 1912. In his *Windows* series, simultaneous contrasts of the flood of colored light, which makes his picture vibrant, became the essential element of his art. The musical qualities of these paintings caused Apollinaire to name the style orphism, after Orpheus. In his *Windows* series, each quite different from the others, planes of color stand for theme and form, and the interplay of neighboring colors suggests the space. The shimmering planes of color of *Windows* replaced aspects of reality and opened the door to a poetic world, free from objective representation. He formulated his theory of painting in "Note on the Construction of the Reality of Pure Painting," (1912), in which he wrote, "Color is form and subject."

Delaunay's use of the dynamic form of the circle in the composition of circularly placed colors in *Simultaneous Contrasts: Sun and Moon* was more than a decorative form. The picture was painted at a time when he was concentrated on the essence of light. To represent the most intense light—the light of the sun—he intensified his colors by contrast with complementary colors. His wife has reported that Robert spent much time observing the emanations of the sun and moon.

Although Delaunay was a member of the group who formed the Section d'Or, as he lived in his own world and was closer to poets than to other painters, he did not participate in the exhibition of the group in 1912.

The first version of the *Cardiff Team* series combines the motion of a leaping soccer player, an airplane, the Eiffel Tower, and letters of advertising. In a letter to Delaunay, Franz Marc expressed his disappointment with this new step. For Delaunay the main point of the picture was color and bodies in motion. In a letter to Marc, who had mystical inclinations, he emphasized that for progress in art, no mysticism is needed.

In *Homage to Bleriot*, the first pilot who flew across the English Channel, he incorporated objective elements—the Eiffel Tower and airplanes—with the rotating forms of multicolored disk of clouds. The picture was exhibited at the Salon des Indépendants a few months before the outbreak of World War I.

At the time of the declaration of war in 1914, Robert and Sonia were in Spain. Robert's attempt to enlist was rejected for reasons of health. The couple and their child stayed in Spain and Portugal until 1921.

The dazzling light of Spain and Portugal, with no sign of the fog of France, permitted Robert to observe a new kind of color vibration and to give free rein to his passion for color, which was musical and poetic rather than plastic. The hues of the blond flesh of the *Nude at Her Dressing Table* are transparent and iridescent like a rainbow. The *Portuguese Markets* painting is built of a moving sea of beautiful colors of folk costumes, fruit, and plants. In Spain, he met Diaghilev and made sets and costumes for the *Cleopatra* ballet.

Back in Paris, he began a second series on the Eiffel Tower, but now the tower was no longer swallowed up by light, but instead stoof erect and often accompanied by a female nude. In 1926 Robert and Sonia made sets for several films.

Delaunay's work after World War I is marked by representational art. About 1930, influenced by that abstract painting that flourished in Paris, Delaunay began his *Rhythm* series, in which he used circular forms but differently from in his *Circular Forms* of 1912 to 1914.

Despite illness that limited his activity, he participated in the design of the air pavilion at the Universal Exposition of 1937 and the decoration of the sculpture hall of the Tuileries Salon. He died of cancer in 1941.

PIET MONDRIAN (1872–1944)

Mondrian was born in Amersfoot, a town in the Netherlands. A Calvinist, his father was the headmaster of an elementary school. After Piet finished school, he decided to study painting. His family agreed, on the condition that Piet first obtain a certificate as a drawing teacher. After he received his diploma to teach drawing in schools, he attended evening courses in drawing at the Academy of Art in Amsterdam.

For the next few years, Mondrian lived in seclusion in the countryside and painted landscapes. His early works followed The Hague school of painting, an offshoot of the Barbizon school. Friendship with a few Dutch painters who had started the Dutch luminist style, a synthesis of Van Gogh's expressive colors and Seurat's systematic brushwork,[17] ended this period of realistic painting.

The blazing colors of *Windmill in Sunlight* and its structure of forms make this picture one of the masterpieces of Mondrian's luminist style. The other masterpiece of this period is *Red Tree*. Its natural branches reduced to expressive lines already show his interest in structural organization.

Exhibition of his luminist work in the Stedelijk Museum of Amsterdam was a great success. Recognized as one of the outstanding figures in the new art of the Netherlands, he was selected as an auxiliary member of the Saint Lucas jury in 1909 and the following year as a full member. The same year he joined the Netherlands Theosophical Society.[18] This break with Christianity, his inherited religion, meant a search for new visions and answers for himself.

---

17 Originally, luminist painting practiced by American painters of the mid-nineteenth century emphasized the effects of light on the landscape. Their work was characterized by a smooth finish and meticulous detail.

18 The Netherlands Theosophical Society believed in a combination of the elements of Plato's philosophy and Christian, Buddhist, and Hindu thought, seeking the knowledge of the presumed mysteries of nature and the purpose of existence.

The first exhibition of international art in Amsterdam, which included cubist paintings of Picasso and Braque, impressed Mondrian. He moved to Paris in 1912, and without imitating, took steps toward cubism. At the beginning the predominance of structure at the expense of color makes his work close to analytical cubism; then his *Oval Composition* (1913), composed of horizontal and vertical lines, with primary colors and touches of blue-gray, coincided with the synthetic cubism period, in which color came back into cubist painting. In 1914, while Picasso turned toward neoclassicism, Mondrian, whose forms at the beginning were derived from objects, moved further away from reality and discarded any objective appearances.

To visit his seriously ill father, he returned home in 1914. The outbreak of World War I enforced him to stay in the neutral Netherlands, where he met Dr.Schoenmaeker, a philosopher and theosophist who deeply influenced Mondrian's concept of art. Believing in a harmonious universe and that art should reflect the underlying spirituality of nature, in a search for purity of forms to reveal the universal and absolute in art, he gradually simplified his forms, to the extent that his art became completely abstract. With compositions of color planes, he moved toward a new concept of painting, different from cubism, whose emphasis was on form.

Mondrian and three of his friends who worked together in concert founded the group De Stijl ("the style"). The group considered art to be a means by which the essence of the mysteries of the universe could be revealed. The group published the journal *De Stijl*, in which Mondrian began writing a series of essays entitled "The New Plastic Art in Painting," defining his theory of neoplasticism. To create a pure art free from any sign of the outside world or individual personality, Mondrian's first neoplastic paintings, composed of rectangles spread over the canvas with no dividing lines, excluded any illusion of space and movement, as well as any impurity such as visible brushstrokes that could disturb the purity of his work. The next step was to frame the rectangles by vertical and horizontal lines, a decision that had metaphysical implications. He saw his verticals and horizontals as representing the equilibrium of the two essential forces: the positive and the negative, the dynamic and the static, the masculine and the feminine. Committed to the right angle, he avoided diagonals and curves. In a few of his paintings, he used a lozenge-shaped composition to give dynamics to the static composition of opposing horizontal and vertical lines. He continued neoplastic paintings, with variations, until 1938.

With the end of World War I, he returned to Paris. Experiments with form and color led him to pictorial solutions that represented the principles of neoplasticism. Léonce Rosenberg, the French art dealer, condensed Mondrian's essays in *De Stijl* and published it under the title *Le Neo-Plasticisme*. In Germany, the book was translated and published as a Bauhaus book. For a while, a close relationship was established between the Bauhaus and De Stijl. But later, on ideological grounds, the relationship did not last.

In 1922, on the occasion of Mondrian's fiftieth birthday, his friends organized a retrospective of his work in Amsterdam. The retrospective and exhibitions of some of his work by Rosenberg did not bring financial relief to Mondrian. Under financial pressure, to get some relief, he painted a few flower pictures in his old naturalistic manner.

Considering the use of diagonal elements by van Doesburg, one of the members of De Stijl group, a departure from the group's principles, he withdrew from the group. As the Munich Agreement of 1938 was a warning of approaching war, he moved to London, and in 1940 the war forced him to go to New York.

The vitality of New York City energized Mondrian's creativity. The rhythm of his painting became the reflection of the rhythms of his surroundings. The architectural effect of his black lines and rectangles of primary color gave way to a musical movement of colorful, interweaving lines. The continuous lines, large planes, and small blocks of colors in *Broadway Boogie-Woogie* give the picture a new tempo.

In 1944, he died of pneumonia. His last work, *Victory Boogie-Woogie*, remained unfinished. Although Mondrian's theosophical beliefs dedicated his art to representing the underlying spiritual order of the universe, his work had a crucial influence on the development of contemporary rt.

EDVARD MUNCH (1863–1944)

Edvard, the son of a medical corps doctor, was born in Loten into an intellectual Norwegian middle-class family. He lost his mother when he was five years old and his sister when he was thirteen.

After studying engineering at the technical college, he left the college to study at a school of design. Munch's creative life can be divided into three distinct periods:

- From 1880 to 1892, he frequented circles of the Norwegian intelligentsia and became interested in literature and philosophy. After a short visit to Paris, he painted the first version of *The Sick Child* in a naturalist-impressionist manner. A four-month scholarship to study painting in Paris exposed him to a wider range of knowledge about painting. Impressed by Gauguin's art, he started to give form to his inner vision.
- From 1892 to 1902, through a synthesis of the elements of art nouveau, symbolism, and primitivism, Munch's work assumed its own characteristics. In this period, after the traumatic

effects of witnessing the death of his mother and his sister, he painted many death scenes. In *Death Chamber*, each member of the family, wrapped up in his own grief, has no communication with the others. He also started *Frieze of Life*, a cycle of painting and prints in which he expressed the anxieties, tensions, and joys of life. Of his famous picture, *The Scream* (1893), which represents the anxiety of modern man, he said, "One night I was walking along a path...I felt a scream pass through nature; it seemed to me I could hear the scream. I painted the picture, painted the clouds as the real blood." The anxiety experienced by a single being in this picture, in *Anxiety*, is represented collectively. *The Voice* (1893), a picture of a woman standing in front of a harmonious landscape, is a counterpart to his pictures depicting anxiety. An intense serenity, free of any anxiety, emanates from her immobility; it seems she is listening to her inner voice.

- Exhibitions and critical art reviews made him an international artist. Excessive drinking led to frequent quarrels with friends and artists. After passing several months in a clinic in 1908, he was stabilized, and he broke with the expressionist components of his art, a reorientation that points to inner causes rather than seeking an aesthetic change. In 1909 to 1911, he decorated the assembly hall of Oslo University, consisting of eleven murals in a neoclassical style. The central mural, *The Sun*, as a symbol of purity shining upon the earth, is one of the great achievements of modern mural painting.

GEORGIO DE CHIRICO (1888-1978)

De Chirico was born in Greece into an Italian family, and he learned drawing in Athens. After the death of his father, the family moved to Munich. The years that De Chirico lived in Germany coincided with beginning of German expressionism, and theosophy was gaining ground among artists and writers. The symbolic paintings of Arnold Boecklin and extensive reading of the philosophical writings of Nietzsche and Schopenhauer deeply influenced De Chirico. In 1910 he moved to Paris, where he met Picasso, but De Chirico was already in possession of an imaginary world that had taken shape in Munich and did not care for cubism.

In De Chirico's apparent realism, logic had no place. He was haunted by the urge to reveal secret ties between unrelated objects, similar to the unusual relationships expressed by images in dreams. The exaggerated tilted perspective and sharp chiaroscuro of an arcade, a distant train, and a clock in *The Delights of the Poet*, or the endlessly diminishing arcades, a girl rolling her hoop toward a looming shadow in a deserted street, and sharp contrasts of dark and light areas in *Mystery and Melancholy of a Street* communicate the feeling of a disquieting dream. He said that Nietzsche's poetic interpretation of autumn afternoons in northern Italian cities had been the source of such pictures, in which the created image comes close to the world of dream. He termed this manner of painting metaphysical painting.

He wrote, "We experience the most unforgettable movements when certain aspects of the world, whose existence we completely ignore, suddenly confront us with the revelation of mysteries lying all the time within our reach, and we cannot see because we are too short-sighted and cannot feel because our senses are inadequately developed."

In 1915 he went to Italy. There he met Carlo Carra, one of the leading figures of the fturist movement that, with the advent of World War I, had started to paint in a style of simplified realism. For a while, they worked together, he taught Carra to paint in the metaphysical manner, and they formed the short-lived metaphysical school. After 1920, he reverted to an academic classical style.

Though De Chirico was not a surrealist painter, his pictures, closer to being images of the world of dreams than reality, influenced the surrealist movement.

HENRI ROUSSEAU (1844–1910)

Rousseau, the son of a tinsmith, was born in Laval. After high school, he worked for a lawyer. In 1863, for appropriating stamps and a few francs from the law office, he was sentenced to a month of imprisonment. To avoid scandal, he volunteered for seven years of military service. Assigned to a regiment supplying reinforcements to Mexico, there he met and listened to soldiers coming back to France from expeditions in Mexico. Their stories of exotic landscapes left an everlasting attraction to faraway lands on the mind of this simple and naive man with poetic imagination. After four years of service, after the death of his father made him the sole supporter of his mother, he left the army.

In 1869 he was employed in the Paris *octroi* municipal service to collect tolls at the gates of Paris. Although posterity called him *le Douanier* ("the customs officer"), he was never entitled to that rank. A self-taught painter, he obtained permission to copy at national museums, and fascinated with plants, he made frequent visits to the Jardins des Plantes. From 1886, he began to exhibit at the Salon des Indépendants, and in 1893 retired from the Paris toll service to devote himself to painting.

Lacking technical knowledge, he used his intuition; therefore, customary technical analysis of a painting does not apply to Rousseau's poetic approach to art. This painter of beautiful trees and foliage was a clumsy painter of the human figure. As he had difficulty painting the position of a figure's feet on the ground, he mostly concealed them from view. To solve the problem of perspective, he painted a large proportion of trees in the foreground, reduced the heights of trees and volumes of tree trunks in the middle ground, and in the background painted vague masses of foliage. He achieved astonishing nuances from a palette limited to few colors.

Dedication of a special section of the Paris World's Fair of 1889 to the Exposition Colonial, where flora and fauna of Africa and Mexico were represented in an exotic village, and his reading of Pierre Loti's novels[19] aroused his interest in exotic lands.

Rousseau's imagination, his passion for plants, and his creativity free of any barrier compensate for the lack of technique of *Storm in the Forest* (1891). *The Sleeping Gypsy*, one of the most fascinating paintings in modern art, was exhibited in the Salon des Indépendants of 1897. The picture and its strange subject of a lion sniffing at a sleeping gypsy became the object of irony of visitors and critics.

In 1905 he sent *The Hungry Lion* to the Salon d'Automne. An accompanying note explained the subject: "The hungry lion throws himself on the antelope and devours it; the panther waits anxiously for the moment it too will have its share. Carnivorous birds have pecked out a piece of flesh from the back of the animal, which weeps. Sunset."

Rousseau's last work, *The Dream*, was exhibited at the Salon of 1910. A nude woman is stretched on a sofa among beautiful orchids, colorful birds, two lions, and a dark-skinned flute player. Rousseau's explanation was that the woman dreamed she was transported to the middle of the jungle.

Rousseau's life was not an easy one. After twenty-two years of painting, the sales of several paintings in 1907 brought some relief to the old man. Although he was consistently ridiculed by the public and critics, master painters of the twentieth century admired his works.

19 Pierre Loti was a naval officer and a gifted observer who had turned his experiences of exotic lands into novels. Rousseau's *Portrait of Pierre Loti* (1891) could be evidence of his reading of Loti's novels.

Picasso, Apollinaire, Leger, Delaunay, and his wife were among his friends. He had no direct influence on the development of modern painting, yet his poetic imagination impressed modern painters.

Section 5

UMBERTO BOCCIONI (1882–1916)

Umberto Boccioni was born in Reggio, Calabria. His father, a minor government employee, was frequently posted throughout Italy. After Umberto finished his schooling, he attended drawing courses in Rome. Living in a period of social upheaval and social struggle and reading Marx's books, he proclaimed himself an "atheist-skeptic-materialist philosopher" and in a letter to his friend denounced the art of the past.

In the studio of Giacomo Balla's, a painter imbued by a love of nature and the ideas of impressionism, he learned the technique of divisionism, and in his later works, he exploited Balla's attention to composition and the arrangement of planes.

In 1907, during a short visit to Munich, he saw a secessionist exhibition. A few month later, he saw an exhibition of Italian divisionism painting in Paris. Obsessed with discovering new forms of painting, he was deeply impressed by the exhibition. As he saw the need to break away from Balla's realistic and impersonal painting, he went to G. Prevati, one of the proponents of Italian divisionism and a painter with a passion for light. Besides Prevati, to find solutions to the ideas of his restless mind, he also turned to Edvard Munch's inward analysis. He continued in this vein until his encounter with

F. T. Martinetti, the Italian poet, who had initiated the literary and intellectual movement of futurism as a rebellion against the cultural torpor of Italy of the nineteenth century.

Martinetti, in his manifesto of 1909, had rejected the past, celebrated change and originality, and advocated the modernization of Italy. Boccioni and his friends suggested to Martinetti that his movement should also cover visual arts. Martinetti welcomed the suggestion, and they published the first "Manifesto of the Futurist Painters," in which they rejected the past and every form of imitation, instead exalting every form of originality and magnifying modern-day life tultuously transformed by science. In the "Technical Manifesto of Futurist Painting," published the same year, they specified the importance of movement in the modern world, the persistent effect of movement on the retina that multiplied things in motion, and they emphasized the intellectual need of our time to reject the past as motives for their rebellion. At this point, futurism was a movement based on theories. While the case for the impressionism, postimpressionism, fauvism, and cubism movements was different: those movements were generated from the interaction of practice and theory.

In 1910 Boccioni worked almost a year to create a symbolic image of the dynamism of modern life in his large painting of *The City Rises*, in which light, and a whirlwind of color that disintegrate solid forms, gives the impression of speed. The dynamism of work in the modern society is symbolized by the movements and labor of men, the maddening speed of horses dragging loads, and a puffing locomotive. To introduce the futurist's art, this picture was exhibited throughout Europe.

His visit to Paris at the end of 1911 permitted him to see the works of Picasso and Braque. The work of the cubists impressed him, but the futurist's dynamic vision of reality contrasted with the static cubist compositions. Though the futurists did not follow the concepts of cubism, they made use of its analytical procedures.

In 1911 he painted the trilogy of *States of Mind*: *I. Farewells, II. Those Who Go, III. Those Who Stay*. The interpretation of the trilogy is as follows: In Part I, the undulating lines and a combination of abstract forms and a train ready to move of *Farewells*, translate the confusion of departure. In Part II, oblique lines and their cool colors represent *Those Who Go* and their sensation of loneliness. The different shapes and colors of the picture indicate the landscape through which the train passes. In Part III, perpendicular lines represent *Those Who Stay*, and the cool color of the picture reflects their melancholy.

Exhibition of Boccioni's works in Paris received a cold reception by the critics. Then the exhibit moved London, Berlin, Brussels, and other major cities, where numbers of works were sold. The first exhibition of futurist painting in Rome became a stormy evening, that pevented Boccioni from commenting on the theories of the new school.

In 1912 Boccioni revealed a great interest in sculpture. Obsessed by a complete renewal of sculpture, he wrote the "Technical Manifesto of Futurist Sculpture." At the beginning his various experiments with various nontraditional materials did not respond to his desired dynamism. His letters to his friend Servini show the extent of his struggle to make sculpture come alive within its environment. After continuous effort to express continuity in space, he succeeded at arriving at the monumental expression of dynamic movement in *Unique Forms of Continuity in Space*. The forms of the body in motion of this sculpture recall the spread of wings and draperies flowing out behind her of the ancient Nike of Samothrace. This sculpture became Boccioni's greatest contribution to the world of art.

As he did not consider the planes and volumes of an object as absolute, he was attracted to the concept of simultaneity of vision, in which the painter does not see the need to preserve the exact relationships of the features of a face. After 1914, he moved toward a geometrization that showed the influence of Cezanne.

Boccioni's concept of dynamism differed from that of other futurists. His book *Futurist Painting and Sculpture* received a mixed reaction within the group.

At the start of World War I, Italy was neutral. Nationalists, with the hope that intervention might benefit Italy economically and politically, favored entering the war. In 1915, after Italy declared war against the Axis powers, Boccioni and Marinetti enlisted in the Volunteer Cyclist's Battalion, which was dissolved at the end of the year. In 1916 Boccioni was declared fit to join the regular army. That same year he died, following a fall from a horse.

MARCEL DUCHAMP (1887–1968)

Marcel Duchamp, one of the most controversial and influential figures of modern art, born in Blainville in Upper Normandy, grew up in a cultured family environment. His two elder brothers, Jacques Villon and Raymond Duchamp-Villon, and his sister, Suzanne Duchamp, were artists. At the age of fifteen, he started painting. After painting three works influenced by impressionism, he stopped painting to develop his drawings. After graduating from school in Rouen, he joined his brothers in Paris and enrolled at the Académie Julian.

In the course of 1907, the influence of the Fauves replaced the impressionist influence on him, followed by an interest in the structure and color of Cezanne. That he rapidly tried his hand at various contemporary trends in painting shows he was mainly experimenting and demonstrates his dissatisfaction with prevailing approaches to artistic creation. Duchamp, an intellectual person with a dynamic and poetic personality, basically thought in terms of permanent revolution and believed that no movement should stop the progress. Aware of the contradictions of the human mind, he was cynical about common sense, and he rejected conventional reasoning.

Portrait of the Artist's Father (1910) was influenced by Cezanne, while the slightly bent posture and direct look of the father at the spectator show more concern with the personality of the sitter than with image making. *Portrait of Dr. Dumouchel* is another of his psychological portraits. In a letter Duchamp wrote, "The portrait has a note of humor, which indicated my future direction to abandon mere retinal painting."

At Jacques's house in Punteaux, a Sunday gathering of the leading cubist painters, and critics began. The group came to be known as the Punteaux group, or the Section d'Or. But the discussions did not fit with Duchamp's temperament.

The year 1911 was a turning point in Duchamp's art activity. Not satisfied with prevailing styles, he began to assert his own concept of art. *The Young Man and Girl in Spring* is of two young people with Y-shaped arms lifted to the sky. The figures, standing on two separate semicircles from which light emanates, are symbolic interpretations of the opposite worlds of man and woman. This picture, with reference to various esoteric symbols, anticipates the complex conception of *The Large Glass*. The same year *Coffee Mill*, his first machine painting, is an antecedent of his *Chocolate Grinder*.

Duchamp, with his dynamic temperament, loved movement. He watched the futurism movement with interest, but intrigued by the concept of a fourth dimension, he did not approve of the representation of movement as one of the forms of the three-dimensional world. At the end of 1911, he painted *Sad Young Man in a Train* and *Nude Descending a Staircase, No. 1*, followed by *Nude Descending a*

Staircase, No. 2. The difference between *No. 1* and *No. 2* is that in *No. 1*, the human silhouette in motion can be distinguished. He said, "The reduction of a head in movement to a bare line seemed to me defensible. A form passing through space would traverse a line; and as the form moved, the line it traversed would be replaced by another line—and another and another." Cubists, to suggest the fourth dimension, painted multiple views of a subject. Instead, Duchamp's picture, a static representation of movement, shows multiple moments of a moving subject from a single viewpoint.

He sent *Nude Descending a Staircase, No.2* to the Salon des Indépendants. As the representation of movement of this painting conflicted with the static concept of painting of orthodox cubism, one day before the opening of the salon, the committee, composed of his friends, asked for a change of title. Duchamp, instead of changing the title, took away his canvas. No doubt this rejection played a considerable part in deepening his dissatisfaction with the prevailing art. This painting initiated discussions of the relationship of Duchamp's art to futurism. Futurist, saw the movement as a point of destination, while for Duchamp movement was one of the stages of his intellectual research.

In 1912 he painted *Passage from Virgin to the Bride*, and *Bride*, his last painting in the traditional concept of painting. Realizing that to paint in conventional painting was to repeat himself in the service of cultural conventions, he turned his back on all avant-garde styles and conventional subject matter. In 1913, in order to avoid depending on painting for a living, and to have time to ponder, he took a job as a librarian.

An intellectual painter, disillusioned with what he called "retinal" art, he decided on a journey into unpaved areas of art.

Attracted to science, Duchamp found mechanical drawing a proper means to avoid old idealistic expressions in painting, and said, "A mechanical drawing has no taste in it." He painted in a precise style, like an architectural drawing, the first version of *Chocolate Grinder.*

An intellectual painter disillusioned with what he called "retinal" art, he decided on a journey into an unpaved area of art. Interested in representing the fourth dimension, the two-dimensional surface of a mirror reflecting a three-dimensional infinity led him to the thought that he could represent higher dimensions through lower ones.

In an interview to clarify his concept of the relationship between the fourth dimension and *TheBride Stripped Bare by Her Bachelors, even*, he said, "Anything that has three-dimensional form is the projection in our world from a four-dimensional world...my Bride... since it's on the glass it's flat...is a two-dimensional representation of a three-dimensional Bride, who also would be a four-dimensional projection on a three-dimensional world of the Bride."

For the *Larg Glass* he chose the subtitle of *The Bride Stripped Bare by Her Bachelors, even*. He said: "The titles are not the pictures nor vice versa, but they work on each other." The subtitle of *The Glass*, that describe it as an agricultural machine, is referring to the mythical concept of agriculture as a symbolic wedding of Eart and Sky.

In 1913 he made a general layout of *The Large Glass*, a project that occupied him for ten years; growing tired he abandoned it in 1923. *The Large Glass* is composed of two large plates of transparent glass mounted in a frame, holding various liquids and pieces of various materials and a grinder between the two glasses. The upper half of the glass panel is the bride's domain, and the lower glass panel is the bachelor's realm. The bride's domain is composed of ten elements. Its first element is the bride; below her are the bride's garments, the horizon, and a second version of *Choclate Grinder*. On the top of the bride's domain is the Milky Way. The bachelor's realm is composed of twenty-five elements, including a chocolate grinder. The subject and enigmatic objects with symbolic suggestions of *The Large Glass* depict the interaction of unseen opposite abstract forces.

Duchamp also speculated on expanding his rejection of conventional painting to language and social conventions. His mistrust for language as a proper means of communication led him to search for an appropriate form of expression, similar to poetry that expresses itself through metaphor.

Over the course of years, Duchamp frequently resorted to puns and double meaning in his work. Consequently, he developed a noncommittal attitude toward opposites that affected his position toward a work of art. To break from artistic tradition, and to engage the mind of observer instead of his eye, he began to select and designate pieces of everyday manufactured objects, which he called *readymades*, as an art work, on the basis tha tselection of an ordinary object by artist promote it to the status of art work. His first work in this group was *Bicycle Wheel*, a combination of a wheel and a stool. In 1961 he said, "A point that I want very much to establish is that the choice of these readymades was never dictated by aesthetic pleasure. The choice was based on a reaction of *visual indifference* with a total absence of good or bad taste.

In 1915 Duchamp went to United States of America. The exhibition of *Nude Descending a Staircase No. 2* at the Armory Show and at the International Exhibition of Modern Art in New York in 1913, had already made him a famous painte among art circles, and sales of four of his pictures in the exhibition had financed his trip. In New York, he received a warm welcome from intellectual circles. The art collector Walter Arensberg arranged a studio for him in his own house, and Duchamp, to support himself, began giving French lessons.

In 1917, while living in New York, he sent a urinal—which he entitled *Fountain*—to the Society of Independent Artists in New York. As he was a member of the board of the society, he signed it "R. Mutt." It seems that Duchamp, remembering the rejection of his *Nude Descending a Staircase, No. 2*, desired to test the openness of the society to artwork. Following the rejection of the urinal, Duchamp resigned from the board of the society. An article published at the time, which is thought to have been written by Duchamp, claimed: "Whether Mr. Mutt [his pseudonym in this instance] with his own hand made the fountain or not has no importance. He 'chose' it. He took an ordinary article of life, placed it so that its useful significance disappeared under the new title and point of view—created a new thought for that object."

Always rejecting conventional reasoning, in 1917, he published a magazine with dadaist[20] character, and in 1920 he participated in the first dada manifestation in Paris, to which he sent a reproduction of the *Mona Lisa*, to which he had added a mustache, a goatee, and an inscription of "L. O. O. Q." that, when read aloud in French, sounds like *elle a chaud au cul*, meaning "she has a hot ass", possibly referring to Leonardo's alleged homosexuality. Duchamp often traveled between America and France. As his revolutionary spirit drew many artists to him, he had many friends and felt at home in the United States; he became a US citizen in 1955.

He had learned to play chess at the age of thirteen. In America, he played regularly. Soon he became a member of a club's team. In 1925 the French Federation of Chess proclaimed him a chess master. It seemed he had given up art in favour of chess, but in fact he continued his artistic experiments.

---

20 - Dadaism = An anarchchic movement against art, literature, politic, and morality. The movement started in Zurich during WWI.

In 1923, with the intention of turning his attention to other ideas, before leaving for Europe, he abandoned the unfinished *Large Glass*, which he had sold to Arensberg in 1918. Since during the transfer from an exhibition to its owner, the *Large Glass* was damaged, Duchamp went back to repair it in 1936.

His interest in movement and 3-D film led him to collaborate with Man Ray in the production of a few films. The first experiment with a 3-D film in 1920 was not quite successful. Then he built *Rotary Glass Plates*, a machine to exploit the fact that the eye retains an image for a fraction of second after the disappearance of the image. Five years later, he built *Rotary Demisphere*, a more elaborate apparatus, which also created the impression of three-dimensional depth when it was set in motion. The same year he tried his hand in the short 3-D film *Anemic Cinema*. *Discs Bearing Spirals*, a series in cardboard, revolving at the speed of thity thirty-third of a revolutions per second, created the illusion of depth and pointed to the future CinemaScope.

In 1920, with Man Ray and Katherine Dreier, he founded the Société Anonyme, which collected the works of modern artists, and he arranged modern art exhibitions and lectures through 1930. From 1930 onward, he collaborated with the surrealists but did not join the movement. In 1954 he married Alexina "Teeny" Sattler.

His largest painting, with the nonsense title *Tu m'*, combines varied and contradictory kinds of reality. Katherine Dreier had asked him to fill the space above the shelves of her library. Duchamp judged the work too decorative. Nevertheless he accepted it with reluctance. The title of *Tu m'*, a polite contraction of *tu m'emmerde*, meaning "you bore me," politely refers to the pressure he received to paint this work. The delicately shaded background suggests empty space, an illusion reinforced by the series of overlapping lozenge shapes receding toward the upper left corner; we also see the shadows of three readymades: a bicycle wheel, a corkscrew, and a hat rack.

Duchamp's final art work, called: *Étant donnés: 1. La chute d'eau, 2. Le gaz d'éclairage*, was an assemblage of material done in absolute secrecy from 1946 to 1966. In 1969, in accordance with the instructions of Duchamp's manual, it was set up in the Philadelphia Museum of Art. It is an old massive Catalan door set in a frame made of bricks, of a town in Cadaqués. Two small holes in the door make it possible to see the other side. On the other side beyond the breach in a wall, one sees a realistic tableau of a nude woman on her back with her face hidden, legs spread, and one hand holding up a gas lamp against a richly painted landscape.

In the late 1950, young American artists realized the importance of Duchamp's research. Retrospectives of his works were organized in America and Europe. On October 1968, he died of heart failure at his home in Neuilly-sur-Seine.

In an interview, he said, "I believe that art is the only form of activity in which man as a man shows himself to be a true individual and is capable of going beyond the animal state, because art is an outlet toward regions which are not ruled by time and space."

Duchamp was one of the most refined spirits of the twentieth century and one of the artists who created an atmosphere of freedom for art. By insisting that art is about ideas, not the representation of the physical world, he promoted conceptual art. He said, "I want to put painting once again in the service of mind." His intellectualism turned him to a skeptic, which led to his rejection of absolutes and consequently his concepts of art became a mixture of refusal and acceptance. Although he refused to be a follower of any artistic movement, he has been associated with dadaism and surrealism.

DADAISM

The new trends of art in the nineteenth century, neglected by the bourgeoisie, reduced the communication between artists and the public. Avant-garde artists, progressively considering themselves to be outsiders, began to challenge the prevailing values of society.

During World War I, Zurich became a place of escape for a number of young artists, writers, poets, and refugees from the war that was sweeping over Europe. In 1916 Hugo Ball, a philosopher and poet, founded the Cabaret Voltaire as a meeting place for intellectuals and artists from both side of the war. Soon the cabaret became a place of every sort of manifestation. The review *Cabaret Voltaire* contained articles by avant-garde poets and modern art reproductions. The group judged that the interests and logic of the bourgeois establishment had led to World War I, and they believed the only way to salvation is to glorify irrational, political anarchy and the rejection of all values related to a bourgeois society. Disgusted with all bourgeois values, in nihilistic, anarchic, and destructive ways, they also rejected traditional modes of artistic creation. To show their protest through nonart creations, they chose collage techniques. With the end of the war, eliminating the need for a common platform in exile, the Zurich dada group dissolved, but the movement spread to Germany, Paris, and New York.

After the war, the first manifestation of dadaism outside of Zurich, took place in Berlin, where military defeat and general misery offered an ideal atmosphere in which dada could flourish. There, the movement quickly became a political and social protest. In Cologne, it took the form of an aesthetic rebellion; Max Ernst began his collage and photomontage. In Paris, it became more of a literary interest. In 1918 André Breton, Aragon, and Soupault, joined by Elourard and Tzara, founded the review *Litterature* in Paris. In the United States, Duchamp, Picabia, and Man Ray became the center of a dadalike movement.

Although dada came to an end in 1922, its preoccupation with the irrational reinforced a trend away from the reasoned requirements of cubism and abstract art. Yet dada was not quite a completely negative movement. By shattering the remnants of optical world, it set free the imaginations of artists.

Section 6

Expressionism

Until the formation of the German Empire in 1871, Germany was divided into numerous independent states. Lacking the centralized political and art activity of France, it fostered isolated artistic trends and movements.

With the formation of the German Empire, Berlin, as its capital city consolidated the political forces of Germany, and as a growing metropolis attracted artists to Berlin. During the empire, members of the Academy of Arts, supported by the Emperor Wilhelm II, prevented any new movements in art. The forced closure of an exhibition showing the paintings of Edvard Munch, and the rejection of a painting by Walter Leistikow, a leading figure among young artists open to modern ideas, led to the formation of an art association called the Berliner Secession in 1892, whose first exhibition took place in 1899.

The rejection of the works of expressionist painters by the jury of Berlin Secession in 1910, divided the association into two groups. The younger artists who established the Neue Secession, in the preface of their third exhibition declared that their aim was a personal perception of objects, rather than reproducing the outward forms of nature in their fleeting aspects. In 1911 the Die Brücke painters considering most members of the Neue

Secession not gifted enough, left the association. With their departure, the Neue Secession fell apart.

In 1910 Herwarth Walden launched *Der Sturm*, a weekly magazine featuring new art movements. He opened a gallery devoted to avant-garde painting, and exhibitions were followed by articles in *Der Sturm*, broadening his activities. Walden's salesmanship became a decisive factor for promoting German expressionism.

*　　*　　*

The loose term *expressionism* designates an attitude of mind with no stylistic unity or common aesthetic perception among expressionist artists. They expressed their emotional sympathy with their subject, be it portrait, landscape, or still life, through exaggeration and distortion of form and the use of strong colors.

The art of Germany, following Germanic traditions, was pervaded by a poetic interpretation of the world, aimed at expressing emotions rather than logical organization of forms. The expressionist movement that developed mainly in Germany had its roots in the works of Gauguin, Van Gogh, Rouault, Munch, and Ensor. The principal wave of expressionism began with the four young artists who founded the group of Die Brücke and based their work on pure colors.

In Germany, expressionism as a reaction of the critical spirit of youth against the economic system of the upper class of the bourgeoisie who shared power with the aristocracy, became a dominant style in which most German artists expressed their angst, disgust, and discomfort with modern life. The movement spread into other European countries. Kokoshka in Austria and Rouault in France developed their own expressionist styles.

Book burnings by the National Socialists after they assumed power in Germany were an alarming sign for artists. Hitler's speech condemning modern art, delivered at the opening of the exhibition of Nazi-approved art in Munich in 1937, initiated a virulent campaign against modern art.

The Nazis opened *Entartete Kunst* ("Degenerate Art") as a contrast to the nearby exhibition of Nazi-approved paintings and sculptures. The Degenerate Art exhibition contained more than sixteen thousand works of the German expressionists, confiscated from German museums. The chaotic installation and derogatory slogans painted on the walls of the exhibition swayed the majority of visitors unfamiliar with the aims of avant-garde artists. The exhibition made a tour of thirteen cities in Germany and Austria, and much of the art in the exhibition was ultimately lost or destroyed.

DIE BRÜCKE

In 1905 four young architectural students in Dresden founded the group known as *Die Brücke* ("The Bridge"), symbolizing a bridge between nature and emotion. The formation od Die Brucke coincided with various exhibitions of Gauguin and Van Gogh being held in private galleries of Dresden. What brought together these young sons of bourgeois families was their common interest in painting and their intention to bring art and life into harmony. The nucleus of the group was composed of Ernst Ludwig Kirchner, Fritz Bleyl, Erich Heckel, and Karl Schmidt-Rottliff. In Die Brücke's program, in which no aesthetic principles were laid down, they stated, "We call on all youth to join together, and as youths ourselves, bearing the future within us, we wish to create our own freedom of life in the face of long-established older forces."

After two years of working together on painting, woodcut, and lithography, the result of the common experiments of the group appeared in 1907. Opposed to the concept of art as imitation of objects, but without renouncing it, they sought to depict subjective responses to events and objects that arose within a person. To escape from the constraints of the values of bourgeois society, they aspired to a primitive state of mind from which might emerge a new kind of man.

They worked together and exchanged ideas. The chosen themes of the early Die Brücke years were scenes of the everyday life surrounding them: landscapes, street scenes, portraits, and nudes. Kirchner thought that as art is made by man, thus the human form should be at the center of all art. Their efforts were centered on nude figures in landscapes. To study the nude in motion, they drew from nude models in rapidly changing poses while themselves changing places, thus reducing the forms of figures to a style that Kirchner defined as hieroglyphs. Having discovered the emotive qualities of color, it marked the starting point to building their pictures. Broad surfaces of pure color were bounded by flowing outlines. From the outset, the expressive potentialities of harsh black lines and strong contrasts of woodcuts made it a valued medium for their artistic expression, and printmaking was an effective means of reaching a wider public. As in their program, they had called upon young artists to join them, the group did not remain limited to the four friends. A few other painters joined the group for a short time. During the years of working in common, the individuality of each member of the group had been strengthened, so after they moved to Berlin, each member began to follow different trends of evolution. Rejection of Kirchner's proposal to publish *Chronik derBrücke* led to the breakup of the group in 1913.

Kirchner, the dominant personality of the group, was interested in all aspects of life; he painted scenes of the restless life of Berlin streets and prostitutes dominating night streets as symbol of aimless and wasted lives. In 1915 he was called to military service; after six months he had a nervous breakdown. After he went to a sanatorium, first in Germany and then in the highlands of Switzerland, he was released from the army. Dependent on painkillers and with trembling hands, he was not able to paint for a while. When he went back to painting, the nature of the highlands of Switzerland and living among peasants gave him the ideal primitiveness he was longing for. In 1918 he made two series of woodcuts. In the second series, in the story of Absalom, King David's son, he illustrated the struggle, hopes, and downfall of his generation.

BAUHAUS

The city of Weimar elected Walter Gropius, an architect, to organize an advanced school for creative art. The new school was a merger of the Grand Ducal Saxon School of Art and Craft, and the Academy of Fine Arts. The opening of the new school, named Staatliches Bauhaus, took place in 1919. The school became a center that combined crafts and fine arts. In 1925 the school moved to Dessau, in 1932 it moved to Berlin, and it was closed in 1933. Three architects were the directors of the Bauhaus: Walter Gropius from 1919 to 1928, Hannes Meyer from 1928 to 1930, and Ludwig Mies van der Rohe from 1930 to 1933.

The goal of the Bauhaus was a unity of architecture, fine arts, and crafts. To synthesize craftsmanship with the formal requirements of art, Bauhaus instructions were based on a series of workshops, each dedicated to a particular craft under the supervision of a fine artist. After attending a preliminary course, the training was followed by workshops. Gropius wrote, "Art comes into being above all methods. Art itself cannot be taught, but craftsmanship can. Architects, painters, sculptors are all craftsmen in the original sense of the word; thus it is a fundamental requirement of all artistic creativity that every student undergo a thorough training in the workshops of all branches of the crafts." The participation of a number of leading painters in the Bauhaus gave the school an exceptional importance, from which rose some forward-looking thoughts, which impacted architecture and art of the twentieth century. The foundation of the Bauhaus after World War I was at a time when Germany had turned away from expressionism and moved toward rational matters. But the aesthetic ideas of Johannes Itten, a Swiss painter, and Kandinsky influenced the school.

WASSILY KANDINSKY (1866–1944)

Kandinsky was born in Moscow to a wealthy and cultivated family. His father, a successful tea merchant, supported his son during his many years of study. Kandinsky as a child played cello and piano and liked to paint. At an early age, he acquired the German language from his maternal grandmother and aunt. In 1885 he began to study political economy and law at the University of Moscow. To investigate the uncodified legal system of the peasants, he traveled to the isolated Vogada region. The old Russia left its mark on Kandinsky's imagination, and like many Russian intellectuals of the nineteenth century, he disapproved of the effects of the West on Russian culture. After he graduated, he was appointed as a lecturer at the university. In 1895, in an exhibition in Moscow, he saw Monet's *Haystacks*. The paintings, glowing with light and color, appealed to his Slavic affection for color and fascinated him to a point that it changed the course of his life. Financially secure due to the wealth of his family, at age thirty he went with his wife to Munich to study painting.

In those days Munich represented one of most important centers of activity of young avant-garde artists in Germany. The German style of art nouveau, called *jugendstil*, dominated Munich art. Shortly after arriving in Germany, Kandinsky enrolled in the well-known private art school of Anton Azbe, where he met Alexi von Jawlensky. After two years he tried to enroll in the Munich Academy. His first attempt being refused, in 1900 he succeeded in enrolling in Franz von

Stuck's painting class. When he left the academy, his work showed no sign of his later originality. He cofounded an artists' association called the Phalanx. In 1902 the Phalanx opened a painting school at which Kandinsky was chairman, director, and teacher. At the school, he began a long and complicated relationship with Gabriele Munter, a young and talented student. The Phalanx and the school were both short-lived. But the Phalanx, by organizing twelve exhibitions of the works of avant-garde foreign painters, provided Kandinsky with international recognition and the inclusion of his work in the 1904 exhibition of the Salon d'Automne in Paris.

His early paintings or prints from woodblocks were narratives of fairy tales or sentimental stories. His visits to other centers of Western art between 1903 and 1908 helped him to expand his knowledge and to form his personal style. In Paris, he visited the exhibits by the Fauves; the liberation of color that he saw in their art encouraged him to incorporate the same freedom in his art and to direct his attention to finding a new pictorial language.

Back in Germany, he spent the summer with Munter at Murnau, a rural retreat in the Bavarian Alps. The colorful traditional costumes of inhabitants of Murnau revived his memories of Russia. He began to assimilate the different stimuli that had gone into his work. He painted expressive, dynamic, and relatively naturalistic landscapes of Murnau, with stronger tones. Soon after, he moved toward nonobjective painting.

In 1909 he helped the organization of the exhibition society of Neue Kunstler Vereinigung (NKV), whose members included Jawlensky, Kubin, Munter, and later Franz Marc. The intention was to exhibit works of younger artists. But as NKV artists refused to accept his move to nonobjective painting, he split off from the group, and in 1911 with Franz Marc formed *Der Blaue Reiter* ("The Blue Rider"), named after one of Kandinsky's work.

Der Blaue Reiter, one of the most seminal groups of the twentieth century, marked the culmination of a development initiated by Kandinsky and his friends Munter, Jawlensky, Marc, and Macke. The group emphasized that good art consists of expressing the inner self in an entirely original form. They organized exhibits of their own work and of other modern painters. To demonstrate that behind diversity are similarities, in their *Der Blaue Reiter Almanach*, they emphasized their receptivity to all kinds of the art of mankind, past or present. They reproduced children's sketches, primitive and medieval art, Asiatic and African works, pictures of modern artists, and articles on music contributed by Schönberg and Weber. This almanac, now considered one of the important manifestos of twentieth-century art, marked the end of the group.

The relationship between art and music had always fascinated Kandinsky. A brilliant art theorist, in 1911, he gave expression to his concept of art in the theoretical treatise *Über das Geistige in der Kunst* ("Concerning the Spiritual in Art"). As he was concerned that an emotion aroused by any association with the natural world would obscure pure art, he expressed his longing for the independence of painting, similar to that of music, from natural phenomena, in order to be devoted only to the expression of the artist's soul. Still, for a while, he based his pictures on visual motifs, until by 1913 the last traces of the visible were eliminated. Exhibition of his first entirely nonobjective canvases attracted controversy.

Kandinsky's marriage, which from the beginning seemed more a friendly arrangement, ended in 1911, although he maintained a close relationship with his ex-wife. After Germany declared war on Russia, in 1914, Kandinsky, his ex-wife, and Gabriele Munter moved to Switzerland. Then after three months, he returned alone to Russia.

In Russia. he married Nina Andreevskaya. The confiscation of all private assets by the revolutionary government deprived

Kandinsky of all his personal sources of income. But hoping that the revolution would free Russia from the influence of the West, and knowing that his organizational abilities would be in demand, he did not leave Russia. From 1918 to 1921, he was in charge of successive administrative posts, and he helped foundation of the Institute of Artistic Culture (Inchuk). With the fading of liberalism of the first years of the revolution and faced with increased attacks, Kandinsky resigned from Inchuk and returned to Germany. Although he had never joined the Communist Party, his activity in Russia was later interpreted by the Nazis as evidence of his communist inclinations.

Despite hostility of the political atmosphere in Germany to a Russian involved in the Soviet government's activities, Gropius, aware of Kandinsky's management capabilities, wanted him on the Bauhaus staff. Charged with the mural painting workshop, Kandinsky became one of the main figures of the Bauhaus. In Dessau, Kandinsky and his wife shared one of the Gropius buildings with the Klee family. *Off Balance* (1929) and a few other paintings of the Dessau period are reminiscent of Klee's work.

The suppression of references to the external world, disciplined distribution of lines and shapes, and dominance of geometric elements are characteristics of Kandinsky's Bauhaus paintings. This controlled self-expression reflects Kandinsky's romantic inclinations and the rigorous discipline he was subjected to.

In 1926 he published *Point and Line to Plane*. A section of this book contains his observations about the psychology of line and its importance as a means of communication. He explained that in the human imagination, horizontal lines correspond to a cold supporting base. In contrast to horizotal lines, vertical lines correspond to warm movement. The third type of straight line are diagonals, which diverges from both horizontal and vertical lines, therefore have the same inclination to both of them, and correspond to cold-warm movement.

After the closure of the Bauhaus in 1933, he went on holiday to the South of France. In France, he heard on the radio Hitler's speech condemning modern artists. Although he had already obtained German citizenship, he decided not to go back to Germany, and he moved to Paris.

The growing international crisis and French artistic circles giving a cool reception to his abstract art increased his concern about the future of his much younger wife. In 1837 he participated in an exhibition of the Jeu de Pomme (Musée Nationale d'Art Moderne, Paris). Two years later the Jeu de Pomme purchased Kandinsky's *Composition IX*.

The images that dominated the Kandinsky's work in Paris are geometric forms with many irregular and organic marks that resemble living cells under a microscope. His intention was to create forms without associations and precedents, only following their own internal rhythm, not other law. The dark palette of his last works mirrors the mood of the old master. A few months after the liberation of Paris in 1944, Kandinsky died at age seventy-eight of arteriosclerosis.

PAUL KLEE (1879–1940)

Klee was born in Bern; his father was a German, his mother a Swiss, and he had German nationality like his father. He grew up in a family of musicians. His great-grandfather was an organist, his father was a teacher of music, and his mother had had voice training at Stuttgart Conservatory. He began to play the violin at the age of seven and was soon playing it so well that, at the age of eleven, he became an associate member of an orchestra. The study of Greek left a lasting impression on him. Throughout his life he continued to read Greek poetry in the original and to play music. While at school he drew caricatures. Encouraged by his grandmother, he decided to study painting and devote his life to art. To realize his goal, he chose to go to Germany.

In Munich, his principal teacher was Franz von Stuck. Klee excelled in drawing and like a child let the pencil lead him until the image began to emerge. His main creativity moved toward satire. Then he studied etching, a technique that increases the expressive quality of line. In the domain of color, although he became one of the masters of color, he had no natural gift for it.

At that time Paris was the center of art activity, but to broaden his experience Klee chose Italy for his first travels. Deeply impressed by Leonardo, he wrote, "All the greatest achievements in art derive from this man." Back in Bern, to learn more about technique, he attended lectures on anatomy and drew from the nude. During his short visit to Paris in 1905, in the Louvre once again, Leonardo attracted his attention. He met impressionists, but he did not see works of the painters of his generation.

Between 1901 and 1906, the years that he lived in Munich, he married Lily Stumpf and devoted his time to etching. His *Virgin in a Tree* represents social prejudice that denies one the right to live. In *Perseus, Wit Has Triumphed over Grief,* his concern is not the myth but the concept of good and evil and the truth that lies in the combination of them. His *Hero with a Wing* tell us that both materialism and spiritualism are needed for flight. Klee's command of anatomical detail reveals the benefits of his study in anatomy. He sent his etchings to his teacher, Franz Stuck, and the jury of the Secession Exhibition. Stuck was pleased, but critics ridiculed his work.

For his pictorial creation, Klee had to find a bridge between nature and the inner self. His encounter with the impressionists led him to work from nature; his intention was not to make a copy of nature, but to find a method of transferring his visual impressions. In the works of that period, one notices his preoccupation with the problems of structure, tonality, and light. Naturalistic studies also fortified his psychological improvisations.

Desiring to expand the variety of his work and to work from nature, he began to draw and paint on glass, where his focus was mainly the contrast between light and dark, not the color. The distorted drawing of these glass paintings, more naturalistic than his etchings, were thematically more grotesque than satirical.

Candide, the satirical novel of Voltaire, was about the reactions of a disillusioned young man to the hardships of the world. Candide was, like Klee, a person concerned with gaiety, mingled with a deep pessimism. From 1906 he began a series of comic drawings for *Candide*. Repeatedly laid aside, he completed them in 1912. The vehemence of actions described in these drawings is the same as Voltaire's *Candide*.

With an extremely varied culture, Klee was a wise, modest painter who, by studying the paintings of masters and the art of other cultures, slowly developed his vision of art. He composed scrupulously, paying utmost care to details and the relationships between parts of the composition. He taught himself in the medium of watercolor, but he did not approach color until he was sure of his control over the expressive possibilities of line.

In 1911 he met Kandinsky, who was a theorist and a more advanced painter than Klee. Despite a difference in temperament, a close relationship developed between them in the Bauhaus, and with mutual influence, their methods of instruction complemented each other. Being introduced to Kandinsky's friends broke Klee's isolation, and particularly his friendship with Franz Marc was crucial.

At the first Der Blaue Reiter exhibition, organized by Kandinsky and Franz Marc in 1911, Delaunay's chromatic investigations impressed Klee. During his second visit to Paris, he arranged to visit Robert Delaunay, who had started his *Window* series. This time he saw the works of Picasso, Braque, Derain, and Vlaminck. With the assimilation of new influences, his painterly abilities grew, and his impulse to satirize diminished.

In 1914 Klee took a journey of twelve days to Tunis and Kairouan with Macke and Moilliet. The colors under the sun of Africa helped him to have a breakthrough in painting and become a painter in the truest sense. In the early watercolors of this trip, the geometric shapes of colors translate the landscape, but soon color distanced him from nature, and he painted more abstractly. In *Vor den Toren von Kairuan*, one of the last painting of this trip, to form the view of the town, he applied delicate shades of colors on top of each other. He painted most of his Tunisian watercolors after his return to Munich. In these paintings colors, not lines, separate areas. After the Tunisian trip, painting became the core of his art, while drawing remained an important component of his work.

The outbreak of World War I dispersed his friends. Marc and Macke both were killed in the war, but he was not called to duty until 1916. Recent legislation exempting artists from combat spared him from front-line duty. Remaining in Bavaria, he continued to paint, and in his journal, he wrote, "The more horrifying this world becomes, the more art becomes abstract; while a world of peace produces realistic art."

In 1920 he was appointed to the faculty of the Bauhaus in Weimar. His teaching was essentially on painting, but he also taught glass painting and weaving. With the necessity of teaching, he had to clarify in his own mind artistic procedures that he had adopted almost unconsciously. Contact with his colleagues and his own theoretical lessons strengthened Klee's constructive powers, without replacing the power of intuition. At the Bauhaus, his teaching was theoretical in a highly personal manner. For thirteen years his time was divided between teaching and his own creative work.

Rendering space on a flat plane is one of the important elements of artistic creation. Through overlapping and color, Klee produced the impression of depth, but there are numbers of his perspective pictures that could have been used for the teaching of perspective.

The designations *abstract* and *representational* cease to have application to Klee's art. His forms and pictorial elements expressing ideas, without being abstract, are mostly remote from nature. Among his many types of compositions are pictures made of flat colored rectangles. Around this time the composition of rectangle of flat color was being developed by a few painters, but Klee, himself a musician and nourished by the music of Bach, Mozart, and modern music, conceived the color rectangle as analogous to musical compositions. The repeated geometrical forms and color give these paintings a rhythm, as if they were elements of a polyphonic composition [21]. He also produced a group of pictures on the basis of fugal imitation. (Fugal imitation means to carry the same theme through all the voices).

Klee considered art a language of signs. The fantasy subjects of some of his pictures prove that logic was not always everything for Klee; he remained a lyrical poet and never stopped dreaming. To link the poetic and pictorial, he built up an imaginary world around ordinary objects and often combined disparate elements, such as primitive art and the drawings of small children. The title has an indispensable role in revealing the evocative quality of Klee's works. *Twittering Machine* is a watercolor with delicate pen drawing of four mechanical creatures with the heads of bird standing on a crankshaft

---

21 - Polyphony consists of two or more simultaneous lines of independent melody, as opposed to a musical texture with just one voice, Monophony, or a texture with one dominant melodic voice accompanied by chords, which is called homophony.

over a rectangular abyss; with a turn of the crank the birds twitter. The picture is an allusion to man's life and his final destiny.

In 1928 Klee made a trip to Egypt. Although the impression of the six-thousand-year-old culture was profound, and it inspired monumental pictures with brighter colors than before, he considered Tunisia much purer. On *Monument in Fertile Country*, he wrote, "The polyphonic interplay between earth and atmosphere has been kept as fluid as possible." In *Legende vom Nile* (1938), a reminiscence of his journey to Egypt, he used the hieroglyph signs for *boat*, *men*, *fish*, and *plant* on various shades of blue.

Before the final closing of the school in 1933, Klee ceased to be a member of the teaching staff of the Bauhaus. Although sales of his pictures supported him, he was accepted to teach a painting class at the Prussian State Academy in Dusseldorf from 1931 to 1933. Officially, he was supposed to lecture on the technique of painting, but the academy director's primary interest in Klee was to stimulate the artistic life of Dusseldorf.

Klee's paintings and drawings are small-scale pictures. In 1932 he painted *Ad Parnassum*, one of his largest and most complex works, in the pointillist style. The background is composed of rectangles of various colors. Over the rectangles, which are made of carefully organized tiny, mosaiclike, luminous color dots, he drew a mountain and a gateway; thus he created polyphony through color and depth. The title refers to Mount Parnassus, the home of Apollo and the Muses of the fine arts.

In 1933 Klee was attacked by the Nazis, who called him a Jew and a foreigner. With the political upset in Germany and its impact on his freedom to teach, he decided to go to Switzerland. The closed eyes, tightly shut mouth, and large X next to the head of his self-portrait, in *Von der Liste Gestrichen* ("Struck from the List"), painted in 1933, pictured the lack of freedom in a totalitarian society.

He went back to Bern, his hometown, and devoted his efforts to his own creative work. As the result of an exhibition of Klee's work in Bern and Basle, he enjoyed prominence among Swiss artists. In 1935 the first sign of a little-known disease, scleroderma, appeared. For a while, the illness hindered him from working. But in the final years of his life, he increased his productivity.

Revolution des Viaduktes was among the pictures that he painted after he started to work again in 1937. At the beginning critics believed that the single-bridge arches with legs like men moving forward showed a totalitarian mass movement, but the differing thickness and colors of these arches represented more individuality than uniformity of the masses.

To give abstraction to the representation of objects or figures, he used hieroglyphiclike elements in his pictures. One of these pictures, *Insula Dulcamara* ("Bittersweet Island"), just as the name implies a conflict, consists of delicate plants and flowers surrounding the white face of death in the center of the picture.

In 1939, after living in Switzerland for five years, he applied for naturalization. The political implications of his art instigated the scrutiny of Swiss authorities; nevertheless, his application was approved.

In *Tod und Feuer* ("Death and Fire"), a heavily outlined whitish death's head with features that could be letters raises his hand toward the sun. On the left of the picture, a figure with an indefinable object in his hand—possibly a staff—is approaching. The red and blue colors evoke water and fire in the ever-changing alternation of life and death.

Five years after the beginning of his illness, he died in June 1940. He was a withdrawn man to the point that no one dared trespass upon his private world. His pictures are a blend of the opposing forces that made up his personality. Music was a part of his daily life. He was an avid reader of literary masterpieces. A shy man who avoided long discussions, he said little about his contemporaries. In 1951, when Picasso was asked about his visit to Klee in 1937, he responded, "Pascal-Napoleon." Presumably he meant the strange mixture of wisdom and excessive energy.

Klee's culture and experiments were extremely varied. To expand his knowledge of art, he studied the works of visionary painters, Byzantine mosaics, Persian art, pre-Colombian art, and Chinese paintings, and he touched on almost every aspect of twentieth-century painting.

FRANZ MARC (1880–1916)

He was born in Munich and began his studies with theology, but he suddenly resolved to become a painter and studied at the Munich Academy for three years. In his visits to Paris, he admired impressionism, but it was the work of Van Gogh that influenced him. Like Klee, Marc developed his vision of painting slowly.

He had no interest in theories. A painter with intense mysticism, he simplified forms to use them as symbols to convey the mystery of nature and express his emotions. After Macke drew his attention to pure colors, he worked on the expressive value of colors. Always fond of animals, and believing that humans have destroyed nature, his attention was turned to the intact vitality that animals embodied.

In 1912 Marc and Macke met Delaunay in Paris. As he realized that his animals in nature had reached a point that could not be carried any further, and influenced by Delaunay's work, he moved toward abstraction. From 1914 till his death at the Verdun front in 1916, he served in the army. He said, "Traditions are all very well, but what matters is creating a tradition, not living in one."

OSKAR KOKOSCHKA (1886–1980)

Kokoschka was born in Pochlarn near Vienna. His father, a silversmith, due to the availability of industrial products at a lower price, lost his business, which forced the family to move to Vienna. After elementary and high school, Kokoschka studied at the School of Applied Art in Vienna, where he learned a variety of craft techniques, among them drawing and lithography, but not painting. Interested in painting the human figure, he taught himself to paint in oil, so his approach to the medium had no regard for the traditional way of painting.

In 1897 a group of artists aspiring to a renaissance of art revolted against the academic tradition, moved toward a decorative art similar to art nouveau, and founded the Vienna Secession, a movement that paralleled the direction of other European modernist schools. In the first decade of the century, critics attacked its decorative language. One of the standard-bearers of this criticism was the architect and theorist Adolf Loos. Kokoschka's disdain for the prevailing decorative aesthetic impressed Loos, who provided support to the young artist and secured him commissions for paintings.

During his first Viennese period, he expanded his activities to literature, in which he expressed humanistic ideas. In his early portraits, he goes beyond the expression of psychological states of the sitter to projecting his own mental torments to his sitter. As the Viennese aristocracy and the bourgeoisie considered his expressionist dramas and portraits outrageous, he moved to Berlin in 1910.

In Berlin, he began to provide illustrations for the art magazine *Der Sturm*, one of the main promoters of the expressionist movement, and he painted portraits of the Austrian and German intelligentsia. Though his name became widely known through *Der Sturm*, he remained as poor and tormented as before.

After his return to Vienna in 1911, he continued to take part in all exhibitions at the *Der Strum's* gallery and the secession in Berlin, and was represented in *Der Blaue Reiter Almanac*. From 1913, through expressive forms of hands, distortion of faces, violent brushstrokes, and the effects of color, he moved into the intimate world of his subjects.

Between 1912 and 1814, Kokoschka maintained a passionate relationship with Alma Mahler. Alma, daughter of a painter and the widow of the composer Gustave Mahler, had grown up surrounded by art and artists, and during her lifetime became friends with numerous artists, composers, and writers. His passionate love for Alma was followed by many drawings and single portraits of Alma, and double portraits of Alma with himself. The famous *Bride of the Wind* (1914)—also known as *Tempest*—a work of intense pathos, features Alma sleeping peacefully beside Kokoschka, who with open eyes stares into space. The large and swirling brushstrokes he used in this picture reflect his intense emotions at that time. This turbulent relationship ended in separation.

With the beginning of World War I, he volunteered in the Austrian army. Before the end of the year, he was seriously wounded on the Russian front. Demobilized in 1916, he settled in Dresden, where he was appointed to a professorship of fine arts at the Dresden Academy.

Kokoshka's World War I pictures all have in common nervous, almost fidgety, brushstrokes—evidence of his struggle to overcome the physical and psychological effects of his wound. A group of portraits such as *Emigres* (1916) projects his disgust with war. In a landscape with a few bare trees and branches sit two men and a woman. They have lost their home; they seem to consider with obvious perplexity their future. Upon leaving Dresden in 1924, by traveling throughout Europe, North Africa, and the Middle East, he led a wanderer's life for ten years.

The lively tonalities of joyful children, painted during the decade of the 1930s, reflect his optimistic views of a better world to come. In 1934 he went to Prague, where he met Olda, his future wife. From Prague, he protested against the Nazi regime in Germany. With the Munich Agreement, he fled to England with Olda and married there. After the war, he was honored with exhibitions of his work throughout Europe and in the United States. In 1953 he and Olda settled in Switzerland, which became their home.

Disillusioned with World War II, he expressed his distress at the human suffering in a number of large canvases such as *That for Which We Fought* of a dead woman holding her dead child. During the 1960s, seeing the world once more rising up from the ashes of World War II, and hopeful for the future, by painting pictures such as *Herodotus* and *Myth of Prometheus*, he looked back to Greek origins as the foundation of Western values.

He said, "The creative man has to identify and determine what it is that darkens the human spirit and then set this spirit free."

Section 7

Painting in Russia

During the rule of the tzars, Russia maintained a close relationship with the art of Western Europe. The political atmosphere that followed the abortive uprising of 1905, demanding constitutional monarchy and social reform, brought Russia closer to other European countries and revitalized Russian art. The collections of two Russian art lovers, Shchukin and Morosov, of impressionists, postimpressionists, fauvists, cubists, and futurists, making them accessible to Russian painters, opened up new areas of exploration to the imaginations of young artists.

* * *

KAZIMIR MALEVITCH (1878–1935)

Malevitch was born of humble Polish-Russian stock settled near Kiev. He received little education as a boy, but as an intelligent person and avid reader, he acquired a great deal of knowledge. At the age of nineteen, he entered the Kiev School of Art. In 1905 he moved to Moscow to study painting in the avant-garde studio of Roerburg. The visiting collections of Shchukin and Morosov introduced him to new trends in painting.

Determined to look for a new aesthetic to liberate painting from the bondage of representation, he explored different aspects of cubism and worked in a variety of styles. *The Woodcutter* (1911) was his first mature cubist work. In paintings after 1912, the figure merged into the background and became a series of geometrical forms, which recalls Leger's work.

In 1915 he exhibited thirty-five abstract pictures of compositions of simple geometrical forms; heading the list was the *Black Square*. His writing "From Cubism to Suprematism" laid down the foundation of suprematism, one of the earliest developments in abstract art, and his pictures became a complex relationship of various forms and colors.

After the revolution of 1917, he was chosen as a member of the Commission for Protection of Monuments and Museums. In 1926, his *The Non-Objective World* was published in Munich.

MARC ZAKHAROVICH CHAGALL (1887–1985)

Chagall, whose art was not typical of the Russian artistic world, was a rare modern painter who presented old themes in unprecedented expressive forms. He was born into a poor Jewish family, in Liozna, near Vitebsk in Belarus. The Chagall family followed Hasidim, a Jewish sect that sought the mysteries of the Kabbala. Hasidic tradition is made up of countless anecdotes, stories, fables, and the importance of joy, happiness, dancing, and singing. In the Russian Empire, Jewish communities, segregated from the rest of Russian society, lived in their own quarters. As a Jewish boy, Chagall was not allowed to attend the school of his choice, and painting was a taboo according to his religion. The support of his mother enabled him to sidestep these restrictions. After a short time at school and a few months of studying painting at the studio of Jehuda Pen in Vitebsk, in 1906 he went to Saint Petersburg to study painting for two years at the Art School of Saint Petersburg. Eager to learn more, and supported by a small scholarship paid by a patron, in 1910 he went to Paris.

When he arrived in Paris, he was nearly destitute and spoke no French. He moved to live in La Ruche, a group of studios, where he met Fernand Leger and a few other painters. He also became friends with Apollinaire and Cendrars, the poets who were the first to discover the importance of the art of this wanderer between orient and occident. He was a lyrical man with a store of childhood memories and the details of the lives of simple people of his hometown. He juxtaposed reality with the world of dreams, where nothing was bound by logic, everyone and everything could float in any direction, and he ignored natural color and relative size. He had no concern for the rules of composition and no interest in theories; nonetheless, he could not remain untouched by the color contrasts of fauvism and the poetic side of cubism. But Chagall's cubism was his own; his use of geometric structure was to increase "the expressive force of his images."

Chagall always carried with him his Jewish mysticism and the memories of his hometown. A pictorial storyteller, he was one of the exceptional painters of modern times to not reject subject matter. Faithful to his memories, he painted the people and wooden houses of his village, donkeys and goats, dancing fiddlers, and legends.

Chagall exhibited his works at the Salon des Indépendants, but as he was still unable to earn enough from his painting, Apollinaire introduced him to Helwarth Walden, a German art dealer, who invited Chagall to exhibit in Berlin. The exhibit coincided with the breakout of World War I.

The war made him hasten to go back home to marry Bella and then return to Paris. But the war closed the borders, making a return impossible. In Vitebsk, echoes of cubism became limited to folds of clothing and architectural elements. He toned down his color contrasts, and the delicate light that suffused his tones enhanced the weightlessness of his subjects. He married Bella, and their daughter was born the following year. From now on Bella became a dominant motif of his pictures. In *Double Portrait with Glass of Wine*, love and happiness have made him weightless and caused him to float on the shoulder of Bella.

After the October Revolution, a friend in Paris who became chief commissar for education appointed Chagall responsible for organizing art schools, museums, and exhibitions. He also opened an art school in Vitebsk and summoned leading Russian avant-garde artists to teach there. Among these teachers was Malevich, the founder of suprematism, who believed the revolution should sweep away all traces of the past. Malevich lost no time in openly coming into a confrontation with Chagall, and he gathered others around him. Chagall resigned and moved to Moscow. Summoned by the Moscow Jewish Theater to design scenery and costumes for a play by Sholem Aleichem was an opportunity to make contact with a large public. He repeated settings and characters of the play in a series of paintings on the walls of the theater. Following increasing hostility toward himself and his art, in 1922 he decided to go back to France.

In France, his choice of new motifs reveals his happiness at the changes in his life. Motifs of lovers, mother and child, and bouquets of flowers are intertwined with the beautiful nature of Côte d'Azur and the countryside of France in the background, replacing Vitebsk scenes. The contours of his motifs became more sinuous; a gradual emphasis on the importance of color as the basis of expression reduced the importance of metaphorical elements and form in his pictures. The art dealer Ambroise Vollard commissioned him to illustrate Gogol's *Dead Souls*. Chagal's originality in translating the text into etchings attracted more commissions to illustrate books. He became a prolific painter. His work was exhibited in Paris, Germany, and New York.

Rejection of his application for French citizenship because he had served the Soviet regime as fine art commissar and confronting a menacing shape of anti-Semitism in Poland were the beginning of growing worries. His palette lost its brilliance, the theme of crucifixion became a symbol of atrocities to human beings, and Jewish religious motifs dominated his work. With his triptych *Resistance*, *Resurrection*, and *Liberation*, he expressed his concern about the growing violence and injustice.

In 1941 Chagall and his family emigrated to the United States, where exhibitions of his work had already established his reputation. He designed sets and costumes for the ballet of Tchaikovsky's *Aleko* and for Stravinsky's *Firebird*. He said, "I wanted to penetrate the spirit of *Firebird* and *Aleko* without illustrating them...I want color to play and speak alone. There is no way of equating the world we live in with the world we enter in such a way." Upset by horrifying news from Europe, in his pictures Chagall lost the joy of life. After an illness, Bella died in 1944. Chagall's grief was so profound that for nine months he did not touch paint.

He returned to France in 1948. He was given a retrospective in the Musée d'Art Moderne. He settled in Saint-Paul-de-Vence on the Côte d'Azur. In 1952 he married Valentine Brodsky, who gave him back his serenity. Although memories of Vitebsk were still alive, during 1952 to 1954, Paris became one of his motifs. Disregarding form, color became the dominant medium of expression in his works. He used painting knives and his fingers to lay on colors. He also began to opt more for gouache.

Chagall was asked to illustrate the pastoral romance of *Daphnis and Chloe*. While he was working on the illustrations, he received a commission for the set and costumes of a ballet based on Ravel's *Daphnis and Chloe*. The Metropolitan Opera's commission for sets and costumes for Mozart's *Magic Flute* was another opportunity to participate in an intermingling of music and painting.

He was commissioned to design stained glass windows for Metz Cathedral, the synagogue of Jerusalem University, and the Reims cathedral. In 1963 André Malraux requested that Chagall paint the ceiling of the Paris Opera, the enormous edifice dedicated to music and ballet. Deeply touched by the trust of Malraux, and to show his gratitude to France, Chagall made the painting of the dome represent the apotheosis of his vision of color. He divided the ceiling into five areas, each with a dominant color dedicated to the artists of Chagall's choice: blue for Moussorgsky and Mozart, green for Wagner and Berlioz, white set off by yellow for Rameau and Debussy, red for Ravel and Stravinsky, yellow for Tchaikovsky and Adam. Inside the dome of the opera there is a circle. In this circle, he painted four groups to pay homage to Gluck, Beethoven, Verdi, and Bizet.

He executed two murals with vibrant colors for the Metropolitan Opera. *Triumph of Music* is composed of a torrent of swirling circles and weightless dancers floating in the air, in a predominantly red color. In *Source of Music*, the predominant color is yellow and the rhythm of movement gentler.

The Musée Nationale Message Biblique Marc Chagall, created by the suggestion of André Malraux, was inaugurated in 1973. The museum, built in modern architectural style on the hill of Cimiez close to Nice, houses a series of Chagall's paintings that illustrate biblical messages. The central part of the collection is seventeen pictures donated by Chagall.

In the 1970s, during the cultural liberation of the Soviet Union, Chagall was honored by an exhibition at the Tretyakov Gallery. He was offered to visit his hometown, but he refused and said, "It might turn out that the very thing that is one the deepest elements of my painting exists no longer. That would hurt..." He died in 1985 at Saint-Paul-de-Vence.

Section 8

Surrealism

Cubist painters, by breaking the visible forms of human beings and objects and depicting them from multiple viewpoints, paved the way to see the world differently from the traditional way and gave painting an unprecedented freedom to search out new forms to picture the material world and unseen realities. Futurism set out to represent the images that are gone rapidly before the human eye can catch them. At the other end, the desire to bring to light the mysteries beyond the appearances of the material world instigated poetically minded painters to find an appropriate style for their fanciful imaginations.

André Breton, who had participated in the publications of dadaists, disillusioned with dada and influenced by the works of Sigmund Freud, believed that to enable the subconscious to reveal itself, logical processes had to be suspended. He cofounded, with Louis Aragon and Philippe Soupault, the review *Littérature*. He met regularly with a group of French writers, poets, and artists to explore the world of dreams and the Freudian subconscious, and an aesthetic of the nonrational arising from Rimbaud's poetry. From these meetings emerged Breton's *Manifeste de Surrealism* in 1924. He wrote, "We are still living under the reign of logic...But logical proceedings of our time apply no more than to the resolution of problems of secondary interest." He defined the form of automatic writing "thought-dictation without any control exercised by reason," as a descent into ourselves. Automatic writing, taken up by painters, was regarded as a method to liberate poetic inspiration and open it up a field of pure imagination. The second *Manifeste de Surrealism*, published in 1930, explored the philosophical implications of surrealism.

Contrary to negations of dadism and its involvement in the immediacy of the present, surrealism was a positive experience and concerned with the future of man. It aimed to eliminate the distinction between objectivity and subjectivity, to combine the real and the unreal. The movement, a foster child of French symbolism and late romanticism, began in Paris and soon developed into an international movement.

To bring to light the unseen has a long precedent in the history of art. In ancient times the magical purpose of art made invisible a concrete reality. In modern times paintings that mirror the subconscious and could be regarded as the forerunners of surrealism specifically are the following: the mysterious scene of Henri Rousseau's *Sleeping Gypsy* of a lion standing next to a gypsy sleeping beneath a full moon in the silence of a desert, in a style more akin to a dream world than reality; and some of De Chirico's works, such as the unreal perspectives of arcades and pool, a clock, a distant train, and the intense contrasts of light and shade in *Delights of a Poet*, which creates a disquieting mood of loneliness.

The first surrealism exhibition was in 1925. Since at the core of Breton's ideas was individualism, from the beginning the works of the surrealists, with little stylistic similarity, took two directions: one group, like Juan Miro, by moving their brush automatically without control of the mind, followed writers' automatic writings; other group, like Salvador Dali, explored the symbolic meaning of objects and scenes in the distorted forms of dreams, to suggest an evocation of the subconscious. But surrealist images of neither group took its rise in the unconsciousness - as it was supposed to be. The fact was that images were controlled by conscious thoughts. In 1933 Albert Skira founded the journal of *Minotaure* to emphasize the role of the surrealism.

MAX ERNST (1891–1976)

Max Ernst was born in Bruhl, six miles from Cologne, in a forested area on the banks of the Rhine. Cologne is a city at the crossroads of diverse cultures of Europe, especially a meeting ground of the cultures of France and Germany. His father was a teacher of sign language for the hearing impaired and an amateur painter. He liked painting in the forest, and he used to take young Max along. These excursions left a lasting effect on the mind of Max.

Max enrolled at the University of Bonn to study philosophy and psychiatry. Near Bonn was an asylum with a building that housed a collection of the art of mental patients. Fascinated by these works, he started painting. In 1911 he met August Macke, a poet and member of Der Blaue Reiter, and joined his expressionist group. The Sonderbund show in Cologne was an opportunity for Ernst to see works by Cezanne, Van Gogh, Gauguin, Munch, and Picasso. His *Crucifixion* (1913) combines two different styles: the foreground of the painting is in the expressionist manner, while its background landscape setting derives from cubism. His paintings, alongside those of Klee, Chagall, and Arp, were exhibited at the Fall Salon of 1913 in Berlin.

With the start of World War I, Ernst was drafted into the German army, and he served on both the western and eastern fronts. When he was demobilized, he returned to Cologne. Experiences in the trenches of World War I alienated him toward European values.

With the extension of the activity of the dadaists of Switzerland to the rest of Europe, Ernst founded a dada group in Cologne.

In 1919 he began to make collages of cut photographs and engravings. The technique enabled him to create a new reality from two unrelated realities. A few years before the first "Manifeste de Surrealism," his collages attracted the attention of André Breton, who invited Ernst to exhibit his collages in Paris. This exhibition marked his move from dada activity to surrealism. Ernst had already met Paul Eluard. They become close friends, and he settled into a ménage à trois with Eluard and his wife, Gala.

By painting *Aquis Submersus* (1919), a picture with a dreamlike quality inspired by De Chirico's works, Ernst became one of the early adherents of surrealism. An inventive artist, in an attempt to reproduce in painting the principles of the automatic writing of surrealism, he combined collages of unrelated elements with frottage. The process of frottage involves placing a piece of paper on a textured surface and rubbing over it with a pencil, thus obtaining chance shapes and texture. Ernst did not limit the frottage to paper; *Two Sisters* is frottage on canvas. Ernst's automation is the kind of chance-taking of forms that are not anticipated. These images, produced by chance, are not products of the unconscious, but by association with things and events they provoke a mental response in the spectator.

Ernst's participation in surrealism did not mean a total visual dependency. There were points of contact —and differences —in Ernst's art and the principles of surrealism. While he used his art to explore the world beyond consciousness, he remained an eclectic painter, and brilliantly adapted his works to the kind of art he admired.

In 1927 the bird as a symbol of freedom became the basis of Ernst's series *Birds*, a collection of forms that float in a vacuum. In

1938, with Eluard and Man Ray, he published *The Man Who Lost His Own Skeleton*, a denunciation of Breton, followed by his withdrawal from surrealism. In some paintings, such as *Barbarians Marching to the West*, he presents the threat of fascism. With the outbreak of World War II, on account of his German citizenship, he was interned in French concentration camps. Branded as a degenerate by the Nazi government, he emigrated to the United States in 1941. He married Peggy Guggenheim, the American art collector—a marriage that did not last long.

His early paintings in the United States reflect his pessimism. *Europe after the Flood*, is a landscape of a world in which all traces of the life of mankind have been erased. To obtain his desired effect, he used a "decalcomania" technique—a technique consisting of spreading diluted black gouache over a sheet of paper, then laying a second sheet on top of it, applying a light pressure, and then peeling it off—but to be able to use the technique with oil painting on canvas, instead of paper he used a sheet of glass. During his exile, he invented drip-painting: the painter holds a pierced can over the canvas and lets paint trickle down. This process, which attracted young American artists, is an application of the principle of automatism to painting.

After returning to France, Ernst resurrected techniques of his earlier phase. In 1954 he received the Grand Prix of the Venice Biennale. In 1976 successive aretrospectives celebrated his work.

Ernst occupies a special position between the branches of surrealism. What mattered for him was the method of creation, not following a uniform style of surrealism.

JUAN MIRO (1893-1983)

Miro was born in the old town of Barcelona. His father was a prosperous goldsmith and watchmaker. Although he grew up in the center of Barcelona, having a poetic nature, he was attracted to the countryside. From his earliest years, he liked to draw. In his drawing he often simplified objects, but sometimes he recorded with extreme precision. He was sent to a commercial school and also attended the La Lotja School of Fine Arts. At the art school, he had two teachers. One of them encouraged him to practice a sensitive approach to nature; the other was for modern discoveries and techniques. After three years of study at the commercial school, he worked as a clerk in a drugstore. To convalesce from a serious illness, parents sent him to their farm at Montroig, a place that became the heart of his connection with the rural lifestyle. After he recuperated he devoted his time to painting.

He enrolled in the Academy Gali in Barcelona. Francisco Gali, who provided art of contemporary foreign painters in his academy, advised Miro that to acquire a feeling for form, he had to touch the objects and draw without looking at them.

His preferred domain of art was landscape. Landscapes such as *Rut* and *Vegetable Garden with Donkey*, in their precise style, are products of the long summers spent in the family farm of Montroig. While in his earlier painting there is no sign of abstraction, a tendency to abstract forms is marked in *Olive Grove*.

After his first visit to Paris in 1919, he determined to alternate his time between spending summers in Montroig and end of the year in Paris. Despite Maurice Raynal's enthusiastic preface to the catalog, his one-man show in the Galerie La Licorne was not a success.

Returning to Montroig he began the large landscape *Farm* (1921), a celebration of the eternal values of nature. All elements of this magnificent picture are treated meticulously. Specifically, plants recorded minutely are the balance between detailed observation of nature and a personal vocabulary of signs. To emphasis that there is hardly any difference between the near and the far, he eliminated the three-dimensional depth of the square paving in the foreground. A black circle over which is floating a great eucalyptus tree is the symbol of the earth as the source of all life.

Neighboring André Masson in the winters of 1920 to 1925, Miro entered into the circle of young artists who were experiencing André Breton's idea of painting automatically without control of the mind. Following the surrealist approach to automatic creativity, he let his brush move over the surface, avoiding the direction of his conscious mind. In this phase, which lasted three years, color has the substance of a living being; but at the end of the phase, simple lines suggest forms.

A few works painted at Montroig in 1923 mark the beginning of the change. Under the influence of surrealism, he broke free of nature and amalgamated reality with dreams. Losing their natural context, objects became flat shapes—organic and geometric forms. In *Tilled Field*, a painting that followed *The Farm*, the tree has an eye and an ear. In *Maternity* (1924) he isolated the most significant details of the subject. The mother's breast and child are seen from front and profile in two opposite angles of the picture.

In 1928 he began to experiment with collage, which led to dessin-collage. To create forms free of the effects of memory, he used collage as another form of painting. First he made a preliminary collage on cardboard, and then he used it as a model to paint a picture of it. When the pictures and the preliminary collages are compared, the juxtaposition of irrelevant items of the model has found coherence and a new meaning. Intensive work in collage led Miro to a simplification of forms that seem to float in an immaterial space.

His marriage to Pilar Juncosa in 1929, and the birth of his daughter, made him stay longer in Catalonia. The unrest leading to the disasters of the Spanish Civil War shattered Miro's peace of mind. His work of this period indicates his angst. In 1937 he made *The*

Reaper, a mural of a militant peasant, for the Spanish Pavilion at the Paris Exposition. *The Reaper*—now lost—figured alongside Picasso's *Guernica*.

From 1938 to 1940, Miro and his family lived at Varengeville, on the coast of Normandy. With the German invasion of France, the family moved to Palma de Mallorca. In Varengeville he began his *Constellations* series and continued it in Palma and Montroig. A tremendous amount of creative concentration limited his production to only twenty-two pictures of the *Constellations* in the course of two years. These pictures, unaffected by the tragic events of war, are all the same size of human and celestial bodies and are the coherent development of an initial conception progressed from picture to picture without a change of mood. At first, the figures and certain celestial bodies are recognizable; then the pictures become denser and move toward geometric signs. Miro considered this series as one of the most important works he had done. When it was planned to exhibit the *Constellations* series in New York, he specified that they must be shown together in chronological order.

Settled down in Barcelona in 1942, he began to experiment with pastel, gouache, and watercolors to make a series of small works that are remarkable for their freedom of execution.

In 1947 he traveled to the United States; he made a mural for the University of Harvard and a mural for the Terrace Plaza Hotel skyscraper in Cincinnati. The mural for the hHotel was a fulfillment of a wish to reach great masses of people.

He used to model small rudimentary figures in clay. Instructed by his old friend Joseph Llorens Artigas, he mastered ceramic techniques. In 1955 he was asked to decorate two walls of UNESCO's new building in Paris. After studying Altamira's frescos in the Barcelona Museum and Gaudi's decorations, in collaboration with Artigas he decorated the walls in ceramic. Among his experiments with various media was sculpture. The great importance of color to Miro led him to combine sculpture with color.

Some of Miro's works are carefully composed and meticulously painted of the most characteristic side of a subject; others are spontaneous pictures. The title of each painting defines its theme. Pointing out that his motifs correspond to something concrete, he denied being an abstract artist.

SALVADOR DALI (1904-1989)

Salvador was born in the small, rural town of Figueras, near Barcelona. His father was a respected local government notary. Salvaror had been named after an elder brother who died three years before his birth, and he was told that he was the reincarnation of his brother. He said, "All the eccentricities which I commit, all the incoherent displays, are a tragic fixture of my life. I wish to prove to myself that I am not the dead brother but the living one."

Dali's family, who had a vacation home at Cadaques, became friends with Pichot family, who lived in Barcelona and had a summer house at Cadaques. Ramon Pichot was a painter and cultivated man; all the family were artists and possessed great gifts. The friendship of Dali's family with Pichot's intellectual and artistic family developed the interest of twelve-year-old Dali in diverse cultural pursuits and his later wide readings of Voltaire, Nietzsche, Kant, Spinoza, and Descartes.

At school Salvador learned the basics of drawing and watercolor painting, and at the age of thirteen, he attended Juan Nunez's drawing course at the municipal School of Drawing in Figueras. After passing the school examination, Salvador's determination to go to the Madrid Academy of Art, backed by Professor Nunez and the Pichot family, persuaded his father to let him go to Madrid.

At the age seventeen, he was accepted as a student at the famous Academy of San Fernando in Madrid. He lived at the residencia de estudiantes, where he met Luis Buñuel and Federico García Lorca. In this period, he benefited from the lectures of eminent international figures, visits to the Prado Museum, and extensive readings, which acquainted him with the art of modern movements. Outside of his academic training, he developed an admiration for the meticulous drawings of Vermeer and Meissonier, and to experiment for his pictorial research, he painted cubist and pointillist works and briefly imitated futurism.

His participation in a student protest against hiring an unqualified lecturer led to his temporary suspension by the council of the Academy of San Fernando. While on suspension, he attended drawing classes of Julio Moises at the Free Academy in Madrid. After the temporary suspension, he returned to the Academy of San Fernando, but refusing to be examined in fine art theory, he was permanently expelled from the academy.

Reading Freud's *The Temptations of Dreams* gave new direction to his art. He began to paint pictures in a realist manner that represented a consciously imaginary world, with the juxtaposition of irrelevant objects in unexpected situations. He described these pictures as products of his "paranoiac critical."

Luis Buñuel approached Dali to make a surrealist short film. They cowrote the scenario and directed the silent film *Le Chien Andalou*. Adopting the automatic writing of the surrealists, they juxtaposed irrational images. The film, released in 1929, provoked a harsh reaction of the public, but it granted Dali and Buñuel admittance to the surrealist community.

During his trip to Paris, he met all the leading surrealists of the time. Before his return home, a number of surrealist friends promised to visit him in Catalonia. As promised, in the summer of 1929, a group of his acquaintances from Paris, including Paul Eluard and his wife, Gala, descended upon him. Dali had already met Paul in Paris; as for Gala, she was known to all as the surrealists' muse. This encounter was the beginning of a paradoxical love that lasted more than fifty years. Her death in 1982 accelerated Dali's decline in health.

The introduction of the catalog for Dali's first one-man show in Paris, written by André Breton, assured Dali's fame, and *Persistence of Memory*, an image of melting watches in a landscape, as an allegory of the end of time, made Dali famous in America.

Considering himself a surrealist since birth, Dali could not accept Breton imposing limits on the aesthetic of the unconscious. From their side the surrealists, with their revolutionary inclinations, considered Dali's political views a serious matter. Dali had honestly confessed, "Very rich people have always impressed me; very poor people, like the fishermen of Port Lligat, have likewise impressed me; average people, not at all." The surrealists, who were devoted to Breton, expelled Dali. But as they needed Dali's magnetic presence, his art was not banned from their exhibitions.

Dali's encounter with Gala led to the breakup of Gala and Eluard. Dali's father, upset by Salvador's liaison with Gala, expelled him from the family. But Salvador refused to leave Cadaques, and with the proceeds of the sale of *Old Age of William Tell* he bought a fisherman's hut at Port Lligat near Cadaques, and he moved there with Gala. Port Lligat was to remain their favorite place; over the years they bought the neighboring huts to extend their house. In this retreat, the couple welcomed many visitors, including King Umberto of Italy and the duke and duchess of Windsor. In 1934 they married in a civil ceremony in Paris. Gala became Dali's guide, business manager, protector, and above all his most important source of inspiration. Dali's devotion to Gala went to the extent that he added her name to his signatures.

In 1933 he painted *The Enigma of William Tell*, a picture motived by the reaction of his father against Salvador's liaison with Gala. He explained, "William Tell is my father, and the little child in his arms is myself; instead of an apple, I have a raw cutlet on my head. He is planning to eat me." But the picture went beyond his relationship with his father; he deliberately gave William Tell the features of Lenin with a long arse supported on a crutch. Exhibited at the at the 1934 Salon des Indépendants, the picture angered André Breton and his communist-sympathizer circle.

Fascinated by Jean-Francois Millet's painting of *The Angelus*, in which he saw a metaphor of the battle of the sexes, he wrote *Mythe Tragique de l'Angelus de Millet*, and painted numerous versions of the subject. In *Archaeological Reminiscence of Millet's "Angelus"* (1935), the male tries to protect his genitals with his hat.

The outbreak of the Spanish Civil War forced Dali and Gala to leave Spain. While they were traveling around Europe, Dali's family home was bombed, his sister was imprisoned and tortured, and his friend Garcia Lorca was shot.

Meeting Sigmund Freud was the dream of any surrealist. In 1938, through arrangement of Stefan Zweig, Dali met Freud, who had emigrated from Vienna and was living in a suburb of London. After the meeting, in a letter to Zweig, Freud wrote, "I was inclined to think that Surrealists, who have taken me as their patron saint, were absolute fools. The young Spaniard...has prompted me to assess this differently."

With the outbreak of World War II and the Nazi invasion of France, the couple left for New York, a visit that lasted eight years. In New York Dali became the talk of the town. His works covered diverse areas such as painting pictures, creating jewelry, designing sets and costumes for ballets, designing Helena Rubinstein's apartment, and doing work for leading magazines such as *Vogue*. In 1941 the Museum of Modern Art in New York arranged a retrospective of Dali's paintings, drawings, and jewelry creations. The exhibition traveled to eight cities in America. Dali's making a great deal of money led to Breton's famous anagram of Dali's name, *Avida Dollars*.

Deeply shocked by America's dropping of the atomic bomb, he succumbed to mysticism. Fascinated by the movement of particles of matter that seemed to him to organize themselves into a logarithmic spiral, he imagined that the world is governed by a mysterious order. This thought and his interest in religion caused a turn of mind that led him to paint beyond the personal modes of the past and in a new technique. Dali was a devoted Catholic, and the religious remarriage of Dali and Gala in 1958 shows the depth of his religious conviction.

Among his prominent works of this period are the monumental picture *The Discovery of America by Christopher Columbus* (1958); *Tuna Fishing* (1966), combining all various styles he had worked in; and the *Hallucination Toreador* (1969), in which he used a bullfighting arena as a kind of visual autobiography, with his memories of childhood, art school experiences, bullfighting, his cubist rendition of Venus de Milo, and Gala, who is looking from above on all of this.

In 1975 Dali began to show sign of Parkinson's disease. Devastated by the sudden death of Gala in 1982, he moved into Pubol Castle, which he had presented to Gala as a gift.

Dali's diverse artistic and intellectual activity involved painting, sculpture, collaboration on making films and several ballets and operas, designs for jewelry and fashion, and writing articles and diaries that provide insight into his art. Dali's penchant to please and to surprise led him to always make an exhibition of himself. At the age of fifteen, he wore long hair with long side whiskers, and he carried a gilded cane. Later he grew an outlandish mustache, which became his trademark.

Section 9

Armory Show

At the opening of the twentieth century, American art lagged behind Europe. The photographer Alfred Stieglietz, was the first to organize exhibitions of works of modern painters and sculptors in America, in his Gallery 291 on Fifth Avenue in New York City. In 1907, he organized an exhibition of sculpture and painting with sixty drawings by Rodin. In 1908, he included work of Matisse in a large exhibition. In 1909, he held the first Toulosuse-Lautrec exhibion in America. Gallery 291 organized more exhibitions until it was closed in 1917 due to declining attendance. In 1913 the American Association of Painters and Sculptors organized an exhibition of more than eleven hundred works of modern artists at the spaces of the US National Guard Armory. The American public, for the first time exposed to modern art on such a large scale, showed a wide range of reactions to the show. After New York the exhibition was moved to the Art Institute of Chicago and then to Boston. Despite hostile reactions, the consequences of the Armory Show were considerable, and new galleries dealing in modern art began to appear.

The warm welcome given to Marcel Duchamp in 1915 was a sign of the spiritual freedom of Americans and the complexity of their reactions to modern art. After the opening of the Museum of Modern Art in New York in 1929, on the path to determining what American art would be, the Great Depression turned attention to domestic situations. A kind of nationalism led to the rejection of European influences and adaptation of a realist style known as American regionalism. The movement, which lasted until the end of World War II, chose as its theme the depiction of scenes of urban and small-town life in America.

Section 10

Abstract Expressionism

During the Great Depression, which began in 1929 and lasted for a decade, American artists, considering modern art incapable of expressing deep social values, chose realistic styles for their themes. In 1933 a painter named George Biddle, a childhood friend of President Franklin D. Roosevelt, in a letter to the president suggested that government should consider an art program based on the example of the Mexican mural movement of 1920, a program in which the government paid artists wages to decorate the walls of the country. At the end of 1933, the US government started the Public Works of Art Project. In 1935 the small scale of PWAP was enlarged to the WPA's Federal Art Project. The underlying concept of the project was that the artists were the employees of the government, and their products were the property of the government. To qualify for a job, an artist had to prove that he or she was poor. In 1941 the government cleaned out a storage closet containing watercolor paintings, and in 1943 thousands of oil paintings were removed from their stretchers and sold by the pound.

Escaping World War II and the occupation of France, most of the leading figures in European art took refuge in New York. Among the influential immigrants was Peggy Guggenheim, the daughter of a copper magnate, who had moved to Paris in 1920 and had become a friend of avant-garde artists and writers. In Europe, she began to collect works of art, and she opened a gallery in London. In 1941, just before the occupation of Paris, she moved to New York and opened a gallery called The Art of This Century. Among her advisors were A. Barr, the director of the Museum of Modern Art in New York; Marcel Duchamp; and Mondrian. In 1947 she closed the gallery and returned to Europe.

As a consequence of the immigration of leading avant-garde European artists between 1939 and 1942 to the United States, New York became a scene of great artistic activity, similar to the activity of the 1920s and 1930s in Paris. The impact of the art of Matisse, Picasso, and Braque—and particularly Kandinsky's non-representational expressionism, and Max Ernst's automation—led to abstract expressionism as a new movement. The greatest impact of abstract expressionism was to reject regional realism, an isolationist aesthetic that had created a gap between the art activities of the United States and those of Europe. As a consequence of a closer relationship with Europe, American art joined the activities of the art of Europe.

Abstract expressionism was not an organized style, but in spite of its diversity, the works of artists who had little in common could be distinguished by three general approaches:

1. A dynamic handling of painting similar to the drip style of Jackson Pollock, called action painting.
2. A style consisting of the expressive use of large, flat color shapes with undefined edges, represented by Mark Rothko's work.
3. The third approach was a combination of elements of action painting and an expressive use of color.

JACKSON POLLOCK (1912–1956)

Pollock was born in Cody, Wyoming, into a farming family of Scotch-Irish origin. Ten months after the birth of Jackson, the family moved to San Diego, and over the next sixteen years, they moved nine times around California and Arizona.

In 1928 Pollock began to study at the Manual Arts School of Los Angeles. His teacher, Schwankovsky, was a friend and follower of the Hindu philosopher Krishnamurti, who had founded a camp in the Ojai Valley. At Schwankovsky's request, one afternoon Krishnamurti talked to the students. Pollock, impressed by the philosopher, visited the Ojai camp and read theosophical writings, but after a year he became tired of religion.

Inspired by the decision of his older brother Charles, who had decided to become a painter and had moved to New York, in 1930 Pollock also moved to New York to study art, where enrolled at the Art Students League. His teacher, Thomas Hart Benton, a dominant figure among American regionalists, believed that art should appeal to the man on the street and was against modern art movements. Soon, a reciprocal sympathy bound Pollock and Benton's family. Benton helped him to obtain an exemption from the school's monthly tuition and to receive a scholarship.

A few weeks after the death of his father, Jackson left school. For the next two years, he lived in poverty with his brothers—first with Charles and then with Sande. After Jackson's brothers left New York to settle in Kansas City, Benton cared for Pollock like a son. In 1935 Pollock joined the WPA Project. At the beginning, he signed on for the mural division, but as he did not like teamwork, he switched to the easel division.

Having become a heavy and violent drinker, in 1938 at his own request, Pollock was hospitalized for a few months. But four months after his release from the hospital, he was back to drinking heavily again. Realizing Jackson's need for professional help, his brother Sande took him to Dr. Henderson, a psychotherapist with Jungian training. As Pollock was a reticent patient, Henderson, a follower of Jung's theory that art reflects primordial images buried in the unconscious, began analyzing Pollock's work and encouraged him to paint as a way of giving access to his unconscious. This fact led later critics of Pollock's art to read specific Jungian meanings into his works.

From the start of working for the WPA, Pollock was uneasy about painting in the regionalist manner. The abstract power of Picasso's *Guernica* in its exhibition of 1939 in New York attracted Pollock to modern art. *Birth* (1941), a painting influenced by Picasso and Alaskan Eskimo masks, was included in an exhibition and was his first step out of obscurity. Another unknown artist participating in that show was Lenore (Lee) Krasner, who became Pollock's life partner. It was a union of two painters, in which their differences complemented each other. The encouragement and support of Lee helped Pollock move toward his artistic maturity.

Exhibitions of the surrealists in the Museum of Modern Art in New York had already familiarized American artists with the movement. The arrival of leading figures of surrealism as refugees in New York, coinciding with the fading of the social realism of regionalism and providing direct contacts with the pioneers of the movement, influenced American artists. The similarity of the "automation" of surrealism with the element of intuition in expressionism attracted American painters. Pollock, an admirer of Miro, in 1942 joined a group of American artists dedicated to surrealism. But Pollock's surrealism was short-lived; he produced only three surrealist paintings.

In 1943 Peggy Guggenheim decided to hold a competition and exhibition of young artists. Pollock submitted one of his surrealist paintings to the competition. Mondrian, one of the judges, found the painting interesting. Pollock was offered a contract for his entire output and a commission to paint a mural for the hallway of Guggenheim's apartment. Pollock's first show attracted favorable criticism, but his second was less successful, and the third one was disappointing. After the return of Peggy Guggenheim to Europe, Pollock exhibited at the Patterson Gallery.

In 1947 Pollock produced his first drip painting. For these paintings, he laid out a large canvas on the floor and let the pigment run down from a stick onto the canvas, thus creating a picture of countless lines—without defining any shape and with no beginning or end. Considering painting a self-contained unit detached from the spectator was a departure from the traditional concept of easel painting.

Agonized by self-doubts that pushed him further into alcoholism, he abandoned his drip style, limited his colors predominantly to black, and began to explore problems of the human figure in painting. In 1956, driving recklessly, he lost control and crashed into trees, and was killed.

MARK ROTHKO (1903-1970)

Rothko, an American painter of Russian descent, was born in Dvinsk, Russia. His father, Jabob, was a pharmacist with comfortable living standard. When mark was seven years old, his father to get away from the hostile environment of Russia decided to emigrate to America, where his brother had an established business. In 1910 Jacob with his two elder sons went to Potland, Oregan, and in1913 he sent for the rest of the family to join him. Jacob's death, a few months after arrival of Mark, plunged the family into financial prblems. Marko working after school, had no time to enjoy his childhood.

Mark Rothko, at an early age he attended social discussions that took place in the Jewish community center. From those discussions, he maintained revolutionary ideas all his life. After he was graduated from high school with briiliant records, he was granted a scholarship by Yale University, where he followed courses of liberal arts and science for two years. After the freshman years, he had to work again to support his life.

In 1925, he went to New York and enrolled at art classes of Max Weber at the Art Student League, and remained there until 1929; in that year he took a part-time job of teaching children at a school run by a synagogue, and continued to teach children until 1952.

In 1935, he became one of the founding members of the groupe of *the Ten*. The groupe regraded themselves as progressive artists, exhibited frequently, and were invited to exhibit in France. Rothko' painting in *the Ten's* exhibitions, between 1935-39, were expressionist in style. In 1932, Rothko married Edith Sachar, and he became United Sates citizen in 1938.

Before the end of 1930s he painted scenes of streets and subways. These pictures rather to represent city life were more interested in the abstract arrangement of the space of his pictures. Stylistic simplification of *Entrance to Subway* (1938), stress individual isolationin in a silent world. During 1940s, he became influenced by works of surrealist painters, who had emigrated to New York.

Rothko was an intellectual and restless man, as changing subjects and techniques provided him no satisfaction, he turned toward pondering on his *self*, and sought answers in mythlogy. Reading Greek's mythlogy led him to Nietzsche's *The Birth of Tragedy from the Spirit o Music*[22]. Nietzsche relating music to mythlogy responded to Rothko's interest in music and in the matters of myth-

---

22 - The central thesis of *The Birth of Tragedy from the Spirit of Music* is to establish origin of Greek tragedy, as well as the interdepdence of myth and ritual in all primitive cultures.

logy. Nietzsche's interest in Greek tragedy turned Rothko toward Aeschylus for answers, and sought to express clash of forces that he found in the Greek tragedies.

Rothko, who had moved through many artistic styles, influenced by Nietzsche writing searched to give his pactures the suggestive capacity of music. By the end of 1940s his art evolved from figurative to abstract. He began to eliminate linear elements, and to paint floating color shapes that their undefined edges gave them a sense of movement. Over next few years he reduced the numbers of floating colors, but played color and shape variation on them.

He painted fourteen murals for *Rothko Chapel* (1965), set on the campus of St. Thomas Catholic University. Sombre colors of the murals reflect Rothko's melancholic mood of his last years. For the design of the building Rothko worked closely with architects.

Phsycally ill, and depressed he commited suicide in 1970.

Section 11

In the early 1950s in London, a group of young artists, called the Independent Group, discussed various intellectual subjects in their meetings. One of their topics was American mass media, such as motion pictures, comic strips, and advertising, which had flooded England after World War II. Lawrence Alloway, one of the members of the group, in reference to mass media coined the term "pop art," without envisioning it as a fine art. Later, Richard Hamilton, also a member of the group, by sending his first pop art work to the exhibition "This is Tomorrow," redefined the term and became the initiator of pop art in England.

In the United States in the 1950s, a few painters, by representing ordinary objects and figurative images, challenged the dominance of abstract expressionism and in general the concept of the picture as essentially "a flat surface covered by color assembled in a certain order."

Pioneers of pop art in America, some from the world of painting, and some out of the advertising world, realized that the astonishing effects of advertising representing familiar objects, the instant communicability of comic strips, and the taste for news photography represent the demand for a facile and unconcerned art by a public tired of the hardship of World War II. To create an art with immediate effects became the primary concern of these painters. In 1963 the organization of a series of exhibitions by American museums was an attempt to look at and examine pop art as a new movement.

The misconception of pop art as an art of protest, led to its being compared to dada and called neodada. But dada was motivated by a negative attitude against the established values of bourgeois society and its idea of art, while aesthetic freedom after World War II, which made possible the positive and aggressive attitude of pop art, was different from in dada's time.

Some critics approved the very essence of pop art in its complete break from aesthetic tradition and its elevation of everyday objects to the level of fine art. Other critics pointed out that the concept of reality depends on a philosophical interpretation of the outside world—that realist painters, such as Chardin and Courbet, through their aesthetic concepts changed the reality of their subjects and created a world of their own, while the work of pop artists is a shallow and passive representation of reality. Consequently, a piece of pop art does not require an intellectual effort—neither from the artist to create it, nor from the spectator to enjoy it.

Modern art lasted until 1960s, when it was replaced by postmodern art.

A few Considerations of the Process of Painting from 18th to 20th Century

A painting, figurative or abstract, indicating art for art aesthetic or social concern, is painted to reveal the painter's sense of beauty, or his concept of reality.

Definition of beauty and of reality, are not fixed conventions. Definition of beauty, a phenomenon established by Greeks, has been changed several times, and concept of reality, has changed age to age.

In pre-Renaissance artists were called artisans. In Renaissance artist had the status of an employer, and patron had right to specify the end product, which means painter had to give form to a reality imposed on him by a patron. Gradual weakening of patron power, along with glorification of individualism by the Enlightenment philosophers had a profound effect on the development of painting. Painters began to paint images indicating their own sense of reality. Spread of individuality, which isolated painters from each other, led to contradictory approaches to painting: Ingres's interest for Qutrocento art differed from David's interest, his teacher, who favoured Greek art. Constable and Turner, chose oppsite concepts of landscape painting. Constable painted naturalist landscapes, while Turner searched sublime in his paintings.

In general, it is supposed that economy and social movements that effect life of artist, should effect also his work. But despite turbulent years of the nineteenth century, art of few painters showed any social awareness. Cezanne an intellectual person searched permanence hidden beneth appearances, and Gauguin, in search of the engma of life, travelled to far away places. These painters, considering art a highly intellectual activity, did not want to preoccupy themselves with ephemerals; for them art was not to represent, but to create.

Diversity of individual concepts of art and of art movments, made the first half of the twentieth century an exceptional epoch, full of surprises: Henri Matisse's intellectual approach to paing and absorved to solve technical problems, Pablo Picasso's inventive power, poetical imagination of of Henri Rousseau and Marc Chagal, unusual approach to art by Marcel Duchamps, and Paul Klee's sophisticated art beyond any lable, are highlights of paintings of those years.

Importance given to study and research gave rise to new movements: Expressionism's aim to give form to emotions was a counterpoint to Impressionism. Surrealim attempted to go beyond conscious level. Abstract movement using line and color to suggest, not to represent, was revival of Schopenhauer's remak that all arts should aspire to the condition of music.

Bibliography

Auguste Renoir – Pete H. Feist – Benedikt Taschen.

Cezanne – Maurice Raynal – Skira

Cezanne – A Study of His Development – Roger Frye – The Macmillan Co.

Chagall – Andre Pieyre de Mandiargues – Maeght.

Concerning the Spritual in Art – Wassily Kandinsky - Dover Publication.

Corot -Jean Lemarie – Skira

Delacroix – Maximilian Gautier – Larousse.

Dialogue avec Le Visible – Rene Huygue – Flammarion

French Eighteenth Century Painters – E. and L. de Goncoure -Phaidon Book.

From Baudelaire to Bonnad -Maurice Raynal – Skira

From Picasso to Surrealism - Raynal, Lassaigne, Schmalenbach, Rudlinger.

Gauguin - Charles Estienne – Skira.

Gauguin - Rene Huygue – Crown Art Library.

Gauguin a Retrospective – M. Prather and C.F. Stuckey – Park Lane.

Georges Braque – F. Ponge and P. Descagues _Harry n. Abrams, Inc.

Goya – Enrique Lafonte Ferrari – Unesco

Goya, San Antonio de la Florida – Enrique Lafonte Ferrari- Skira.

Goya – Pierre Gassier -Skira

Gustave Klimt – The R. S. Lauder and S.S. Sabarsky Collection.

Henri Matisse- J. Lemarie, H. Read, W.S. Liebermaan – University of Cal. Press.

Henri Matisse – John Jacobus – Harry N. Abrams, Inc.

Histoire de l'Art Modern -Elie Faure -Le Livre de Poche.

Impressionism -Jean Lemarie - Skira.

Ingres et l'Ingrisme – Jean Alzard – Albain Michel.

Landscape into Art – Kenneth Clark -Pelican Books.

La Peinture aux XIXe et XXe Siecles – Henri Focillon – Librairie Renouard.

L'Art et l'Homme -Rene Huygue – Larousse.

L' Esprit des Formes – Elie Faure – Le Livre de Poche.

Le Nu – Kenneth Clark – Le Livre de Poche

Les Voix du Sillence – Andre Malraux – *nrf.*

L'Intemporel – Andre Malraux – Gallimard.

Looking at a Picture – Kenneth Clark- Beacon Press.

Manifestes du Surrealime – Andre Breton – Gallimard.

Marcel Duchamp – Arturo Schwart – Harry Abrams, Inc.

Matisse, His Art and His Public – A. H. Barr – The Meusem of Modern Art, NYC

Matisse, Mmch, Rouault – Raynal,.Rudlinger, Bouliger, Lassargne- Skira

Modern Art – Meyer Schpiro – George Braziller.

Monet – William Seitz – Harry N. Abrams, Inc.

Paul Cezanne – Meyer Schapiro – Harry N. Abrams, Inc

Paul Klee -Will Grohmann – Harry N. Abrams, Inc.

Picasso, Fifty Years of His Art – Alfred H. Barr Jr. – Secker & Warberg.

Picasso, Metamorphoses et Unite – Jean Lemarie – Skira.

Point and Line to Plane – Wassily Kandinsky – Dover Publications, Inc.

Rouault – Lionello Venturi – Skira.

Saturne – Andre Malraux - *nrf*

Seurat – Roger Fry – Encyclopedia Britannica.

The Life of Forms in Art – Henri Focillon – Zone Books.

This I Saw, Life and Time of Goya – Antonina Vallenti – Random House

Theory and Philosophy of Art: Style – Meyer Schpiro – George Braziller.

The Romantic Rebellion – Kenneth Clark – Harper & Row, Publishers

Van Gogh – Rene Hughe – Crown Publishers, Inc.

www.ingramcontent.com/pod-product-compliance
Lightning Source LLC
Chambersburg PA
CBHW060821170526
45158CB00001B/51